Adam's Contract with Satan

Adam's Contract with Satan

THE LEGEND OF THE CHEIROGRAPH OF ADAM

Michael E. Stone

INDIANA
University Press

Bloomington & Indianapolis

This book is a publication of
Indiana University Press
601 North Morton Street
Bloomington, Indiana 47404-3797 USA

http://iupress.indiana.edu

Telephone orders 800-842-6796
Fax orders 812-855-7931
Orders by e-mail iuporder@indiana.edu

Library of Congress Cataloging-in-Publication Data

Stone, Michael E., 1938–
    Adam's contract with Satan: the legend of the cheirograph of Adam /
Michael E. Stone.
       p.   cm.
    Includes bibliographical references and index.
    ISBN 0-253-33902-2 (hardcover : alk. paper)
    1. Adam (Biblical figure)—Legends—History and criticism. 2. Devil—
Legends—History and criticism. 3. Legends, Christian—Eastern Europe—
History and criticism. I. Title.

    BS580.A4 S83 2002
    229'.911—dc21

                                                                00-054099

    1 2 3 4 5 07 06 05 04 03 02

CONTENTS

PREFACE

I have long felt a keen interest in the Adam literature and first observed the tradition about Adam's contract with Satan many years ago. As evidence came together in my files documenting the spread and significance of this tradition, I felt impelled to present it in the form of a book. I lay it here before the reader with some misgivings, for its composition has led me into areas into which I have never ventured before. I can only hope that, like Rabbi Akiba, I "entered safely and left safely."

The last generation has taken a growing interest in the history of apocryphal traditions. This makes it particularly interesting to trace a legend such as the one presented here across geographical and cultural boundaries. When, as is the case here, the legend also reveals and reflects varying attitudes to basic aspects of the human condition, the quest for it becomes more gripping.

Two sections of this book were written by others. Alexander Kulik assembled and translated the Slavonic texts and supplied the bibliographical references relating to them. His work is acknowledged in the relevant chapters. Beatriz Moncó prepared a study of the term χειρόγραφον in the papyri, which forms appendix 3 of the present work. If her conclusions are correct, the legend's use of the term "cheirograph" cannot be later than the mid-first millennium c.e. and comes from the Byzantine Greek area. She also made the translations of the modern Greek texts. Work done by two students has been incorporated here: K. Koblentz prepared the translation of the passage from Pseudo-Macarius in chapter 7, and Steven Smith the translation of "On the Apostle's Discourse" in the same chapter.

Learned colleagues and friends have tried to save me from some of my own inadequacies. In addition to Alexander Kulik's help, I acknowledge that of Constantine Zuckerman in matters Slavonic. Nicolae Roddy was kind enough to review the chapter on Romanian sources and made a number of most helpful suggestions. Nicholas Constas made many important remarks about the modern Greek texts. Gary Anderson provided much stimulus, particularly in the early stages of this study. David Satran read some sections of the book, which is the better for his insightful comments. The work of my research assistants is here gratefully acknowledged, particularly that of Beatriz Moncó and of Erica Martin. All mistakes are mine.

The cited texts are reproduced by permission of the various authors and publishers. All nonattributed translations were made by the author. Odigia Foundation in Den Haag kindly made photographs of their icon available. The Matenadaran in Erevan, Armenia, has given me permission to reproduce miniatures from their manuscripts. The research for this book was supported by a grant from the Israel Science Foundation; the major part of its composition was done during a year I spent at the Netherlands Institute of Advanced Studies in Wassenaar. Both of these organizations have made much scholarly research possible, and that is gratefully acknowledged here.

Michael E. Stone
Jerusalem

INTRODUCTION

R. H. Charles's *Apocrypha and Pseudepigrapha of the Old Testament* (1913) was a summary of the nineteenth century's research into the Jewish background of the New Testament. He assembled translations of most of the then known ancient Jewish apocrypha and pseudepigrapha, with the basic aim of explaining "the course of religious development between 200 B.C. and A.D. 100."[1] In this work, L. S. A. Wells presented three narrative versions of the life of Adam and Eve: one in Greek (*Apocalypse of Moses*), one in Latin (*Life of Adam and Eve*), and one in Old Church Slavonic (*Slavonic Life of Adam and Eve*).[2] Wells expressed his view of the work's importance when he stated that "St. Paul and the . . . author of Apoc. Mos . . . moved in the same circle of ideas; profoundly modified in St. Paul's case by his Christian convictions."[3] In other words, the books of Adam and Eve were thought to preserve ideas about the protoplasts that were part of the religious thought of the age of Christian origins. These ideas were related to those evident in Christianity's basic documents.

The three versions of the *Life of Adam and Eve* that Wells published were closely affiliated. Thus, he could present them in three parallel aligned columns (i.e., in synoptic form). An examination of his synopsis quickly reveals that, although there is quite a lot of text that is peculiar to each version, they share a very substantial amount of material. Since Wells's time, two further complete versions of this book have been discovered and published, one in Armenian and the other in Georgian. These two new versions are closely related; they are designated the Armenian *Penitence of Adam* and the Georgian *Book of Adam*. Moreover, the existence of a fragmentary Coptic version has been noted.[4] All these versions were translated from

Greek (or survive themselves in Greek), and a new synoptic presentation gives all five in parallel columns.[5]

Today, scholars are less certain than Wells was in 1913 about the date and Jewish provenance of this work. They debate the character of the source from which the known versions of the Adam books derive, and questions of its Jewish or Christian provenance, original language, and date remain unsolved. It is safe to say, however, that all contemporary experts regard this writing to be definitely as old as the fourth century C.E., and perhaps considerably older than that, and they have concluded that Greek was the original language of all the surviving versions.[6]

In the Second Temple period, Adam and Eve are mentioned a number of times. Previously we referred to Paul's use of traditions about them in the *Epistle to the Romans,* and Adam and Eve are prominent in further New Testament writings as well. They also figure in other Jewish writings of the age, such as Ben Sira, *Jubilees, 4 Ezra, 2 Baruch,* and the works of Philo Judaeus.[7] This shows that exegesis and development of Genesis 1–3 were rather important in the age of Christian origins. Nonetheless, the particular narrative traditions found in the *Books of Adam and Eve* are not paralleled extensively in the writings of that period.

In current terminology, "primary Adam book" or "books" refers to the narrative known to Wells as *Apocalypse of Moses* in Greek and *Life of Adam and Eve* in Latin and Slavonic, as well as to the *Penitence of Adam* in Armenian and the *Book of Adam* in Georgian.[8] In later centuries, throughout the Christian world, the stories of the protoplasts were retold in a variety of literary forms, including poems, narratives, dramas, and epics. These numerous later retellings of the Adam and Eve stories are called "secondary Adam books."

As our discussion proceeds, it will become evident that the Slavonic *Life of Adam and Eve,* although designated above as a primary Adam book, is rather different from the other four primary versions. It has been greatly changed from them, either at the Slavonic stage of its transmission or in the particular form of the Greek text that was translated into Slavonic. With its very distinct, even "aberrant," views and its additional narrative material, it is not unlike the secondary Adam books previously mentioned. Its overall text, however, resembles that of the other four full versions at very many points. The intermediate position of the Slavonic version, part primary and part "secondary," causes some inconsistency in our discussion of it, but we strive to be clear at each point.

The present work is devoted to tracing one particular tradition, a distinctive form of the idea that Adam signed a contract or cheirograph with Satan. This particular tradition is not found in the Bible, nor in the primary Adam books, but it occurs in a number of secondary Adam books, in a variety of languages. The story, its diffusion, and the way it was used make the fascinating tale that we will tell here. Its unique character can readily be seen when we compare it with the biblical narrative and with the primary Adam books.

The present study, then, will concentrate on that legend. However, where appropriate, the relationship between the legend and the New Testament verse Colossians 2:14 will be considered. Some samples of patristic exegesis are gathered in chapter 7 for the sake of illustration, and the reader who consults them will readily see the distinction we are drawing here. Most of this book is devoted to the presentation in English of the various sources conserving the legend and discussion of them, including consideration of the interrelations between the cheirograph story and the various primary and secondary books of Adam and Eve. Many of the sources transmitting the legend are given in full in their original languages in a separate appendix.

ABBREVIATIONS

We have attempted, as far as possible, to avoid abbreviations, because the range of subjects discussed would have made them so numerous. However, in addition to standard abbreviations, we have used the following:

Col.	Colossians
CSCO	Corpus Scriptorum Orientalium Christianorum
JJS	*Journal of Jewish Studies*
JSJ	*Journal for the Study of Judaism*
JTS	*Journal of Theological Studies*
SVTP	Studia in Veteris Testamenti Pseudepigrapha
ZNW	*Zeitschrift für die neutestamentliche Wissenschaft*

Adam's Contract with Satan

CHAPTER ONE

The Legend of Adam and Eve

The Cheirograph and the Deceit
and Fall of Adam and Eve

The legend of Adam's contract with Satan is an apocryphal tale. Through-out the ages, Jews and Christians embroidered and filled out the biblical narrative with stories and legends. Some such stories had already come into being in the period of the Second Temple, soon after the end of the writing of the Hebrew Bible. Others were composed over the ensuing centuries.[1]

The legend of the cheirograph of Adam is a later representative of this fecund creative impulse. It is to be found neither in the biblical corpus nor, for that matter, in the mainstream ancient apocryphal literature.[2] It does not occur in the primary Adam books, which are conventionally included in collections of biblical apocrypha such as that of Charles, nor in such rich repositories of Adamic traditions as the somewhat later (perhaps fourth century C.E.) Syriac work titled *The Cave of Treasures.*[3]

Studies have been devoted to tracing the history of such apocryphal traditions, which frequently took on a vigorous life of their own in the Byzantine and medieval Christian worlds. Thus investigations of the development of the themes of the Quest of Seth,[4] the Fifteen Signs before the Doomsday,[5] the Horned Moses,[6] Enosh,[7] and a number of others have been published.[8] Moreover, medievalists have explored some Adam and Eve traditions in the course of their study of medieval texts dealing with Adam, such as the Old Irish *Saltair na Rann*,[9] the Middle High German Genesis poems, and others.[10] Scholars of Milton have addressed the issue of his sources for the Paradise stories.[11] Thus, the character of these traditions and how they functioned over the centuries has been investigated to some extent (indeed, more than we have mentioned here). Yet much more remains to be said about them.[12]

The apocryphal narratives associated with the first created people, Adam and Eve, are widespread. The biblical story of Adam and Eve was a foundational story for the Christian view of the world as well as for Judaism and Islam. It had an enormous impact on Western and Eastern cultures: Jewish, Christian, and Muslim.[13] It stimulated the creation of numerous works of literature and art, theology, and biblical exegesis. The stories of Adam and Eve took on many forms and shapes; one of them found in the East, but less known in the West, is the legend of Satan's third deception of Adam and Eve and the agreement Adam made with him. This story is dubbed the legend of Adam's cheirograph, or contract, with Satan.

The legend of the cheirograph of Adam occurs in a wide variety of sources, chiefly of Greek and oriental Christian origin. Certain of its elements surfaced by the late first millennium C.E.,[14] and the story is still alive in the twentieth century in Greek, Bulgarian, and Romanian literature.[15] The sources that transmit it include narratives, poetry, and artistic representations as well as popular songs and folk tales. We will present a number of them in detail.

The reader may well wonder why we have called this story the third story of the deception of Adam and Eve. The first, of course, is the biblical one, recounted in Genesis 2–3. The second time Satan deceived Adam and Eve is told in the primary Adam books. Pericopes 2 and 4 of the primary Adam books (comprising Latin; Armenian, and Georgian 1.1–4.3 and 5.1–11.3; Slavonic 28–32 and 35–39) relate the incident in which Adam and Eve resolved to repent, standing fasting in the Rivers Jordan and Tigris. Adam was to repent for forty days and Eve for thirty-four days (per Armenian and Georgian). On the eighteenth day of Eve's repentance, Satan appeared as a glorious angel and convinced Eve that her penance had been accepted. She therefore ceased her fast before its due time and thus negated the effect of the whole penitential exercise. Adam reproaches her, "O Eve, O Eve, where is the work of your penitence? Have you again been seduced by our adversary, through whom we were alienated from the dwelling of the Garden and spiritual happiness?" (Latin 10:3).

The story we are discussing in this work is the third story of Satan's deception. It usually does not occur in works that relate the second deception, just described.

The Legend of the Cheirograph

According to the third deception story, Satan tempted and deceived Adam and Eve again (the first deception, in Paradise, resulted in their fall, expulsion, and curse). How did this happen? After they left the Garden, they encountered an obstacle: darkness. They had lost the paradisiacal light. In the Garden, it had always been light, and they had never experienced darkness.[16] Outside the Garden, the sun set, and when the world grew dark, Adam and Eve became afraid. Satan came and promised them that if they agreed to the terms of a contract or cheirograph (χειρόγραφον) that he proposed, he would bring the light.[17] Adam and Eve accepted his offer, and Adam signed the contract with Satan. In this contract, in exchange for the light, Adam and Eve agree that "until the unbegotten is born and the undying dies, we and our children will be subject to you," or another similarly formulated condition. Initially, this agreement seemed to establish, or strengthen, Satan's rule and dominion.

Satan brought a flat rock and recorded the contract on it. Adam pronounced the terms of the agreement out loud and put his hand on the rock to sign the contract so made.[18] The oral reading of the contract was a part of its ratification.[19] Satan then placed the rock in the river Jordan.

A very prominent dimension of this legend is deception, and the legend contains a double tale of deception. Satan is the great deceiver, and the Greek word δόλος, like the Armenian *բանսարկու*, has exactly this association. These are the words regularly used to describe Satan and his action.

The first level of deception was that Satan tricked Adam and Eve, and as a result Adam signed the cheirograph. Satan promised to bring the light, but of course it was not Satan that brought it; it came in the natural course of events. Thus, Satan's very promise was false. On the basis of this deceitful promise, he convinced Adam to accept his conditions and his domination. This is one level of deception.

The legend, however, is more subtle than that, for Satan's ploy backfired. He set conditions he thought were impossible to fulfill in order to guarantee his perpetual dominion over human beings, that "until the unbegotten is born and the undying dies, you and your offspring will be my servants." In this way, he thought, he was deceiving Adam and his offspring. Actually he deceived himself, for the very conditions he thought were impossible to meet were exactly those that Christ would fulfill in his incarnation and crucifixion. The birth of the unbegotten and the death of the undying are the very events that will bring about the end of the contract and of Satan's dominion over humans.[20] He sought to deceive Adam through the terms of the contract, but was himself deceived by them and thus condemned to failure; he succeeded in subjecting humanity only for a time, and then was himself bound. In this way, Satan became the deceived deceiver. That is the second level of deception.

Adam and Eve quickly discovered that Satan had deceived them: although the morning light came, evening and darkness followed it once more. They mourned and wept, and God sent an angel to reveal to them that, although they had been duped, in the long run it was Satan who had been deceived. They had been deceived for a limited time, while Satan had condemned himself for eternity. God told them of this in a divine promise, often mediated by an angel. In some versions of the legend, God even writes them a document, his own contract, to this effect.

Satan placed Adam's cheirograph in the Jordan River, thus preparing the way for the final stage of the drama. According to the legend, at the time of Christ's baptism, the waters of the Jordan turned back and revealed the stone cheirograph, sometimes guarded by demonic serpents or dragons.[21] Christ smashed the cheirograph and trampled the dragons that guarded it (Psalm 73:14).[22] Thus, Adam and Eve's subjection to Satan was brought to an end. This concluding stage of the drama focuses a number of different themes: stones in the Jordan, Christ or God crushing the heads of serpents in the water, and Satan's relationship to serpents or dragons are the most prominent among them.[23]

The Slavonic Form of the Legend

Another version of the legend, preserved in the Slavonic *Life of Adam and Eve,* differs in a number of features from that just recounted.[24] After their fall, when Adam and Eve were plowing, Satan took up his stand in front of the oxen and would not permit them to continue their work until they acknowledged the dominion of the "lord of this world."[25] In this Slavonic version, then, the obstacle Adam and Eve encountered was the need for food, while in most forms of the legend it was lack of light.[26] In all versions of the legend of the cheirograph of Adam, the obstacle provides the occasion of Satan's intervention.

According to this form of the story, then, Satan interferes with agriculture. This may be explained in two ways. The first is God's curse upon Adam. According to Genesis 3:17–19, the curse laid upon Adam is related to the tilling of the ground: "Cursed is the ground because of you; in toil you shall eat of it all the days of your life" (Genesis 3:17). In the illustrative cycle of the Old Testament in the Cathedral of Monreale in Sicily (twelfth century), agriculture is the first scene represented after the expulsion from the Garden of Eden.[27] Adam is shown tilling the ground while Eve looks on; this sequence reflects the actual biblical narrative. Thus, there is a certain structural logic in Satan's disturbing agriculture.

According to the primary Adam books, on their expulsion from Paradise Adam and Eve encountered the need to find food, and eventually they were taught agriculture as a response to this need.[28] This is the second way of explaining the curse. Agriculture, though a curse, had to be revealed. Tilling the fields is definitely an intermediary level between the status of the animals who eat grass and the *esca angelorum,* "the angelic food," which the protoplasts had eaten in the Garden. In this context, the picture of Adam plowing and Satan standing in his path is a natural one.[29] It represents Satan's disruption of a basic necessity of the post-expulsion Adam and Eve.[30]

A different form of the idea of deception may be observed in the Slavonic *Life of Adam and Eve,* Variant A. According to the Slavonic story, Adam deliberately worded his contract so that Satan thought he himself was being granted eternal dominion, whereas Adam knew very well that was not the case. By this means, Adam repaid in kind Satan's attempt to deceive him. Of the many differences between the two versions, the agricultural obstacle and Adam's deceit of Satan are the most striking.

Some Implications of the Legend

The legend of Adam's contract with Satan has a fascinating implication, which will emerge repeatedly as we proceed to analyze it. The present condition of the world is due to a mistake: Adam and Eve *were* duped, but not into disobeying a direct divine command. According to the Bible, Eve, and apparently Adam, disobeyed God's explicit command, and "because you . . . have eaten of the tree about which I commanded you, 'You shall not eat of it,' cursed is the ground," and so on (Genesis 3:17–19). In the legend, there is no deliberate transgression; there is a mistake, an error, and the error will be rectified in Christ's baptism. The promise of rectification is given to Adam and Eve from the beginning.

It is as if the great transgression in the Garden and its rectification through Christ's Passion bracket a rather more mundane event: Adam and

Eve's mistake. Their mistake explains the present state of the world. It is not presented as a sin; guilt does not ensue. Its undoing is promised *ab initio*.

This view contrasts starkly with the ideas of original sin and human guilt, expiated by the death of Christ on the cross, which so dominate Western Christian thought. Those ideas were present in the Eastern Christian traditions that cultivated the cheirograph legend, but it was Adam and Eve's mistake in signing the contract with Satan that explained the day-to-day state of humans. The people for whom the legend played a great role must have perceived the world very differently.

CHAPTER TWO

Contract, Penance, and Redemption

Colossians 2:14, the Cheirograph, the Legend, and the New Testament

So far, we have used the terms "cheirograph" and "contract" interchangeably. In most, but not all forms of the legend of Adam's contract with Satan, the contract is called a χειρόγραφον, "cheirograph," a Greek word meaning literally "a hand writing." In many versions of the legend in other languages, the contract is also called a "hand writing," usually a mechanical translation of the two parts of the Greek word. According to the great Greek dictionary of Liddell-Scott-Jones, the Greek word χειρόγραφον means "manuscript note" (inscription of the second century B.C.E.; Polybius and Septuagint Tobit 5:3); "note of hand" (papyrus of the second century B.C.E; Plutarch).[1] In the texts of the legend, however, it means "contract" or "signed agreement." The developed legal meaning of the Greek word in the late antique world is similar, as is shown in appendix 3, where its use in Greek papyri is examined.

Colossians 2:14 is the only place in the Bible where the word χειρόγραφον, "cheirograph," occurs. Its occurrence in this New Testament epistle immediately raises the question of whether its use there is related to its meaning in the legend of the contract of Adam with Satan. A careful consideration of this word's meaning in the two different contexts yields the following result. In Colossians 2:14 and in the literature dependent on that verse, the word χειρόγραφον means "bill of indebtedness." Humans, by their sins, incurred a bill of indebtedness, which Christ annulled or erased by his crucifixion. In the legend of the contract of Adam, however, the word χειρόγραφον designates the document embodying the contract that Adam made with Satan. Christ tears up or smashes Adam's contract with Satan at the time of his baptism. This distinction is crucial.

The whole passage in Colossians reads

> 13. And you, who were dead in trespasses, and the uncircumcision of your flesh, God made alive together with him, having forgiven us all our trespasses, 14. having cancelled the bond [χειρόγραφον] which stood against us with its legal demands; this he set aside, nailing it to the cross. 15. He disarmed the principalities and powers and made a public example of them, triumphing over them in him.

This passage is difficult to understand, particularly the sense of verse 14. Moreover, the word χειρόγραφον, which occurs here, and only here, in the New Testament has aroused the interest of numerous New Testament commentators and scholars.[2] It is beyond our present purpose to trace the understanding of Colossians 2:14 and of the word χειρόγραφον in that verse through the rather extensive patristic and subsequent exegetical literature, much less the influence of such exegetical literature on other aspects of Christian thought and writing. That has been done by others.[3] Nonetheless, it will be helpful to consider a couple of examples of this line of thought.

The idea that Adam incurred a bill of obligation or indebtedness through his sin is a very old Christian tradition. Thus, we can read in Irenaeus (born between 140 and 160 and died in 202), *haer,* 5.17.3: *quemadmodum per lignum debitores facti sumus Deo, per lignum accipiamus nostri debiti remissionem;* that is, "Just as we became debtors of God through a tree, through a tree we receive remission of our debt."[4] In other words, Adam (and thus humanity) incurred a debt by eating the fruit of the forbidden tree, and Christ annulled this debt through a tree, the wood of the cross on which he died. From the time of Irenaeus on, many Latin, Greek, and Oriental Christian patristic sources contain this interpretation. In certain sources, the idea is found that Adam incurred the indebtedness by disobeying the commandment; the people of Israel by disobeying their undertaking at Sinai; and sometimes Christians by sinning after their baptism. This is to be observed, for example, in John Chrysostom and in the Armenian text, "The Cheirograph of Adam."[5]

According to Colossians 2:14, then, the annulment of humans' bill of indebtedness (called a χειρόγραφον) is achieved through Christ's crucifixion.

The legend, however, sets the destruction of Adam's contract with Satan (equally called a χειρόγραφον) at the time of Christ's baptism. The shared Greek term provides an obvious basis for linking the legend of the contract with Christ's crucifixion, for drawing the two cheirographs together and identifying Christ's two redemptive acts. Yet that link is almost never realized, which is a remarkable testimony to the independence and vitality of the legend of the contract-cheirograph.

The Legend and the Biblical Story of Adam and Eve

Before proceeding to analyze the different literary and iconographic creations that have transmitted the legend of the cheirograph, we shall trace some of the implications of the overall form of the legend presented in chapter 1. To do this, we must place it in the context of the other stories of deception in Genesis and in the primary Adam books. For the cultures and churches that preserved them, the Genesis stories were current coinage, and their reworkings in the primary Adam books were widespread and familiar. They formed the underpinning of the conception of sin and redemption. They explained how the human condition became what it is, and how divine beneficence provided a means to escape the human condition and to undo the mistake of the first ancestors. Because of the foundational function of Adam traditions, transformations of them indicate changes in the understanding of sin and redemption. However, although they function similarly, the two narratives differ considerably, and both similarity and differences are significant. Moreover, the third story of deception, the legend of the cheirograph, forms a counterpoint and contrast to the biblical story of the fall that differs in a number of respects from the primary Adam books.

The serpent's seduction of Eve and Adam and Eve's fall according to Genesis are readily compared and contrasted with Satan's deception of Adam and Eve and their self-subjection to the "lord of this world" related in the cheirograph legend. According to Genesis, Eve's seduction leads to the expulsion from Paradise and, in the Christian understanding of the Genesis story, eventually to redemption through Christ's death. Adam and Eve's subjection to death (Hades), the result of the fall, is undone by Christ's death on the cross. In the oldest layer of post–New Testament Christianity we find the idea that between his death on Friday and his resurrection on Sunday, Christ descended into Hades, smashed its doors, and freed Adam, Eve, and the saints and prophets of the Old Testament.[6] In the cheirograph legend, however, Adam and Eve's voluntary subjection to Satan is destroyed in the baptism of Christ, when he breaks up the stone upon which the contract is written.

Functionally, the two narratives are similar. Adam and Eve make some sort of mistake. They become subject to Satan or Hades/death. By a redemptive act, Christ frees them from their bondage. Release from the contract is achieved at the time of Christ's baptism—according to the cheirograph legend; redemption from Adam's sin is through Christ's crucifixion—according to the Christian reading of Genesis and Colossians 2:14. The two events, baptism and crucifixion, thus serve corresponding roles; yet in both the literary and iconographic traditions, this correspondence was rarely, if ever, carried as far as identification.[7] This is very striking and very significant. The strength, independence, and vitality of the legend of the cheirograph hold the two different structures apart.

The Bible, the Primary
Adam Books, and the Legend

The differences between these three stories of seduction and fall are noteworthy. In the biblical story of the first fall, Eve is seduced and transgresses God's command. Although Adam also sins, he does not recognize that he is transgressing; at least that is not stated explicitly. In the story of the second fall in the primary Adam books, only Eve is deceived, whereas Adam immediately recognizes Satan. Eve does not recognize Satan and disobeys Adam's command. Adam completes his penance, but it does not result in a reversal of the curse on food, apparently because Eve did not complete hers. In the cheirograph legend, it is Adam who plays the chief role in the dialogue with Satan, and both he and Eve are deceived.[8] Their deception, however, bears within it the promise of redemption, and the culmination of the legend is the baptism of Christ and the smashing of the cheirograph. In both of these latter stories, it is a lack of perception—not recognizing the Deceiver—that makes the deception possible. No divine command is transgressed; Eve, or Adam and Eve, does not see reality properly and is thus deceived. The human condition is a result of a mistaken perception, not of an intentional transgression of the divine command.[9]

Above we discussed the varieties of redemption in the different versions of the Christian reversal of Adam and Eve's fall. In the case of the eating of the fruit, it was through Christ's crucifixion and descent into the underworld, while according to the cheirograph legend, at the time of his baptism, Christ annulled the contract signed between Adam and Satan.[10] The functional similarities have been noted. Yet, if these three stories are regarded from the perspective of the problems of which they are the etiologies or of the difficulties to which they are responses, the differences are very stark. The first fall is the explanation, in the final analysis, of how humans came to live under the curses of Genesis 3:14–19, which comprise central features of the human condition: death, the labor of childbirth, and agricultural toil.

The idea of another fall, after the expulsion, is shared by the primary Adam books and the legend of the cheirograph. In the primary Adam books, it is directly related to the problem of food, which resulted from the loss of the paradisiacal state.[11] The archangel Michael's revelation of agriculture partly redresses this problem. Thus, the toilsome situation inferred from the Genesis curse is softened, and perhaps it is the difficulty of agriculture, rather than agriculture itself, that is the curse.

The primary Adam books bear the promise of redemption within them, albeit in a less focused and precise fashion than in the cheirograph legend. It is explicit in the angelic responses to two quests or requests. One is the archangel Michael's response to Seth and Eve's quest for oil to relieve Adam's pain. Michael promises them that, "at that time when the years of the end are filled," the oil of joy will be granted and resurrection will ensue (*Life of Adam and Eve* 42:3–4 = *Apocalypse of Moses* 13:3–5).[12] Thus, bodily illness, also a result of the fall, will receive eschatological healing. The other quest comes to the fore when Adam and Eve are expelled from the Garden. It is then that Adam is promised the fruit of life at the time of the resurrection: "when again the Resurrection has come to pass, I will raise you up and then there shall be given to you from the Tree of Life and you will be without death forever" (*Apocalypse of Moses* 28:4).[13] The import of this promise is not completely clear, referring only in general terms to a future resurrection in which Adam will participate. It presumes that his children also will have a part in this resurrection. The paradisiacal fruit will be given to them.

These answers were thought to be unsatisfactory by the later Christian tradents of the Latin text of the primary Adam book, and they reworked parts of the narrative. Thus, according to recension III of Latin 43:2, in response to their quest, Seth and Eve receive the branches that eventually become the wood of the cross.[14] Thus, the tree of death becomes the tree of life.[15] In this formulation, redemption is integrally tied into the fall and the quests, and the subtheme of the tale of the Rood Tree is introduced. This is, however, a secondary narrative development in the Latin version of the primary Adam book. Its very introduction witnesses to the tradents' perception that the primary Adam books do not adaquately tie protology to eschatology: the fall does not necessarily imply redemption.

In the primary Adam books, then, the promised future resurrection is not inherent in the deception and the fall. This is true both of the first fall and of the second. In the legend of the cheirograph, however, redemption is guaranteed by the very way the fall happened. Thus, while resurrection may well be original to both texts, the cheirograph legend ties the eschaton structurally into the fall far more tightly than do the primary Adam books.

According to the cheirograph legend, the problem engendered by the second fall is subjection to Satan and release from that. The cheirograph legend bears within it both the creation and the resolution of the problem. The deceiver is himself deceived: the unbegotten will be born, and the immortal will die. Redemption is both foretold and related. This form of the story is profoundly Christian.

In some texts, we find only the story of the second fall without the redemption. This is the situation, for example, in the Armenian *Expulsion of Adam* (see chapter 5 below). Such texts, however, usually form part of longer narratives that commence from creation, and they do not always continue through the biblical history up to the point of redemption. Although the legend of the cheirograph always bears within it the promise of redemption, because of the narrative structure of a particular work, sometimes the promise of redemption or the redemption itself is not mentioned explicitly.

The Second Deception
in the Primary Adam Books

In the primary Adam books, the story of the second deception raises certain difficulties. In *Life of Adam and Eve* 6:1–2, Adam says he will stand in his river for forty days, and that Eve is to stand in her river for thirty-four days. This is, at least, the reading of the Greek, Armenian, and Georgian texts, which explain that the difference in the number of days is due to the creation of Eve. According to Georgian and Greek versions, it is because she was not created during the six days of creation, but subsequently.[16] According to *Jubilees* 3:8, Eve was created from Adam's rib on the second Friday—that is, seven days later than he was.[17] In the Latin primary Adam book, various readings are found, but a main one talks of thirty-seven days, while in the Slavonic *Life of Adam and Eve,* Adam is to fast for forty days and Eve for forty-four.

In *Life of Adam and Eve* 9:1, eighteen days of penance are said to have passed for both of them, which means that Adam has a period of twenty-two days remaining and Eve has sixteen days.[18] On this eighteenth day, Eve was deceived and left the river. As she issued forth untimely from the water, she fell down and remained on the ground without moving for two days.[19] Then Satan led her to Adam. When Adam told her that she had been deceived, she fainted again (11:1). No number of days is mentioned at this juncture. Adam's conversation with Satan and the latter's response ensue, including the story of Satan's fall from heaven.[20]

At this point in the narrative, Adam prays to God to make Satan distant. Satan left, and Adam completed his penance. Then he issued forth from the water (17:1–2). Here again the versions differ. Latin says nothing at all about Eve, but merely that Adam *vero perservavit XL diebus stans in poenitentia in aqua Iordanis,* "truly persevered for forty days standing in penitence in the water of the Jordan" (17:3). Armenian and Georgian both read, "Adam stood from then on in the waters of repentance, and Eve remained fallen upon the ground for three days, like one dead. Then, after three days, she arose from the earth." According to Armenian and Georgian, we have the following timetable:

–Adam and Eve stand for eighteen days.
–Eve faints for two days.
–She goes to Adam and faints again.
–Conversation takes place between Adam and Satan.
–Eve remains in a faint for three days and then goes off. That is on the twenty-third day.
–Adam remains in the water for the remaining period (twenty days) (according to the Latin text).[21]

A final observation about the timetable is that after the birth of Cain, according to Latin, Armenian, and Slavonic, Adam took Eve to the east, "and then eighteen years and two months were completed" (22:2).[22] Perhaps the period of eighteen years and two months, which is a little odd in context, corresponds to the amount of time Eve was in the river according to the other versions: eighteen days followed by a two-day faint.

It is worth noting that in this story Eve is unconscious while Satan reveals to Adam the reasons for Satan's fall. Moreover, Eve's faints form an *inclusio* for that revelation (11:1 and 17:3). Adam is tested and passes the test exactly at the middle point of his appointed period, on the twentieth day. He recognizes Satan, even though the latter is disguised as an angel. Eve has been tested and deceived two days earlier.[23]

The period of the penance and the trial is forty days, a period evocative of Moses' ascent to Mount Sinai,[24] during which period the Israelites sinned with the golden calf (Exodus 32). It is also the duration of Christ's withdrawal to the desert and his successful repulse of Satan (Matthew 4:1–11). In that period, Adam fasted (*Life of Adam and Eve* 6:1: explicitly "fasting" in the Latin and Slavonic texts, "repenting" in the other versions), as Moses did on the mountain (Exodus 34:28) and Elijah did on Mount Horeb (1 Kings 19:8).[25] In the biblical incidents, there is an element of testing: the Israelites failed where Moses succeeded; Elijah recognized God in the small, still voice; and Christ succeeded against Satan. It is very likely that this biblical pattern, including a testing, influenced the formulation in *Life of Adam and Eve.*

Penance and Second Deception

At the heart of the legend lies the tale of the second time Satan deceived Adam and Eve, after they had left the Garden. On the previous occasion, in the Garden, the serpent seduced Eve first, as is related in considerable detail in Genesis 3:1–5, a text that has frequently been analyzed.

> 1 Now the serpent was more subtle than any other wild creature that the Lord God had made. He said to the woman, "Did God say, 'You shall not eat of any tree of the garden'?" 2 And the woman said to the serpent, "We may eat of the fruit of the trees of the garden; 3 but God said, 'You shall not eat of the fruit of the tree which is in the midst of the garden, neither shall you touch it, lest you die.'" 4 But the serpent said to the woman, "you will not die. 5 For God knows that when you eat of it your eyes will be opened, and you will be like God, knowing good and evil."

After that, the biblical text says, "So when the woman saw that the tree was good for food, and that it was a delight to the eyes, and that the tree was to be desired to make one wise, she took of its fruit and ate; and she also gave some to her husband, who was with her, and he ate" (Genesis 3:7). The Bible does not describe how Eve convinced Adam to eat, but simply states that she gave him some fruit and he ate. This first deception is described repeatedly in the primary Adam books, and despite some variation of details and emphasis, the basic structure of the story remains stable.[26]

There is only one deception in the biblical narrative. However, both the primary Adam books and the legend of the cheirograph revolve around a second instance in which Satan deceived Adam and Eve. Although both the primary Adam books and the legend of the cheirograph have a second deception, the actual event is very different in these two sources. According to the primary Adam books (5:1–11:3), after their expulsion, Adam and Eve decide on a penance: they will stand in the rivers Jordan and Tigris for fixed numbers of days, "until we learn that, behold, God has hearkened to us and will give us our food" (Armenian *Penitence of Adam* 6:2). In the *Life of Adam and Eve,* Eve is said to stand on a stone in the Tigris River as an act of penance while Adam stands in the Jordan.[27]

This full story of the penance occurs in three versions of the primary Adam books: the Latin, Armenian, and Georgian versions. In them, the penitence narrative stands at the beginning of the book, which opens with the events directly following the expulsion from the Garden. It is not found in the Greek version, however; while in the Slavonic *Life of Adam and Eve* its position and its outcome are different.[28]

At the beginning of the penance, Adam raised the possibility that Eve would fail: "Perhaps you will begin and be unable to repent and God will not hearken" (Armenian *Penitence of Adam* 5:1). Eve's penance indeed fails, not because her stamina is exhausted but because "[w]hen eighteen days of their weeping were completed, then Satan took on the form of a cherub with splendid attire, and went to the Tigris to deceive Eve" (Armenian *Penitence of Adam* 9:1). He succeeded, and Eve came out of the water, thus voiding the penance. Satan led her to Adam. Adam, however, who was still in the river, recognized Satan and cried out to Eve, "How did you go astray to follow him by whom we were alienated from our dwelling?" (Armenian *Penitence of Adam* 10:3). Adam apparently brings his penitential immersion to a successful conclusion, but Eve fell prey to the deceiver, and so the possible amelioration of the human condition on this earth did not take place. The results of the second deception in the primary Adam books are the continued earthly life of Adam and Eve under the curses of the expulsion.[29]

In the Slavonic *Life of Adam and Eve* 28–29, the penitence narrative does not occur at the beginning of the book, but follows Eve's story of the fall.[30] Strikingly, according to the Slavonic *Life of Adam and Eve,* Satan does not succeed in deceiving the penitent Eve. She recognizes him and does not abandon her penance.[31] This seems surprising until we recall that, alone of all the primary Adam books, the Slavonic *Life of Adam and Eve* also has the cheirograph story, and in that story, Satan's deceit is successful. So the Slavonic *Life of Adam and Eve* avoids Satan's deceitful ending of Eve's penance and instead introduces Satan's deception of Adam and Eve through the cheirograph.[32] Clearly, it was felt that a second deception must have taken place immediately after the expulsion to solve issues arising from it. In that position in the plot, Slavonic had the cheirograph story with its deception, and that sufficed. As a result, the Slavonic version effectively annuls the deception connected with the penance, setting it in the middle of the book and relating that Satan failed in his attempt.[33]

Three versions of the primary Adam books (those in Latin, Armenian, and Georgian) do have the penance story at the beginning. In them, Satan succeeds in stopping Eve's penance. Those versions neither have nor need the cheirograph story. This dynamic is corroborated by a later work, the Armenian *Adam, Eve, and the Incarnation*. Although it has a very full form of the story of Adam and Eve, it does not have the penitence narrative, even though it was readily available in Armenian in the *Penitence of Adam*. *Adam, Eve, and the Incarnation* does have the cheirograph story and, consequently, a second deception.

Thus, we may observe that the cheirograph story plays the same role as the narrative of the penance, but with some differences. According to the cheirograph story, instead of having an intention to repent but being deceived by Satan, Adam and Eve err and are deceived by Satan. Instead of the apocopation of Eve's penance, which justified the continued state of human life on earth, in the final analysis the cheirograph is annulled at Christ's baptism, although until then Satan dominates this world. In terms of the economy of salvation, Adam and Eve's sin in the Garden leads to Christ's crucifixion, while their mistake in signing the cheirograph is reversed by Christ's baptism.

Culpability

The issue of redemption also bears on the question of culpability. According to the legend of the cheirograph, Adam and Eve are both deceived and both guilty. Although Adam is mentioned more often, their roles are not substantially different. Moreover, it is worth considering further the nature of the act that caused the fall. As we have said, in Genesis, God's commandment is contravened, which brings punishment in its wake. This pattern is repeated when the primary Adam books relate the second fall. Eve contravenes Adam's commandment, and the punishment for that is the failure of the penance. He had said, "stand silent there in the middle of the water until [you] have done penitence for thirty-four days" (Armenian *Penitence of Adam* 6:2). Yet, Eve's deception is also a lack of perception, and when Adam upbraids her, "'Where is my command of repentance, which I gave you? How did you go astray, to follow him by whom we were alienated from our dwelling?'" the text relates that "when Eve heard this, she knew [or realized] that he who deceived her was Satan" (10:3–11:1).

In the legend of the cheirograph, however, no commandment and no transgression are involved. Is the very making of the agreement with Satan considered to be the transgression? Perhaps, but that is not stated outright.

The question of culpability has become a major issue in modern scholarship of Genesis 3; the traditional interpretations, however, predominantly teach that Eve bears the brunt of the responsibility. The different versions of the primary Adam books have varying attitudes about the protoplasts' culpability for the first fall, but Eve is unambiguously guilty of the second fall.[34] In the cheirograph legend, the blame is borne equally by Adam and Eve.[35]

Satan's Form and the Baptism of Christ

Satan does not appear explicitly in the Genesis story at all; by the period of the Second Temple, however, it was commonly understood that he was the motivator of the events of the fall.[36] Thus, for example, in Wisdom of Solomon we read, φθόνῳ δὲ διαβόλου θάνατος εἰσῆλθεν εἰς τὸν κόσμον πειράζουσιν δὲ αὐτὸν οἱ τῆς ἐκείνου μερίδος ὄντες, "but through the devil's envy death entered the world, and those who belong to his party experience it" (2:24). This text, from about the turn of the era, implies that Satan is connected with the serpent, since in Genesis the deception and subsequent introduction of death are brought about by the serpent; here, however, we read that they happened through "the devil's envy."

In the first seduction, as it was understood in the Second Temple period, Satan takes on the form of a serpent. Thus, in the primary Adam books, Satan speaks through the serpent's mouth, using it as a musical instrument: "Be you, in your form, a lyre for me, and I will pronounce speech through your mouth" (Armenian *Penitence of Adam* 44[16]:4).[37] According to the primary Adam books, in the second seduction Satan takes on the form of an angel: *et transfiguravit se in claritatem angelorum,* "and he transfigured himself into angelic splendor" (Latin *Life of Adam and Eve* 9:1), "then Satan took on the form of a cherub with splendid attire" (Armenian *Penitence of Adam* 9:1). Here again, there is a difference: in the story of the Edenic fall as told by the primary Adam books, Adam does not see Satan; but in the story of the second fall related in those books, he immediately recognizes him despite his angelic form: "And when Adam saw Satan and Eve who was following him" (Armenian *Penitence of Adam* 10:3). In spite of the glorious attire, Adam sees right through Satan's disguise.

The idea of Satan's angelic guise occurs in a number of the forms of the cheirograph legend; but in the legend, there is no stage at which Adam sees through his appearance. Only after the signing of the cheirograph, when the sun sets and Adam and Eve discover the deception, does the truth about the "angelic" figure emerge. Even then, it is not proclaimed explicitly.

The idea that Satan is in fact an angel, with angelic form but differing in color, is to be found in representations in early Christian art. In a sixth-century mosaic in San Apollinare Nuovo in Ravenna, he is shown just like the other angels and distinguished from them only by his color. The Armenian Gagik Gospel of the eleventh century (Jerusalem, Armenian Patriarchate no. J2556), in the scene of the Temptation of Christ, presents Satan as a blue angel with wings (fol. 244; see figure 1). Another early painting of Satan as an angel is in the ninth-century Paris manuscript of Gregory Nazianzus, which is based on a sixth-century exemplar (Paris BnF ms grec 510). These representations are intriguing in view of the Latin text cited previously, where stress is on the luminosity of Satan, with which we may compare Slavonic *Life of Adam and Eve* 38–39:1a, "the devil came to me in the form and radiance of an angel."[38] In Latin *Life of Adam and Eve* 15:3, Satan describes his fall as being "from our glory." Thus, perhaps, the Latin here preserves the original point, that all Satan lacked to look like a heavenly angel was the glory. He lost the glory when he fell, and he could take it on temporarily in order to deceive Adam and Eve.[39]

There are three interwoven themes here. In the first, Satan, who once had heavenly glory and luminosity, puts it back on temporarily in order to deceive Eve and Adam. When he lost his glory, Satan became a different-colored angel and would have been easily recognized. Provided with the σχῆμα "form" of an angel,[40] he becomes externally angelic. In the primary Adam books, Eve is taken in by this σχῆμα "form," but Adam isn't. According to the cheirograph legend, both Adam and Eve are deceived by it. In the story of the first fall in the primary Adam books, Satan enters another being, the serpent, and there is no scene of recognition at all. This is a much more radical change of his external appearance. He has fallen from his heavenly state before creation and is not included in the curses either.

The idea of Satan's σχῆμα is intriguingly correlated with Adam and Eve's recognition of him. In the primary Adam books, as we have said, there is no recognition scene in the first deception story. In the second one, although Eve is deceived, Adam immediately recognizes Satan for what he is; Adam has special perspicacity. In the cheirograph story, they both are deceived, and both come to know who Satan is not through an act of knowing or of recognition, but by inference when they discover that he has deceived them.

At various junctures of the story in the primary Adam books, Satan be-

1. Satan as a blue angel with wings. Fol 244r, Jerusalem Arm. Patr. J2556 "King Gagik Gospels."

comes invisible. The assumed form is not permanent. In *Apocalypse of Moses* 20:3, the Greek text relates that when Satan had succeeded in seducing Eve and Adam, he descended from the tree (here as the snake) καὶ ἄφανατος ἐγένετο, "and vanished" (literally: "became invisible"). When Adam in the river recognized Satan, he asked him why he was so hostile. Satan responded with the story of his fall (12:1–17:3). At the end of the conversation between Adam and Satan, we read *et statim non apparuit diabolus ei,* "immediately the devil was not visible to him" (Latin *Life of Adam and Eve* 17:2). That is to say, Adam saw through Satan's disguise with no difficulty;

Satan, upbraided about his conduct, simply disappeared. The appearance of Satan, his angelic form, is thus shown to be a mirage. Challenged, he disappears from sight.[41]

It is not only Satan, of course, whose appearance changes as events take place. Adam and Eve also change after committing the sin. Following the first seduction, they are both stripped naked (of glory).[42] After the second deception, according to the Georgian *Book of Adam* 10:1, Eve alone is rendered ugly: "her flesh was withered like rotten vegetables . . . all the form of her beauty had been destroyed."

This theme, which is rather prominent in the primary Adam books, plays a lesser role in the cheirograph legend, but persists in references to Satan's angelic disguise (*Adam, Eve, and the Incarnation*, 23, and other sources). It is related to vision or recognition. In the cheirograph legend, only events, not perspicacity, show up Satan the deceiver.

There are, oddly enough, a number of themes that occur in the primary Adam books related to Eve, which are applied differently in various forms of the cheirograph legend. One we have just mentioned: Eve's falling as if dead for three days. This happens to her upon Adam's reprimand, according to the Armenian *Penitence of Adam* 17:3. The period of three days was apparently a period in which souls were thought to remain close to the body. The same period of three days is to be observed in the case of Paul's vision on the road to Damascus (Acts 9:9). The most prominent instance, of course, is the death and resurrection of Christ.[43]

The odd correspondence of Eve and Christ is accentuated by another striking parallel. The legend tells us that at the time of his baptism, Christ stood upon the stone cheirograph that Satan had put in the Jordan River. This scene is represented in many paintings of the baptism, as we will show below, and is a fixed element of Christ's baptism according to the cheirograph legend. We have pointed out above that as part of her penitential undertaking according to the primary Adam books, Eve stood in the Tigris River on a stone.[44] Only in the Latin *Life of Adam and Eve*, and not in any other version of the primary Adam books, is Adam—who might most naturally be paralleled to Christ—placed on a stone. Eve's stone remains unexplained. We do not know how or why she stood on it nor what function it served. The primary Adam books are indubitably older than the cheirograph legend, and it is unclear how the two are related. There is a symmetry, which may not be accidental, between Eve standing on a stone in the Tigris as a penance for her sins (and being deceived by Satan), and Christ standing in the Jordan River on a stone that contains the contract that Satan had duped Adam and Eve into signing.[45]

Adam's standing in the river in the Latin, Armenian, and Georgian versions of *Life of Adam and Eve* 8:3 is, moreover, like the crossing of the Red Sea by the Israelites and the crossing of the Jordan under Joshua. In the pericope, we find both a stone and the stopping of the waters for Adam. Like the Israelites, Adam remained dry.[46] In Psalm 66:6, the two crossings are drawn together: "He turned the sea into dry land; they passed through the river on foot." As we have noted, it was Eve who stood upon a stone in the Tigris, according to the *Life of Adam and Eve*.

The Jordan crossing also played a role in the typology of the baptism of Christ. The miraculous dryness of Adam and of the Israelites, however, could not be repeated when Christ was in the Jordan, because, of course, it was his very baptism with water that formed the heart of the event. Nonetheless, the play of the biblical traditions and typology is quite clear in those forms of the cheirograph legend in which the Jordan rolls back and the stone with the cheirograph is revealed. In fact, in a number of artistic representations, Christ and/or the cheirograph seems to be standing on the water and not submerged (see chapter 4).

In many Slavonic images of the baptism, Christ is shown standing on a stone in the Jordan. Although this element certainly derives from the cheirograph legend, it does not occur in the Slavonic *Life of Adam and Eve*. Nor is Adam said there to stand on a stone, an assertion made only in the Latin version. Where does the Latin *Life of Adam and Eve* find this feature? It is probably not original to the *Life of Adam and Eve* and might have been introduced by analogy with the story of Eve. According to all versions, she stood on a rock.[47]

In our text, Adam, filled with the Holy Spirit, stops the waters just as the priests carrying the ark did in the days of Joshua. This may be an evocation of typological similarity. "When Adam had said that, all moving things which were in the Jordan gathered to him and stood around him like a wall. And the waters of the Jordan stopped at that time and became stationary from their flow" (*Penitence of Adam* [Armenian] 8:3). The crossing of the Jordan becomes a central image for Christian baptism as well. According to Joshua 4, twelve Israelites, one per tribe, gather stones from the Jordan and set them up as a covenant renewal. In the cheirograph story, Satan takes the stone containing the covenant with Adam and puts it into the Jordan. This is an inversion and one of a number of ways the story in Joshua is used by later sources.

Dragon Heads in the Jordan

According to some forms of the legend of the cheirograph, the stone in the river is guarded by serpents. Their heads appear on many icons showing the baptism. The idea may be derived from the plurals "heads of the dragons" and "heads of Leviathan" in Psalm 73(74):13–14. (see figure 6)

> 13 Thou didst divide the sea by thy might;
> thou didst break the heads of the dragons on the waters.
> 14 Thou didst crush the heads of Leviathan,
> thou didst give him as food for the creatures of the wilderness.

In scenes of the baptism, Christ is sometimes depicted trampling a dragon, clearly evoking Psalm 73:13–14. (see figure 6)

This theme is explicit in a number of versions of the legend (see *Adam, Eve, and the Incarnation* §49). It is quite old, as was remarked by Porfirjev,[48] and certainly older than the eighth-century date implied by its utilization by Cosmas of Maimunsk. In a hymn for the baptism (6 January), Ode 11, Troparion 1 Cosmas writes, Ἀδὰμ τὸν φθαρέντα ἀναπλάττει | ῥείθροις Ἰορδάνου καὶ δρακόντων | κεφαλὰς ἐμφωλευόντων.[49] "He restores corrupted Adam by the streams of the Jordan and the heads of the lurking dragons." An intriguing, but later, formulation of this is to be found in the poem *On the Creation of the World* by the Armenian poet Yovhannēs Tʻlkurancʻi (1320?–1400?). Stanza 35, relating the creation of the fifth day, states —

> First of all there came into existence the marine dragon (*višap*) Leviathan,
> A type of Satan, he is killed on the day of the Coming.

R. Stichel has kindly drawn our attention to an illustration of Psalm 143 in a Russian painting of the year 1584 (Moscow, Historical Museum, Uvarov cod. 2° 592, a. 1548). In this composition, we find both the baptism and the Descensus ad Infernos. In the water of the baptism under Christ's feet are dragons, and Christ on the cross is also piercing dragons with a lance.[50] In a painting of the baptism in the exo-narthex of the church of Gračanica, Yugoslavia, dated to around 1530, Christ is shown standing in the Jordan on the doors of Hades.[51] The doors may have been deliberately transferred from the scene of the Harrowing of Hell. One might think that they were introduced here by iconographical error, in place of the stone, but serpents' heads may be seen emerging from beneath them.[52] This would mean that the artist is linking the baptism and Harrowing of Hell, just as they are connected in some rare forms of the cheirograph legend.[53]

2. Icon by Basil Vamboulis, Athens. 1960 Baptism with Christ standing on crossed plaques resembling the doors of hell, with serpents' heads.

The same iconography is to be found on an image painted by Basil Vamboulis in Athens in 1960 (figure 2). Vamboulis was a student of Photis Kontoglou (1895–1965), "a Greek . . . from Asia Minor who, together with his students, was largely responsible for reviving traditional Byzantine iconography in Greece. Kontoglu spent years prowling around ancient monasteries and chapels filling his sketch-pads with images and motifs that few people at that time had ever seen. . . . A close associate and personal friend of Kontoglou, Constantine Cavarnos," gives the following description of this element: "Sometimes Christ is shown standing on two slabs of stone that form a cross, having underneath them serpents raising their heads. This detail is inspired by Psalm 73(74), verse 13, . . . The dragons symbolize the devil and his evil angels. This idea appears in the hymnography of the Church, as do the rest of the features of the baptism which I have described. In good icons, the serpents are not depicted in large dimensions and with bright colours—they are not emphasized. It is best to leave out this feature, because it causes unnecessary distraction from the essential points of the scene. The great masters who did the mosaics of Hosios Lukas, Nea Moni, and Daphni made no use of it."[54] Clearly Kontoglou and Cavarnos simply do not know the legend of the cheirograph, from which the serpents' heads were drawn. The unfamiliarity with the legend, combined with the perpetuation of its iconography, resembles the situation of the nineteenth-century painter of Esphigmenou described below.[55]

CHAPTER THREE

Adam Plows and Satan Forbids: The Slavonic Story

It is striking that the legend of the cheirograph of Adam—which we presently know to exist in Greek, Armenian, Georgian, Slavonic, Bulgarian, and Romanian sources—occurs mostly in narrative apocryphal texts. Patristic exegetical literature discusses a "cheirograph of Adam," but all the patristic references we have seen in the course of our research deal with a different, distinct tradition, context, and concept.[1] They use the same term, χειρόγραφον, "cheirograph," but its meaning differs.

The primary Adam book, the *Life of Adam and Eve,* survives in full in Greek, Latin, Armenian, Georgian, and Slavonic versions, as well as in a small part of a Coptic version.[2] Its transmission and literary history are complex,[3] and each version (except, of course, for that surviving in Greek) was translated from Greek; however, they differ quite dramatically from one another. Some of the differences between them arose in the course of translation and transmission, while others may be attributed to variations among the Greek originals from which they were made. Naturally, the discrimination of these types of variants is a delicate and complex task, and the preparation of a synopsis of the primary Adam books contributes significantly to it.

The *Life of Adam and Eve* was a most influential document, as is evident from the large number of copies that exist in diverse languages. It formed the basis of many later literary and dramatic works, and is also reflected in artistic representations. The following chief narrative elements occur in it, although no single version contains all of them: the fall of Satan; the sin, the judgment, and the expulsion of Adam and Eve; the penitence of Adam and Eve; the birth of Cain and Abel and the murder of Abel; the birth of Seth; Adam's mortal illness; Eve and Seth's quest to the Garden of Eden and Michael's promise; Adam's death; his burial arrangements and interment; and Eve's death.

A narrative about the contract or cheirograph that Adam signed with Satan is unique to the Slavonic version of the *Life of Adam and Eve.* Scholars have often attributed the presence of this legend in the Slavonic *Life of Adam and Eve* to Bogomil influence. The Bogomils were a medieval heretical group, originating in the Balkans in the mid-tenth century.[4] They particularly stressed dualistic doctrines and the idea of Satan as demiurge, creator of the world. They were reputed to be authors of many apocryphal works.[5] The origin of the legend of the cheirograph of Adam is not Bogomil, in any case, as its spread in Oriental Christian traditions outside the Slavonic makes evident.[6]

Jagić edited the text of the Slavonic *Life of Adam and Eve* in 1893 and translated it into German. This edition became well known in the West. In addition to Jagić's work, another edition, based on a variant, sixteenth-century manuscript, was published by Ivanov in 1925.[7] The version of the legend incorporated in the text of the Slavonic *Life of Adam and Eve* that Jagić chose to publish and translate became most familiar to scholars of the Adam literature. In fact, however, three forms of the legend occurring in the Slavonic *Life of Adam and Eve* have been published, and further unpublished forms of it may lie still undiscovered in Slavonic manuscripts.[8]

The date of the translation and redaction of the Slavonic *Life of Adam and Eve* itself is uncertain, but the oldest surviving manuscripts date back to the fourteenth century. Both Jagić[9] and Fuchs[10] hold the view that the Slavonic *Life of Adam and Eve* was translated from Greek. Ivanov notes that the oldest manuscript of the fourteenth century claims to have derived from the *Historical Palaea.* The *Historical Palaea* is a retelling of biblical history, and such works are known in Slavonic and in Greek. In fact, the Slavonic *Life of Adam and Eve* is found neither in the Greek *Palaea* nor in the Slavonic *Historical Palaea.*[11] Of course, more manuscripts of such works exist than have been published, and it is quite possible that an apocryphal Adam book is incorporated into one or another of them.[12]

The Greek manuscript family with which this Slavonic text of the *Life of Adam and Eve* is associated is attested only as far back as the fourteenth century. This is Family II of the Greek text, identified by M. Nagel.[13] Because the older of the two Greek manuscripts is of the fifteenth century, it seems that Nagel's dating of Family II is actually fixed by the fourteenth-century date of the oldest Slavonic manuscripts. Yet a still older date for the actual *Vorlage* of Slavonic seems likely. The oldest published manuscript containing the cheirograph legend is S, of the fifteenth century (see list in appendix 1). If these dates are correct, and even if the hyparchetype of Greek Family II and Slavonic was somewhat older than the oldest extant manuscript, we are dealing with a text-type that developed no later than the early part of the second millennium C.E.

Here, we give new translations of three published Old Church Slavonic texts of the legend of the cheirograph of Adam; in appendix 1 of this book, the texts themselves are published. The texts and translations were prepared by Alexander Kulik, who presents all of the published evidence clearly. Kulik distinguishes three forms of the story. The first, his Variant A, is based on the text published by Ivanov, manuscript S, to which he adds variants from ten further published manuscripts. The edition of Variant B is drawn from the same manuscript, in which it occurs following the text of Variant A. No further copies of Variant B have been published. Variant C is found in a single manuscript, otherwise unidentified, which was published by Tikhonravov in 1863.[14] At the end of the chapter, another, perhaps secondary, form of the legend is considered, which appears in the Slavonic version of the *Apocalypse of Pseudo-Methodius*.

Variant A

TRANSLATION

1 So he (i.e., Adam) took oxen and began to till in order to obtain nourishment.[15] 2 Then the devil came and stood and did not allow Adam to till the earth [= ground] and said to Adam, "Mine is that which belongs to the earth, but heaven and Paradise[16] are God's. Will you be mine and till the earth? Or will you be God's? Then, go to Paradise!" 3 And Adam said, "The heaven and the earth and Paradise[17] and the whole universe are the Lord's." 4 The devil told him, "I will not allow you to till the earth, unless you write me your handwriting[18] that you are mine." Adam told him, "Whoever is lord of the earth, to him I and my children belong." The devil rejoiced. 5 For Adam knew that the Lord would descend on the earth and would take upon himself the form of a man and would tread the devil under his feet.[19]

6 And the devil said, "Write your handwriting for me."[20] And Adam wrote, "Whoever is Lord of the earth, to him I and my children belong."[21]

STRUCTURE

The text presented as Variant A is substantially the same as that found in the English translation of Wells in Charles's *Apocrypha and Pseudepigrapha of the Old Testament,* although it is based on a different manuscript. This text of the legend of the cheirograph is integrated into the Slavonic *Life of Adam and Eve,* and in order to understand it, we must examine its role in that work.

In the Slavonic version of the *Life of Adam and Eve,* the legend is found in the context of Eve's tale of the fall. This includes her narrative of the deception of Adam, God's descent for judgment, and the uncovering of their sin (Slavonic §§ 18–25). Next, the expulsion is related and Adam's request to take with him something of Paradise, particularly food (§§26–29). For seven days Adam and Eve stood mourning before the gates of the Garden; Eve prayed to God and Adam apologized to her.[22] Most of these pericopes are also extant, *mutatis mutandis,* in the other versions of the *Life of Adam and Eve.* The Slavonic *Life of Adam and Eve,* however, has no narrative about the fall of Satan such as occurs in the Latin, Armenian, and Georgian *Lives of Adam and Eve.*[23]

Following this story of the deception, expulsion, and mourning, however, we find material that does not exist at this point in the other versions: a rather extensive form of the story of the penitence (Slavonic *Life of Adam and Eve* §§28–39:5). This incident occurs at the start of the book in Pericope 4 of the Latin, Armenian, and Georgian versions. It is noteworthy that an abbreviated narrative of the penitence occurs in Greek Family II at exactly the same point at which the extensive penitence narrative occurs in Slavonic (after chapter 29). Yet, the actual text of the penitence narrative found in Slavonic is closer to that in the Latin, Armenian, and Georgian versions than it is to that found in Greek Family II. From this, we may infer that the Greek from which Slavonic was translated had a long text of this passage, which was epitomized in the *Vorlage* of Greek Family II. That long text is what was translated into Slavonic.[24]

Within the penitence story, in §§30–34, a passage occurs relating the instruction given by the angel Joël.[25] Joël teaches the protoplasts about agriculture, the separation of the domestic from the wild animals, and the use of oxen in plowing (§30–32.8).[26] Then comes the story of the cheirograph (§33–34) followed by Eve's entreaty of Adam to pray to God for deliverance from the devil (§35). The rest of the penitence story follows "Joël's in-

struction." Nagel raises the significant question of whether "Joël's instruction" went back to the Greek manuscript from which the Slavonic *Life
of Adam and Eve* was translated, or whether it was produced in Slavonic.
He comments,

> Une importance particulière revient à l'insertion du chapître XXXII (com-
> parer *Vie grecque* XXIX,9), où il est raconté comment l'archange Joël en-
> seigne à Adam à domestiquer les animaux et par là à cultiver la terre. La
> comparaison avec les textes grecs *Va Pl* établit que cette interpolation fait
> un tout avec celle des chapîtres XXX à XXXV.[27]

The passage in Slavonic §§30–35 is to be found neither in the epitome in
Greek Family II nor in the full text forms of the penitence narrative in Latin,
Armenian, or Georgian. It is apparently an expansion peculiar to the
Slavonic *Life of Adam and Eve* as, indeed, Nagel argued, and it is marked
off from its context by an *inclusio* (Slavonic *Life of Adam and Eve* §§30–35
[middle]).

The legend of the cheirograph is embedded in this clearly delimited
Slavonic expansion, and it is completely integrated into it. Moreover, Nagel
observes, the theme and ideas of this passage are taken up at a number of
other points in the Slavonic *Life of Adam and Eve*.[28] Thus, our analysis of
Variant A must take account of the whole of §§30–35, which may be di-
vided into three sections: §30–32 being the story of Joël's instruction of
Adam and Eve, §33–34 relating the cheirograph legend, and §35 giving
Eve's entreaty.

JOËL'S INSTRUCTION

The context of this Slavonic expansion is set forth in §28–29. After the expulsion, Adam and Eve became hungry. They did not find food to eat such
as they had eaten in the Garden; although they searched all over the earth,
they did not find anything to eat "except thorns, a wild grass."[29] This is the
food that God had given the animals to eat (cf. 4:2 in the other versions),
and they did not wish to eat it. They despaired and prayed to God. At this
point, in the Latin, Armenian, and Georgian versions, Eve says something
like, "Arise, let us repent for forty days; perhaps God will pity us and give
<us> food which is better than that of the beasts so that we should not be-
come like them."[30] In these three versions, this statement introduces the
narrative of the penance, which follows directly. Eventually, after the
penance and the deception and all the events that accompanied them, God
sent an angel and revealed the secrets of agriculture to Adam and Eve. In

the Slavonic version, this angel is Joël. This search for food and its resolution are to be found in all those versions of *Life of Adam and Eve* that feature the penance story.[31]

The theme of food appears in different forms in the various versions of *Life of Adam and Eve.* When we analyze it, we see that it refers to three types of food. The first is the paradisiacal food that Adam and Eve ate before the expulsion. This is called *esca angelorum* or, as the Armenian puts it, "our food is that which the angels eat."[32] The second type of food is the thorns and wild grass that form the food which God gave the animals to eat. The third type of food is the produce of agriculture, which God ordered the archangel to teach Adam and Eve. Agriculture is viewed ambiguously: its revelation is an act of divine grace, but the labor of cultivation is part of Adam's curse.[33]

There has been considerable speculation about the paradisiacal food. In *Aboth de Rabbi Nathan,* an early midrashic writing, we read, "Rabbi Judah ben Bathyra says: Adam was reclining in the Garden of Eden and ministering angels stood before him roasting meat for him and cooling wine for him. Along came the serpent and saw him, beheld his glory, and grew jealous of him" (Recension A, chapter 1).[34] Not all the Rabbinic traditions saw the paradisiacal food as roast meat, but the deprivation from whatever food it might have been was regarded as a very grave matter. Thus, a little further on in *Aboth de Rabbi Nathan,* we read (in a discussion of Adam's curses in Genesis 3:17–18), "As Adam heard the Holy One, blessed be He, say to him *And thou shalt eat the herb of the field,* he trembled in every limb [showing he had repented]. 'Master of the Universe,' he cried, 'shall my beast and I eat out of the same crib?'" Adam's repentance was successful, and he was given a concession. "Said the Holy One, blessed be He to him, 'Because thou didst tremble in every limb, *in the sweat of thy face shalt thou eat bread*'" (Genesis 3:19).[35]

Exactly the same process may be observed in the penitence narrative in the *Life of Adam and Eve.* First they refuse to eat animal food; then they repent; after that they learn about agriculture. This development is based on the confrontation of Genesis 3:19 with Genesis 1:29. The curse (Genesis 3:19) reduces them to the level of animals ("and you shall eat the plants of the field,"), but the repentance returns them to the level of the blessing given in Genesis 1:29; "I have given you every plant yielding seed that is upon the face of all the earth, and every tree with seed in its fruit; you shall have them for food."[36]

In order to benefit from the blessing of Genesis 1:29, however, the first created ones needed to learn about agriculture. This knowledge is granted to them in response to a prayer following their fruitless search for the "angelic food." In the Armenian and Georgian versions of the *Life of Adam and Eve,* Michael instructs them in agriculture (20:1). The incidents of Eve's deception by Satan and Satan's story of his own fall separate Adam's prayer for food offered in the river (8:1) from the agricultural instruction in 20:1. Nonetheless, the agricultural teaching clearly remains a response to the search and prayer for food. In the Latin version, the revelation of agricultural knowledge is given even later in the course of events, after the birth of Cain in 22: 1.[37] In the Slavonic *Life of Adam and Eve,* however, Joël's teaching is linked closely with the preceding failure of the search for nourishment, so the problem of food is given an immediate and satisfactory response. In *Adam, Eve, and the Incarnation* §21, we find the same order of events as in the Slavonic *Life of Adam and Eve,* but that work is a rewriting of the Adam and Eve story that does not contain the penance pericope at all.[38]

In the context of Joël's instruction, the Slavonic version alone mentions Adam's naming of the animals (30–32.8), and this is tied directly to the domestication of animals. Thus the naming, the domestication of animals, and Adam's taking the oxen and plowing are all connected.[39] This tightening and increased integration of the story line is presumably part of the work of the editor of the Slavonic *Life of Adam and Eve.*

Just before that unit of text, in §25–27, Eve describes the expulsion.[40] Adam, she says, prayed for incense to take with him. Before making his final decision whether to grant Adam's prayer for incense, God consults the angel Joël. The angelic host begs God to have mercy on Adam. God responds with an assertion of his justice, which is echoed by the angels, but he concludes by granting Adam and Eve the spices they request.[41]

The content of the story in the next pericope of the Slavonic (§28–29) parallels chapters 1–3 of Latin, Armenian, and Georgian (expulsion and search for food). In 4:3, the other versions introduce the penance, whereas the Slavonic produces what is essentially a bridging text. Adam and Eve return to Paradise and beseech God for food. At this juncture, the Slavonic starts a substantial addition, including "Joël's instruction." Adam and Eve pray for fifteen days and hear the archangel Joël also praying for them, a reprise of Joël's role in the preceding section (§25–27).[42]

God responds to the prayers and takes a one-seventh portion from Paradise and gives it to Adam and Eve (§§30–32.4). We must presume that the mysterious phrase "one-seventh portion from Paradise" signifies the instruction about beasts and agriculture that is the content of Joël's teaching. This does not return Adam and Eve to the paradisiacal state, but it resolves the search for food. Adam and Eve have now the information necessary to grow their own food, and thus they achieve a status that is above that of the animals, but not a return to Eden.[43]

It is worth observing that, according to the form of the cheirograph legend in the Slavonic *Life of Adam and Eve*, after their expulsion Adam and Eve encounter a problem related to food. The material dealing with food in the Slavonic *Life of Adam and Eve* differs, in both content and structure, from that in the other versions of the *Life of Adam and Eve*. The passage we have identified as a Slavonic expansion intervenes (§§30–34) between the prayer for food and the act of penance, and the proposal to fast and repent occurs following the Slavonic expansion. In this position, the proposed repentance is not designed to get food, for the problem of food has been resolved by Joël's instruction (§§30–31). Instead, it is a penance intended to undo the results of the cheirograph, as we read in §35–37.2: "But I (Eve), my children, said to your father, Adam, 'Arise, my husband, pray to God, that he deliver us from the devil, for you suffer so on my account.'"

A final observation on this telling of the legend is about the ideas of culpability and deceit. According to Slavonic *Life of Adam and Eve* §38–39, Eve recognized the devil at the time of the trial in the river. She is thus exculpated; this contrasts with the other versions, in which Eve is deceived in the river and only Adam recognizes the disguised Satan. The themes of recognition and culpability are discussed above.[44] Adam, when he issues forth from the water, sees the devil's footsteps and fears lest the devil has deceived Eve, but he has not.[45]

Just as in the other versions of the story, the element of deceit is present in the Slavonic Variant A of the legend of Adam's contract, but with a difference. Usually Satan is the deceiver. In Slavonic *Life of Adam and Eve* Variant A, however, Satan did not deceive Adam and Eve: he blackmailed them. In response to the extortion, Adam deceived Satan; Satan wanted a pledge that "you belong to me," and Adam, who knew that God is owner of the earth as well as the heavens, gave a pledge to submit to "whoever is Lord of the earth." The devil, the story tells us, was *nevertheless* extremely pleased. The phrase "heavens are the Lord's" comes from Psalms 115:16.[46] Adam knew very well that Satan was not lord of the universe, but he formulated the conditions of his undertaking to Satan in such a way that the blackmailer was himself taken in. The text explains, "For Adam knew that the Lord would descend on the earth and would take upon himself the form of a man and would tread the devil under his feet" (§5).

Moreover, there is another literary "oversight" in this text. At no point does it mention explicitly the annulling of the cheirograph. Adam's deception leaves the cheirograph in Satan's hands until the incarnation of Christ. Only until that time does Satan continue to hold power over the human race. But this is not made explicit here, nor is the means by which the cheirograph is annulled. This is doubtless due to the story line of the Slavonic *Life of Adam and Eve*, which extends only to the protoplasts' death.

Variant B

The second version of the Slavonic text occurs only in one single copy, Ms pp, in which it is clearly an insertion. It follows Variant A of the story of the cheirograph and is introduced as an alternative version of the same events. Intriguingly, there is no attempt to integrate it with the context. We have supplied Alexander Kulik's translation with section numbers.

TRANSLATION

1 And there is written differently in the holy writing:[47]
2 Adam was in Paradise glorifying God with archangels and angels in the unfading light. 3 When he was banished from Paradise for his crime (and Adam did not know that before him God had created night and day), he sat opposite Paradise and mourned the paradisiacal living. 4 And night came, and it was dark, and Adam cried saying, "Woe is me who broke God's commandment and was banished from the luminous paradisiacal life and from the supernal, unfailing light! Oh my most luminous light!" he said, weeping and sobbing, 5 "Can it be that I shall not see your radiance and your unfading light, nor shall I regard the paradisiacal beauty? O Lord, have mercy on me, (who have) fallen,"
6 And the devil came to him and told him, "Why do you groan and sob?"
7 Adam said, "For the sake of the light of the most luminous Paradise which is concealed because of me." 8 The devil said to him, "I shall give you light. Inscribe yourself (as belonging) to me by your handwriting and also (about) your family and children." 9 And Adam gave him the handwriting for the sake of light. And he wrote this, "To whom belongs light, to him I and my children belong." And day came and light shone in all the universe.
10 And the devil took Adam's handwriting and hid it (in the Jordan under a stone where Christ was baptized).[48]

This unit of text is introduced by a superscription, which indicates that it is an alternative version. The superscription quotes a "holy writing" (perhaps a religious manuscript; clearly it cannot be the Bible, for this incident does not occur there), which preserves an alternative version of the preceding events.

Variant B differs very considerably from the preceding "agricultural" story (Variant A) and resembles the stories of the cheirograph as they are told in most other languages. Instead of focusing on agriculture and food, this passage focuses on light and darkness. This theme permeates this version. The light of Paradise was unfading (§2), and Adam, when he was banished, did not know that God had created the succession of night and day (§3). According to Genesis 1:14–18, the luminaries were created on the third day, and Adam was created on the sixth day. Nonetheless, at the time of the incident related in Slavonic Variant B, Adam had experienced only the perpetual light of Paradise. Consequently, he had never seen night, even though it had been created before him. Next, Variant B relates Adam's banishment from "the luminous Paradise" (§4) and his lament to the lost Paradise proclaims, "O my most luminous light!" (§4).[49]

The devil asks Adam why he is weeping and lamenting. Adam tells him that it is because the most luminous light is concealed from him (§7). Satan offers to bring the light "in exchange for your handwriting," i.e., an agreement by which Adam subjects himself and his descendants to Satan (§9). Day came, and "light shone in all the universe" (§9). Thus, this telling of the legend is centered on light, thereby resembling nearly all the other retellings of this story, except for Variant A of the Slavonic *Life of Adam and Eve* and its congeners.

A number of particular points should be made about the literary structure of this text. As for the plot, there is no search story such as we find in the primary Adam books: Adam appears onstage, expelled and mourning his expulsion. He prays for restoration to paradisiacal light; the theme of the angelic food is completely absent.[50] Night falls, and the author is careful to inform us why night was a problem for Adam—he did not know about its existence. Nightfall causes Adam to redouble his mourning and opens the way for the devil's deception. The devil offers to bring the light if Adam will make himself and his descendants the devil's property. Adam responds to the proposal by writing, "To whom belongs the light, to him I and my children belong" (§9). Then day comes, and Satan takes the cheirograph and hides it, and, according to a piece of text that has been scratched out but not completely obliterated, he hides it in the Jordan, under a stone, where Christ was baptized (§10).

As it stands, this story lacks a number of elements that would give it coherency. Like Variant A, it accounts only for the enslavement of Adam and his descendants to the devil, but not for their release. On the face of it, the devil seems to strike a fair deal because the story does not explain that his deception is uncovered when the second night comes. The sentence "Adam did not know that before him God had created night and day" implies clearly that, in fact, later Adam discovered Satan's deception, but this is not stated explicitly. Equally, in this narrative, Adam does not learn what the devil's eventual fate will be.

Nonetheless, Adam's undertaking to the devil is ambiguous. It is formulated just like his undertaking in Variant A, which says, "Whoever is the lord of the earth, to him I and my children belong" (§33–34:7).[51] The phrasing is almost identical, and the implication is the same, that Adam is deceiving the devil. Yet Variant B does not have the explanation that Variant A offers, that Adam knew about the coming redemption. An additional peculiarity of this narrative, in contrast with that in Variant A, is the complete absence of Eve. This is particularly striking in light of the reinterpretation of Eve's role in the Slavonic *Life of Adam and Eve,* pointed out above. She is given a very prominent role in Variant A, which avoids inculpating her in any way. However, she is completely absent from Variant B.

The unevenness in the narrative is partly explained by the fact that Variant B is not a complete tale, but only an alternative version excerpted from another source by the copyist of the manuscript. The copyist was interested, apparently, in the most striking difference between the two versions, i.e., the nature of the problem the protoplasts encountered. In Variant B, the problem is light and not agriculture. The scribe has copied the Slavonic *Life of Adam and Eve,* which includes Variant A, and into this he inserts only that part of a second version available to him, the part that is focused on light. This is the most probable explanation for the missing elements, and Variant B is apparently only the first part of a full form of the legend.[52]

The last verse, moreover, is even more unusual. In a number of versions of the legend, such as here, the devil takes the cheirograph and keeps it. Indeed, because it is a promissory note given him by Adam, that is a natural thing for Satan to do. In Variant A, however, this element is not found in the oldest manuscripts, whereas it is more developed in Variant B. There, not only does the devil take and hide the cheirograph, but he hides it under a stone upon which Christ will stand at the time of the baptism.

This detail is in exact agreement with a number of other forms of the legend, which will be related below. It also is exactly what is reflected in the iconography of certain Greek, Moldavian, and Russian representations of the baptism, which are discussed in chapter 4. There seem to be two versions of what Christ stands on at the baptism. One version has him trampling a dragon/snake.[53] Another version has him standing on a stone. Both of these versions occur in artistic representations and in narratives.

The origins of the stone are intriguing. We previously discussed the stone upon which Eve stood at the time of her penance according to the *Life of Adam and Eve*. This stone is not explained at all in the *Life of Adam and Eve*. In various versions of the legend of the cheirograph, a flat stone features on which Adam signs or writes the undertaking itself. In the present Slavonic *Life of Adam and Eve*, Variant B, however, there is no indication that the stone is inscribed, only that the cheirograph is hidden underneath it. Is this form of the story a development of what is told about Eve in the penance narrative in the various versions of *Life of Adam and Eve*, or is it a reuse of the flat stone tradition, in which the flat stone has lost its function as that upon which the agreement is written? This is impossible to determine.

There are some further peculiarities of this form of the story that should be considered. The theme of knowledge, which was so striking in Variant A, is scarcely present in Variant B. It is true that, in §3, Adam's ignorance of the nature of night is the major factor enabling Satan to deceive him, but this is the only point at which Adam's knowledge is mentioned. Satan is not said to present himself as a luminous angel, and thus the question of whether Adam can see through Satan's disguise is not raised. We are led to ask whether the absence of this theme is related to the absence of Eve from the story. In the primary Adam books, this "knowledge" material clusters around Eve, which is natural because the second deception in them is, in a sense, a replay of the initial deception of Eve in the Garden of Eden.

Thus, when we examine this form of the legend as a literary work in its own right, we feel a sense of incompleteness. Most probably this is because the legend is in fact incomplete, although, as we have pointed out, we cannot know how incomplete it is. A further, very significant point emerges from this story as it stands. The form of legend of the cheirograph that included the light as a pivotal issue did exist in the Slavonic tradition, although it was not integrated into the *Life of Adam and Eve*. By which work, we may ask, was it borne and where is it to be found? We cannot answer this question in the present state of knowledge, but it would not be in the least surprising if the "light" form of legend of the cheirograph were to turn up in as yet unpublished Slavonic apocrypha. Considering the spread of the form of the legend of the cheirograph centering on light, it may well be typologically older than the "agricultural" version that is found in Slavonic Variant A. The agricultural form of the legend of the cheirograph in the Slavonic *Life of Adam and Eve,* as is abundantly clear from our earlier discussion, is carefully crafted so as to be integrated into the special material of the Slavonic version of the primary Adam book. It could be a reinterpretation of the light legend in view of the imperatives of the concerns of the translator-editor of the Slavonic *Life of Adam and Eve.*[54]

Thus, this incomplete copyist's insertion into a single manuscript of the Slavonic *Life of Adam and Eve* provides very important information. It teaches us that the "light" version of the legend of the cheirograph circulated in Old Church Slavonic and was available to the editor-copyist of Ms pp or its *Vorlage* so that he introduced it as an alternative tradition to the one he found in his text. This enables us, presumably, to date the "light" form of the tradition before Ms pp, which is of the sixteenth century. This date takes us back to the time before many of the Moldavian and Armenian witnesses to the tradition.

Nothing in this material indicates the provenance of the tradition. More information from Slavonic sources is very desirable indeed to assist in this respect. Only one piece of evidence is known that bears on this question, and it is equivocal. The Slavonic word that we render as "cheirograph" or "letter of agreement" is Old Russian *rukopisanie,* which, as Kulik comments, is literally "handwriting" and has the usual meaning of "official writing," or "registration record."[55] In the cheirograph texts, however, it reflects the Greek χειρόγραφον, "cheirographon," which does have the meaning of "bill of indebtedness" or "contract."[56] Indeed, it means exactly that in both Variants A and B. The meaning assigned to the word is calqued from its Greek sense and is not its usual Slavonic meaning. Thus, this linguistic usage may indicate that the tradition was formed in Greek, translated into Slavonic, and then reworked in Slavonic. In the Slavonic Version C, which is presented below, the word χειρόγραφον, "cheirographon," which is calqued into Slavonic, is given a simple etiological explanation. The agreement is called a χειρόγραφον, "cheirographon," because of the "writing of hands," i.e., the handprints, left on the rock by Adam's bloody hands.

Above we pointed out in connection with the legend that a χειρόγραφον, "cheirographon," was usually pronounced out loud by the person incurring the debt and giving his or her signature.[57] In Variant B, the oral element of this type of agreement has disappeared, and it has become a written document. In Variant A, however, both the oral and written forms of Adam's undertaking are maintained. The ancient process of making a χειρόγραφον, "cheirographon," has left footprints in Variant A, but not in Variant B. As a result of the literal meaning of the Old Russian word, Variant A has actually introduced a written form of the undertaking alongside the oral one, while Version B has lost the oral one altogether.

Variant C

TRANSLATION

1 The holy Apostle Bartholomew asked the holy Apostle Andrew how and in what way our forefather Cain had been born and how our forefather Adam had given a handwriting to the devil.

2 Our forefather Cain was born nasty; his head was like others, <but> on his breast and forehead there were twelve snake heads. 3 When Eve suckled him, the snake heads tormented her stomach, and our original mother Eve was covered by a scab because of this torment and fierce torture.[58] 4 Adam, having seen his wife suffering a lot, grieved for her. The devil came to him in the form of a man and told him, "What would you give me, if I heal your son Cain and deliver your wife Eve from this torture?" 5 Adam told him, "But what would I give you?" And the devil said, "Give me a handwriting concerning yourself." Adam told him, "What handwriting should I give you?" 6 The devil said, "Slaughter a goat and mark on a stone which I shall give you and say this, 'The living are God's and the dead are yours.'" 7 And Adam did as the devil ordered him and (the devil) brought a large stone plaque for him and Adam slaughtered a goat and poured out the blood into a vessel and moistened both of his hands in that blood. 8 He put his hands on the plaque of white stone and Adam's hands were depicted on the plaque.

9 The devil approached Cain and plucked off the twelve snake heads and put them on the stone and on the handwriting and cast it into the Jordan river and ordered the snake heads to guard the handwriting.

10 It was guarded by the snake heads until the advent of our Lord Jesus Christ. And when He came to the Jordan to be baptized for our salvation, the snake heads stood in the streams of the Jordan before him, and he smashed the snakes' heads in the water.[59] 11 The devil saw the snake heads smashed, and then the devil took remainders of the handwriting and brought them to Hell where the saints were imprisoned. 12 When our Lord Jesus Christ arose from the dead, he also tore the remainders of Adam's handwriting to pieces and expiated it. And he bound the devil and released the souls from hell and brought them to the first <kind of>

Paradise, the Paradise,[60] to his Father and according to his own will. 13
From ancient Roman parchment manuscripts of *The Passion of Christ.*

The third Slavonic version was published by Tikhonravov in 1863. He notes
that the manuscript was of Old Believer origin and was new, i.e., apparently
nineteenth-century. This form of the story is of particular interest. It is
difficult to assess, however, because of the absence of further details about
the manuscript. At the end of the text is a small colophon attributing it to
"ancient Roman parchment manuscripts of *The Passion of Christ.*" The word
"Roman" apparently means "Catholic," and *The Passion of Christ* is known
in a West Russian (Catholic) version. This seems to suggest a Western origin for this form of the cheirograph legend, but nothing is known in Latin,
for example, resembling this incident.[61]

The text starts with a strange attribution: the Apostle Bartholomew
asked the Apostle Andrew about the birth of Cain and the cheirograph of
Adam. This very conjunction of subjects is strange and unparalleled although, as we have indicated, one Slavonic text combines the cheirograph
motif with Abel's burial. In the *Life of Adam and Eve,* the birth of Cain is
problematic.[62] It is described as follows by the Armenian *Penitence of Adam*
(21:3): "Then, when she bore the child, the color of his body was like the
color of stars. At the hour when the child fell into the hands of the mid-
wife, he leaped up and, with his hands, plucked up the grass of the earth
near his mother's hut; and infertilities became numerous in that place."
Moreover, Eve's labor and parturition were very difficult and dangerous.

In addition, in the various versions there seems to be a secret surrounding
Cain, for Adam is commanded not to reveal to Cain the mystery that he
knows: "Reveal not the mystery that you know to Cain your son, for he is
a son of wrath" (Greek *Apocalypse of Moses* 3:2a and parallels in Armenian,
Georgian, and Slavonic *Life of Adam and Eve* 23 [3]:2a). Yet the primary
Adam book never reveals what this mystery is. Traditions exist according
to which Cain is not the son of Eve and Adam, but the son of Eve and Satan.[63] This idea is avoided rather carefully in the *Life of Adam and Eve,* but
nonetheless some mystery surrounds Cain's birth. It is interesting to note
that this text knows of the devil's disguise (§4), but he takes on the form
of a man and not of an angel.

Variant C of the Slavonic version of the legend is the most important
literary document we shall examine that has two stages of annulment of the
cheirograph: the first at the baptism and the second at the crucifixion and

Harrowing of Hell. The introduction of the latter incident here is the secondary combination of two distinct traditions. It resembles the Russian painting of the year 1548 referred to above, in which baptism and crucifixion are shown side by side as two parts of Christ's fight against Satan and dragons.[64] Yet no representation of the cheirograph is to be found in this painting. In the Slavonic text "From the Sea of Galilee," quoted in chapter 4, no. 2, Satan takes the cheirograph to hell directly, and the Jordan River and baptism are not mentioned; the Romanian folktale, chapter 4, no. 7 is similar. The Bulgarian tale, no. 10, has Christ destroy the cheirograph on the Jordan. It adds a descent into Hades, but no hint at the cheirograph. According to this tale, the contract is in Hades.[65]

According to Slavonic Variant C, the agreement is called a χειρόγρα-φον, "cheirographon," because of the "writing of hands," i.e., the handprints, left on the rock by Adam's bloody hands. In the final analysis, then, by combining Christ's baptism and crucifixion, this text draws together the two meanings of χειρόγραφον, "cheirographon." It combines the meaning "contract" found in the legend with the meaning "bill of indebtedness" of Colossians 2:14.

The element of the blood on Adam's hands is remarkable. In Slavonic Variant C, it is the blood of a goat.[66] In the Bulgarian folktale cited by Ivanov (chapter 4, no. 7), the devil scratches Adam's thumb so he can sign the cheirograph with his blood. A variant is Megas's Modern Greek story recorded in Thrace, according to which Adam's hand provides ink for the cheirograph written with his blood. It is washed clear in Hades by Christ's blood.

This story fits admirably with the iconography of the baptism, and indeed might derive from it. This ambiguity of derivation is particularly true of the serpent heads. The type of baptism scene in which Christ is standing on a stone from which serpents' heads issue is widespread, as will be seen in the next chapter (see figures 3 and 4). One explanation of the unusual incident about Eve and Cain in the present chapter is that it is a late etiology of the iconography.

A further point is that Satan asks for the dead and cedes the living to Adam. This is to be found in story no. 7 in the next chapter, as well as in the story found in Pseudo-Methodius, discussed below. It surely derives from the development of the idea of Christ's descent into Hades and his freeing of the dead. The story explains how they got there. An alternative form of this statement, with different referents, is that Satan is ruler of this world and of the dead. Because Christ will free the enslaved of this world through baptism and the dead enslaved to Satan through crucifixion, these different formulations correspond to varying forms of the legend.

It is important to note that in the Slavonic version of Pseudo-Methodius, there exists another distinct variant of this story. The devil will not allow Adam to bury Abel until Adam has given his cheirograph (*rukopisanie*) in his own hand that "the living are yours and the dead are mine."[67] It is intriguing that in Pseudo-Methodius, this tradition is tied to a different locus in the Adam stories. The burial of Abel was the subject of speculation in a number of forms, none of which resembles Pseudo-Methodius.[68] Thus, for example, in the primary Adam books we read, "For he had remained from that day upon which Cain the lawless one had killed him and had wished to hide him, and had been unable. For, as soon as his body was in the dust, a heavenly voice came and said, 'It is not permitted to hide him [in] the earth [before] the first creature (i.e., Adam) has returned to the earth from which he came'" (48[40]:4–5a Armenian and Georgian).[69] Clearly some such tradition might have provided a *point d'appui* for introducing the cheirograph incident. Both in the case of the burial of Abel and in the story of Adam's plowing, the cheirograph incident is introduced at a fitting place in the narrative tradition. In both, the issue of the rule over the earth is potentially present; in both cases, it is a matter of the earth being dug up and Satan being regarded as ruler over the earth.

It seems that this confrontation between Adam and the devil became associated with varied contexts in the Adam stories in the Slavonic tradition. Adam's plowing the field was one, and this was readily transferred to the burial of Abel, about which traditions of various sorts existed. The text from Christ's dispute with the devil, mentioned in note 8, is another example of the anchoring of this theme at various points in the Slavonic tradition. There it is a confrontation with the devil that serves the function of *point d'appui*.

CHAPTER FOUR

The Legend in Balkan Art, Folklore, and Tradition

The cheirograph legend spread in an extraordinary way in the Romanian and Moldavian areas. It seems that it reached these regions in a form resembling the Old Church Slavonic, particularly but not exclusively that in Variant A, which is reflected by many of these sources.[1] We start the description of the evidence with folktales from Romania.

Romanian Folktales

1. Kretzenbacher cites the following popular Romanian tale:

> In order to be able to cultivate the earth, which belonged to the Evil One, Adam concluded a pact with the devil after the expulsion from Paradise. According to this pact, Satan permitted Adam to plow, on the condition that Adam abandon to him the souls of his descendants after death. Christ, nevertheless, tore up this pact.[2]

This tale, which bears no date, clearly reflects the version of the cheirograph legend featuring the plowing found in Slavonic Variant A. This we have called the "agricultural" form of the legend.[3] The context in which Christ destroyed this pact is not specified.

2. A sixteenth-century Slavonic text entitled *From the Sea of Galilee* relates the following. It too is clearly linked with Slavonic Variant A.

The Lord sent his archangel Michael to instruct Adam in agriculture. Adam set about tilling the ground and was accosted by Satan, who asked him by whose authority he was acting. Adam said, "The Lord commanded me (to do) it." And Satan said, "The heaven belongs to the Lord, but the earth is mine. If you wish to cultivate the earth, give me a cheirograph about you and all your offspring who come after you." And Adam said, "If the earth is yours, then I am also yours." Adam wrote a contract (cheirograph) subjecting all his descendants to Satan. The latter took the contract to hell, and, on its basis, he seized all of Adam's descendants up to the crucifixion of Christ.[4]

It is notable that the Jordan River and the baptism of Christ play no role in this form of the legend, and that the terminus of Satan's rule will be the crucifixion. The contract's destruction is not described here.

3. In a Slavonic cosmogonic text preserved in an eighteenth-century manuscript, we find the following short passage:

And Satan heard Adam's groans on account of the sin, and, as he was deceitful and envious from of old, he came to Adam and said to him, "I wish to give you a joyful tiding. The Lord will have mercy upon you. Give me a contract (cheirograph) about yourself and all your offspring."[5]

Satan's envy is, of course, a popular theme from antiquity, and is seen as the force motivating his hatred of Adam and Eve.[6] This text is a very partial reference to the legend, and it is impossible to tell whether the cheirograph story was about agriculture or about light.

4. The Romanian *Plaint of Adam,* a popular song extant in many copies, is the history of Adam's expulsion, and the angelic promise and counsel to him to repent.[7] It is connected with the office for the Sunday before Lent, called "the Sunday of the Renunciation of Cheese," which, particularly in vespers, is completely consecrated to the banishment of Adam from Paradise.[8] This is extremely interesting, since the Armenian texts that will be discussed below were also associated with the fast of Aṙaǰawor, which also precedes Lent.[9]

5. Another Romanian poem starts in the same way as the *Plaint of Adam.*[10] Adam bewails his fate. God sends an angel to teach him that he must work the ground and beget numerous descendants. Many copies of the poem survive; the following extracts are based on a copy from the nineteenth century,[11] cited by Turdeanu, and on a new translation of a part of it.[12] Like the

preceding texts, this poem clearly depends on the form of the legend to be found in Variant A of the Slavonic *Life of Adam and Eve*. As Adam starts to work the ground, Satan intervenes (as happens in the numerous retellings of Slavonic Variant A).[13]

> Who has commanded you / to do me these damages
> and ruin [my] land, / being that here I am lord?
> Adam said, / "God has so commanded me."
> Then Satan answered / and said thus to Adam,
> "I am god here, / and the land is mine.
> So flee from here to paradise / for there is your estate.[14]
> I will not allow you here, /neither will I give you the ground."[15]

Adam yields in the end and proposes the agreement. Satan asks Adam to formalize it by a handprint on a brick of sandstone and goes to hide it in the Jordan under a large stone, not too far from the bank.[16]

In another version of the poem, cited by Turdeanu, Satan is said to take mud and make a brick with the cheirograph on it.[17] He dries it and fires it.[18] Then he sets a hundred demons to guard the cheirograph. When Christ is being baptized, he comes to the Jordan and stands on the rock where Adam's contract is hidden, which is guarded by the demons.[19] When he wishes to get out of the water, the stone turns over and crushes the dragon heads. The cheirograph floats to the surface, and Christ takes it and crushes it to dust.[20] Like Slavonic Variant B §10, the cheirograph is not a stone, but under a stone.

6. Another Romanian folktale, included in a collection published in 1944, is clearly a cheirograph narrative.[21]

> The action commences with Adam plowing: Satan comes and denies him permission to plow, saying that the field is his. Adam says that he will go to another field, and Satan forbids this, too. Adam asks what he should do, then, go to the devil to ask permission? And the devil says, with a certain humor, that he already has. He takes off his hat and shows Adam his horns. Satan then says that all can be arranged if Adam will make an agreement with him. Adam does so, and all his descendants belong to Satan.
>
> Satan asks for the contract to be written. Adam says he cannot write, because when he was small there was no school for either Hungarians or Romanians.[22] Satan brings a large brick and inscribes the contract. Adam puts a handprint on the brick. Satan takes the brick to hell and guarantees the subservience of Adam's offspring until Christ's Anastasis.

As it stands, this story is directly dependent on Variant A of the Slavonic *Life of Adam and Eve,* i.e., on the plowing motif. The agricultural form of the legend is to be observed in many of the retellings here (see nos. 1, 2, 5, 6, 9, and 10). It is frequently connected with one or another form of the assertion that heaven or Paradise is the Lord's and earth is Satan's. See Slavonic Variant A §2 and stories nos. 2, 5, and 9 here. The introduction of the brick is a variant found in *Plaint of Adam* (story no. 5), and it is also to be observed in a Greek folktale given in chapter 6. The brick here is put not in the Jordan but in hell, where Christ goes and destroys it in his descent into the underworld. This is a variant found in a few versions, in which the legend of the cheirograph is connected not with the baptism but with the crucifixion, and is combined with Colossians.

Bulgarian Folktales

7. Jordan Ivanov published a Bulgarian folktale, recorded by Filip Janev from the village of Prilep. The story goes as follows:

> When Adam and Eve were expelled from the Garden, they wandered for some hours; and when darkness fell, they sat under a tree affrighted. Adam reproached Eve for seducing him and causing his expulsion from the Paradise of light. Eve sat despairing and covered her eyes against the dark.
>
> The devil heard this and waited until toward dawn. "Why are you afraid? Did the Lord expel you as he expelled me?" he asked. "You are responsible for this, not God, because you tricked us into eating of the tree." The devil said, "Fear not! I am lord of the darkness. I will bring light and if you are in my hands, you will become monarchs of the earth." Adam assented, and the devil insisted that they not regret or deny him. Adam asked the devil for his little finger so that they might become blood brothers. The devil asked him to put his thumb on a rock and that he accept the oath that "the living are yours and the dead are mine." Adam, at Eve's urging, agreed; the devil scratched his thumb with his nail, and Adam signed the cheirograph with his blood. Satan took the stone and hid it at the deepest point of the Jordan River. The devil taught Adam and Eve how to build a hut, which they did.
>
> Thenceforth Adam lived with the devil and obeyed him. After their (Adam's and Eve's) death, all Adam's children belonged to the devil. When Adam died, he was in eternal torments until Christ entered the Jordan to be baptized. The place of the baptism was also that of the cheirograph, and when Christ was baptized he broke the cheirograph. He later de-

scended to Hades and brought all out from there, and all the demons fled. Only one man remained there.[23]

This story reflects the version of the cheirograph legend that is focused on the light. It was the darkness that brought about Adam's willingness to enter into a contract with Satan. Some features are notable. There is no disguise and no deception. Satan is there in his own form; Adam willingly enters into the contract; there is no divine promise mentioned, nor any "anti-cheirograph" given Adam by God. Moreover, here the feature of the cheirograph being written in Adam's blood comes to the fore, blood extracted by Satan's nail. In this respect, this Bulgarian folk tradition resembles a Greek popular tale (see chapter 6). Serpents or demons as guardians of the cheirograph are not mentioned at all. Christ destroys it upon his baptism, and he also frees Adam and Eve from Satan. A further theme of this text is Satan's realm. He is lord of the darkness, and he takes the dead as his possession, while Adam has the living. This is exactly the same expression used by Slavonic Variant C §6 and in no. 8.

8.   Another Bulgarian folktale reported by Ivanov also has its roots in the idea of Satan as prince of this world, and contains a transformation of the legend of the cheirograph. The story is from Panagjuriste. Our summary follows.

> The devil wished to divide the world into two. "Let the earth be mine," he said, "and the heavens yours; let us divide humans and you take the living and I will take the dead." The Lord agreed but demanded that Satan sign a cheirograph so that the matter would be clear. After the expulsion, Adam and Eve started to work the soil, and Satan objected. . . . God regretted his action, for Satan oppressed both righteous and wicked. He sent an angel to get the contract back. The angel deceived Satan by a ruse and took the contract and flew to heaven with it.[24]

Although on the face of it this story is about a contract between God and the devil, in fact, behind it lies the agricultural version of the legend of the cheirograph. We note the elements, although very differently formulated, of plowing, of Satan's self-proclamation as lord of the world, and of the connection between the water and the contract.

9.   In the story numbered 13 by Ivanov, a full version of the "Variant A" type cheirograph legend is to be found. This story is from Prilep, like no. 14, which is a "light" version of the cheirograph legend. Both existed in the same place.

When God expelled Adam from Paradise, he cursed him with the need to labor for his bread. Adam left the Garden, in spite of his fear of the angel, and wandered around Paradise for a long time, hoping to return.

Adam, urged on by Eve, started digging the ground and found the labor very hard. The devil came and reproached him for working his (the devil's) earth. Adam moved to a second place and the same happened, and then on a third spot. "How will I live," Adam asked him, "if you do not allow me to cultivate the earth?" "Make me an oath," Satan said. "The living will be yours and the dead mine." Adam and Eve consented, and Adam made the contract with his hand, a mark on a stone with his body's blood. Satan took the contract and hid it below the boiler of hell. It remained there until Christ descended to hell and broke it.[25]

The presence of the stone and the blood may be noted here, but the Jordan River and the baptism are absent from this tale. Moreover, Adam is assigned the living and Satan the dead. The writing of the cheirograph plays a very minor role, but it is written on stone, as in nearly all the other traditions. It is hidden in hell and not in the Jordan, and so Christ, in his descent into Hades, releases those imprisoned in hell. The "boiler of hell" is a unique touch.

Iconographic Types

10. The patterns of Christian iconography were fixed early. Scenes such as the baptism and the descent into Hades (the Anastasis) were composed of set elements from ancient times. It is possible, however, to discern the influence of the legend of the cheirograph of Adam on certain examples of such scenes: new features are introduced, or traditional ones are given an unusual twist. Moreover, in some instances, artists created new scenes, illustrating elements of the cheirograph legend. Such modified or newly created scenes, however, are not found in manuscripts in connection with copies of the cheirograph legend. Because the legend had universal significance and related to the underlying structure of creation and redemption, most often its elements influenced illustrations of the Gospel stories, which likewise represented events of cosmic significance.

Type 1. The Baptism with Christ Standing on a Stone Holding a Scroll in His Left Hand upon Which Is Written (in Slavonic) "Cheirograph of Adam"
The scene shows the standard iconographic features of the baptism, but with two additional elements. The first is the square or irregular rock on which Christ is standing, in one instance with serpents' heads; the second is that

he is holding a scroll in his left hand upon which is inscribed "Cheirograph of Adam."[26] Such paintings are rare, and they clearly refer to two legendary elements and reflect two understandings of the cheirograph at the same time. The first is the cheirograph as a flat stone or a brick, which is sometimes guarded by serpents. This is the contract written at Satan's behest and signed by Adam, which Satan hid in the Jordan. The second represents the cheirograph as a scroll. Moreover, the painting intimates Christ's destruction of the cheirograph at the time of his baptism. This is shown by his holding the cheirograph in his hand.[27]

This aspect of the presentation of the cheirograph legend is analogous to a scene illustrating stanza 22 of the *Hymnos Akathistos* (literally, "The Not-Seated Hymn"; it was so called because of its solemn character) that is described in the *Painter's Manual* of Dionysius of Fourna.[28] The *Hymnos Akathistos* is one of the great hymns of the Greek liturgy and is generally said to have been written in the fifth or sixth century.[29] Dionysius of Fourna (ca. 1670–ca. 1745) was a Greek monk and painter. He wrote a book that set forth instructions for painters: how to paint each scene and of which elements to compose it. Dionysius describes the illustration of stanza 22 of the *Hymnos Akathistos* as follows: "Christ is tearing a scroll written in Hebrew characters, on the end of which is inscribed τὸ χειρόγραφον τοῦ Ἀδάμ (i.e., "The Cheirograph of Adam").[30] Stanza 22 of the *Hymnos Akathistos*:

> Having desired to give grace to ancient debts,
> He who liberates the debts of all men,
> He came of his own will
> to those who had drawn far from his own grace,
> And having torn the cheirographon,
> Hears thus from all, Alleluia.[31]

Clear lines connect the poem to Colossians 2:14. The term "having torn" (σχίσας) of the hymn might be taken as a mark of the legend, Colossians having a verb which means "to wipe off" or "erase." Yet this is not the case. The language of Colossians 2:14 was very early transformed by its association with Christ's descent into Hades, where he was believed to free Adam and Eve and other saints who were subject to Satan. This idea is not found in the New Testament, but it is present from very early Christian times.[32] This changed the interpretation of Colossians 2:14 and led to the introduction of verbs meaning "cleave," "tear." Satan was thought to hold Adam's cheirograph, the bill of his obligations engendered by his sins, and Christ tore this up when he descended into Hades. Consequently this terminology is found in first-millennium Patristic texts, which are in every other way uniquely connected with Colossians 2:14 and have no relationship with the legend of the cheirograph.[33]

The scene described by Dionysius of Fourna clearly relates to the descent into Hades and Christ's destruction of the cheirograph, which had become the common understanding of Colossians 2:14. This description reflects iconographic type 6 presented below. The iconographic element, the scroll inscribed "Cheirograph of Adam," has been taken over in the representations of Christ tearing a scroll on his baptism.[34] In this form, in the scene of the baptism, the scroll clearly refers to the cheirograph legend. This is unmistakable from the flat stone on which Christ is standing and from the serpents' heads in one of the illustrations.

Indeed, what is extraordinary about stanza 22 of the *Hymnos Akathistos,* quoted above, is that, *prima facie,* there is no difficulty in seeing that it refers to Colossians 2:14. However, once the cheirograph legend becomes known, it imposes itself here as the interpretation of the *Hymnos Akathistos.* There are other passages in first-millennium patristic writings that open themselves to similar retrospective ambiguity, but none of them refers indubitably to the cheirograph legend. Instances such as stanza 22 of the *Hymnos Akathistos* make the search for the earliest attestation of the legend of the cheirograph difficult. Before such passages can be taken as evidence of its existence, they must make direct reference to an unambiguous and unmistakable aspect of the legend; see chapter 7.

In fact, at least these two examples of this scene are known, both from northeastern Romania. They were adduced by Kretzenbacher and Turdeanu. The latter discusses some further witnesses to the cheirograph in the sixteenth century, as well as its spread in iconography.[35]

a. An illumination dated 1609 from the Monastery of Dragomirna, in northeastern Romania, of the scriptorium of Atanasiu Crimca. Some say that this detached sheet was made after a painter's manual of 1602, but it is in fact a copy of Gospel 1/1934, fol. 11, of 1609.[36] In a scene of the baptism, Christ is standing on an irregularly shaped rock at the front of which the heads of three serpents can be seen. They are light-colored. In his left hand he is holding a scroll, partly opened, bearing a Slavonic inscription *RUKOPISA ADAMOV,* i.e., "Cheirograph of Adam."[37]

b. A second example is on a wooden cross dated 1825 from the Church of St. John the Baptist in Suceava, northeastern Romania. Christ is shown standing in the river, with his feet submerged in the water, in which a faint shape of a square stone is barely visible. In his left hand, as in the previous example, he is holding a scroll inscribed *RUKOPISA ADAMOV*, i.e., "cheiro-graph of Adam."[38]

c. A third example of the same iconography is an undated icon reproduced by Cartojan, *Cărţile populare,* 67.

Type 2. Christ on a Rock in the Baptism with or without Serpents
A second iconographic type is actually that of which the above three paint-ings form a striking, special subtype. This type is much more widespread. In it we have a scene of the baptism in which Christ is standing on a stone from which serpents' heads sometimes come forth. This iconography is found in Greek, Slavonic and Romanian sources. A further witness to the tradi-tion of the serpents' heads on the stone is the 1870 account by a pilgrim from Mt. Athos named Arsenius. He records seeing in the Jordan River a stone with Christ's footprints and the serpents' heads imprinted on it. He was a Russian, and his itinerary is preserved in that language.[39]

The stone is represented differently in the various paintings. In some instances it is submerged, but in most cases it is shown clearly. If that is not just an artist's device to make the representation clearer, the dry stone reflects the drying up of the waters at the time of the baptism, which is mentioned in a number of the literary sources (e.g., Armenian *Adam, Eve, and the In-carnation* §49; see chapter 5). It is also possible that the square stone reflects an element found in retellings of the legend in which Satan makes a brick and bakes it. Alternatively, and perhaps more probably, this feature of the legend, which occurs only in late popular retellings, is the result of the rep-resentation of the stone as a square block in some pictures. In many other instances, an irregularly shaped stone is visible. Examples of these types of illustrations follow.

a. One of the oldest witnesses to this iconography is a Russian icon of the baptism, ca. 1408, in St. Petersburg, inventory number 2098. In it we see Christ standing on a stone. Smirnova comments that this iconographic type is found in late-fourteenth-century and early-fifteenth-century Muscovite art.[40]

b. In two sixteenth-century Moldavian manuscripts preserved in the mon-astery of Suceviţa, in Romania, we find baptisms in which Christ is stand-ing on a flat rock. In one of them, the rock is inscribed with four letters.[41] Sirarpie Der Nersessian points out that these two manuscripts are descendants, one direct and one indirect, of the eleventh-century manuscript Paris BnF grec 74. Although both Suceviţa manuscripts show a stone under Christ's feet at the baptism, their archetype, the Paris Greek manuscript, does not have it. This shows the influence of the legend of the cheirograph on iconography in Moldavia. The iconography of that model was modified in light of it.[42]

c. The same scene is shown on a gilded silver book binding done in 1607 for the monastery of Suceviţa; it is perhaps based on the manuscript illuminations from the same place.[43]

d. An icon of the end of the fourteenth century in the Greek Patriarchate of Jerusalem shows Christ on a barely visible square rock. Two horizontal black lines may be seen on the rock. A serpent's head, difficult to discern, extends from the front corner of the rock. The icon is of Greek provenance.[44]

e. A Greek icon of ca. 1600 from Asia Minor presents Christ standing on a square stone with a border around it (see figure 3). The stone appears to be on top of the water. Seven red serpents emerge from under the stone. Their open mouths are oriented toward Christ. The icon is in the collection of Dr. S. Amberg-Herzog, Kölliken, Switzerland.[45]

f. An icon of the seventeenth century, in the Church Museum in Sofia, Bulgaria,[46] shows Christ on a rectangular stone from which at least six serpents' heads emerge. The stone is clearly separated from the water.[47]

g. In an icon of the seventeenth century, Archeological Museum, Sofia, Bulgaria, Christ is on a square stone with seven serpents' heads on the far side of the rock, and with tails, or perhaps more heads, on its near side. It is of Bulgarian provenance.

h. In a Bulgarian icon of the seventeenth century, Christ is standing in the baptism on a square stone with six serpents.[48] See figure 4.

i. The same iconography is also to be found in a fresco in the Church of St. Nicetas (Nikita) near Čučer in Yugoslavia. Christ is standing on a square rock, from both the front and rear of which serpents emerge. The paintings are traditionally assigned a date of 1309–1314, and some of them were restored in 1483–1484, including the scene we are discussing.[49]

j. In three monasteries of Mount Athos, there are fresco paintings that show Christ treading on a rock from which four serpents' heads emerge.[50] Dates for these frescoes are not given. In that of the Laura, Christ is standing on

3. Icon, ca. 1600, Greek, Asia Minor, ca. 1600. Baptism with Christ standing on square rock with serpents' heads (Ristow, frontispiece).

4. Icon by Goma Oryahovitsa, early seventeenth century, Bulgaria.
Baptism with Christ standing on square rock with serpents' heads
(Paskaleva, no. 76).

a red stone, which either is dry or is on the surface of the water, and from which serpents' heads issue. In 1855, Schäfer reported that a painter of Esphigmenou said that although he had painted the scene of Christ on a rectangular stone with serpents' heads, he did not know its meaning.[51]

k. On a double-sided north Russian icon, designated code 9386, of the sixteenth to seventeenth century in the collection of the Odigia Foundation in the Hague, there is a baptism with Christ standing on a red stone (figure 5).

l. A number of further Romanian examples have been adduced by Kretzenbacher and others, from the early seventeenth century up to the nineteenth century.[52] These examples add nothing to our knowledge of the iconography of the scene, but their considerable number strengthens the impression of the popularity of the scene in the Romanian and Moldavian areas, especially in the northeast. The existence of rather early Greek examples and the continued use of the iconography in Greek representations from the fourteenth century shows its relative antiquity. It was not a Slavonic innovation.

Type 3. Armenian Iconography of the Cheirograph in the Baptism
An Armenian scene of the baptism shows Christ standing on (and apparently trampling) a serpent, which is draped over the frame of the picture. The serpent is so placed that John the Baptist appears to be standing on its head. In its mouth, the serpent is holding a white, oblong object, the cheirograph, which has a handprint on it. The lower part of Christ's body is covered by the water, but the serpent with the cheirograph is painted as if on the surface of the river (see figure 6).

The picture bears captions in both the upper and lower margins. That in the upper margin reads, "St. John, who is baptizing Christ. The Holy Spirit in the form of a dove descending from the heavens." Even more interesting is the caption in the lower margin, which reads, "The river Jordan. Satan in the form of the *višap* serpent, who is guarding Adam's cheirograph in the water."[53] The *višap* is the mythical Armenian dragon, but the word is also used in the Armenian translation of the serpents in Psalm 73(74). It also serves to refer to Satan in the poem of Yovhannēs T'lkuranc'i, which was quoted above.[54]

This extraordinary painting is in manuscript M10805 of the Matenadaran, Institute of Ancient Manuscripts in Erevan, fol. 23v, which is a

5. Baptism with Christ standing on a rock, Northern Russia, sixteenth or seventeenth century. Collection Odigia Icon Institute and Museum, the Hague, code AIR 000.9386.

6. Fol 7r, Matenadaran Ms 10805, Karin, 1587. Baptism with
Christ trampling serpent, which has the Cheirograph in its mouth.

Gospel of 1587 from the village of Salajor in the region of Karin (Erzerum).[55] It was copied and illustrated by Aṙak'el Gełamac'i. The manuscript is richly illustrated.

The preceding examples show how elements from the legend of the cheirograph were introduced into well-known scenes, which served their traditional functions. Another type of representation is wholly founded upon the legend of the cheirograph. This is described in the following paragraphs.

Type 4. Adam Signing the Cheirograph

a. A Moldavian mural with a Slavonic inscription from the church at Voroneţ (1547) shows Adam seated, writing the cheirograph on a scroll on his knees, while Satan looks on.[56] The writing on the scroll is described by Kretzenbacher as Greek uncials, although no word can be made out, at least in the copy by Henry. From the reproduction in Drăguţ and Lupan's book, however, it is clear that he is writing "Cheirograph of Adam" in Slavonic characters (see figure 7).[57] The picture has a title that reads, "Here Adam is writing his Cheirograph." This can be contrasted with the Hebrew letters in which the cheirograph was written according to the description by Dionysius of Fourna mentioned in note 31.

This painting is on the northern wall of the church, as part of six registers of scenes representing Paradise, the fall, and events to the Praise and Assumption of the Virgin.[58] In the top register are three pictures that describe the difficult situation encountered by Adam and Eve after the fall. The first picture is of Eve spinning, the second of Adam plowing, and the third of Adam signing the cheirograph. Then comes a painting of Cain cutting corn and Abel with his lambs.[59]

This context shows that the "agricultural" form of the story is being represented. Henry, in his reproductions and descriptions of the Voroneţ painting, does not address the issue of the source of this representation.[60] It is clear, however, that the Voroneţ painting reflects the form of the cheirograph legend found in the Slavonic *Life of Adam and Eve,* Variant A. The literary and oral sources adduced above witness the wide popularity of this story in the Balkans and the Slavonic-speaking area.

b. P. Henry and Turdeanu refer to two further examples of this scene, both in frescoes. One is at Vatra-Moldoviţci (sixteenth century), and the other is at Suceviţa (end of the sixteenth century). It seems that it also exists at Homor.[61] In Suceviţa its location on the north wall is very like that at Voroneţ while the paintings at Vatra-Moldoviţci are almost contemporaneous with

7. Satan instructing Adam to sign the Cheirograph. Fresco, Voroneţ, Romania, 1547 (Drăguţ and Lupan, fig. 198).

Voroneţ.[62] Henry points out that in all three instances this picture forms part of a cycle of sacred history from creation to redemption.

Type 5. Christ Tearing the Cheirograph

Turdeanu refers to two representations of Christ tearing the cheirograph into two strips: one in Ms grec 115 of the Library of the Romanian Academy, and the other in a fresco of the Megiste Laura on Mount Athos.[63] It is likely that this is identical with the scene described in the following paragraph.[64]

Type 6. Christ Holding the Cheirograph in Limbo

Similarly, in a Russian icon of the fifteenth century, Christ descends to Hades. His right hand is extended to Adam, and in his left hand is a rolled-up scroll.[65] In two seventeenth-century Russian icons of the descent into Limbo, Christ appears trampling the doors of Hades, extending his left hand to Adam, and holding a document in his right hand. In one icon, the document is rolled, but in the other it is inscribed, apparently, "Cheirograph of Adam's sin," and is torn in half. Satan is holding the other half of the document[66] (figures 8 and 9). This is parallel to the figure of Christ in the baptism holding a scroll mentioned above (section 8, §1) and to the description by Dionysius of Fourna quoted in the discussion of iconographic type 1. There are also paintings referred to by Megas and Turdeanu (Martin de Voss: death holding the cheirograph) and Christ in Hades. Of course, they mention only a few of the many representations of this scene.[67]

In the course of the preceding discussion, we remarked upon points that are shared by a number of these Romanian and Bulgarian tellings of the legend of the cheirograph. Prominent is the broad influence of the story about the plowing, which is found in Slavonic Variant A and stories nos. 1, 2, 5, 6, 8, and 9. Most of these stories share an assertion along the lines of "the heavens are the Lord's and the earth is Satan's" (Slavonic Variant A §4, stories nos. 2, 5, and 8).[68] On the other hand, light is the problem in only two texts: Slavonic Variant B and story no. 7. The element of blood in the making of the cheirograph may be observed in Slavonic Variant C §7, stories nos. 7 and 9. It is also to be found in a different form in Megas's Greek story (chapter 6). It is striking that although the feature of blood is present, its presentation differs in the various sources.

Hades is the unique repository of the cheirograph in stories nos. 2 and 6, while Hades is involved as well as the Jordan in Slavonic Variant C §11;

8. Harrowing of Hell. Christ, holding a scroll, tramples the gates of hell. Icon, Russian, seventeenth century (Mauchenheim, 157).

9. Christ, tearing a scroll held by Satan, tramples the gates of hell.
Icon, Russian, seventeenth century (Lange, 72).

also compare story no. 6. None of the typical language of Colossians 2:14
is to be found. The cheirograph is a brick or is compared with a brick in
two Romanian sources: stories nos. 5 and 6. Serpents' heads, widespread in
the iconographic tradition, take their origin from Psalm 73 (74):13. The
story of the serpents in Slavonic Variant C is probably etiological and is not
found fully in any of the other literary or folk sources. In story no. 5, demons,
and later serpents, are said to guard the stone. It is remarkable that the serpents are so rare in the stories and so widespread in the iconography.

From this survey, it is clear that the dominant form of the legend in
Slavic and Balkan areas was that unique to the oldest literary witnesses, the
most common manuscripts of the Slavonic *Life of Adam and Eve*. The oldest of these that has been published dates from the fifteenth century. Satan
prevents Adam from plowing, thus causing Adam to recognize him as lord
of the earth (so, also, Slavonic Variant A §4). The version presenting light
as the problem, the only one found in the Greek and Armenian sources, occurs only in Slavonic Variant B and story no. 7. The element of deceit that
is dominant in the other versions, both Satan's deceit of Adam and God's

or Adam's deceit of Satan, is almost totally missing from the Slavonic and Romanian sources. Even in story no. 7, the protoplasts' discovery of the deceit is missing. Deceit is found in Slavonic Variant A alone, and God's deceit of Satan in the reworked form of the story (story no. 9) is at best a dim reflection of it. Instead, the idea of Satan's constraint or blackmail of Adam occurs in nearly all the stories presented in this chapter.

Thus, a very distinct form of the legend of the cheirograph appears to have been current among the Romanians and the Bulgarians. It derives predominantly from the "agricultural" story widespread through the Slavonic *Life of Adam and Eve,* Variant A. The tradition of the light is also present, but in lesser measure. Unique to these stories is the idea of the blood with which Adam wrote the cheirograph. Slavonic Variant C has goat's blood (compare Genesis 37:31). That has no exact parallel, but in stories nos. 7 and 9, Adam writes with his own blood on the stone. Adam's blood is also the ink of the cheirograph in Megas's story, but in a quite different way. Thus, in addition to the features of this form of the legend shared by the Slavonic, Bulgarian, and Romanian sources, we may point out that the blood was shared with these sources by a story written down in the adjoining area of Thrace in the early twentieth century.

The following table summarizes some shared elements.

Blood	Slavonic C	nos. 7, 9, Megas's story
Under rock	Slavonic B	no. 6
Brick		nos. 5, 6
Cheirograph to Hades		nos. 2, 6
Cheirograph to Jordan and Hades	Slavonic C	cf. no. 9
Agriculture	Slavonic A	nos. 1, 2, 5, 6, 8, 9
Light	Slavonic B	no. 7
Heavens Lord's; earth Satan's	Slavonic A	nos. 2, 5, 8
Living Lord's; dead Satan's	Slavonic C	nos. 7, 8, 9
Serpents	Slavonic C	no. 5

CHAPTER FIVE

Armenian Apocryphal Tales

The Armenians preserved and transmitted apocryphal writings that they created, not only in biblical manuscripts,[1] but in other types of manuscripts as well.[2] The quite numerous and varied texts published to date clearly exemplify the rich creativity of the Armenians in the field of apocrypha. Furthermore, they illustrate the way apocryphal traditions and interpretations have penetrated many aspects of Armenian literature, religion, and art.

No better example of this can be found than the very numerous Armenian works dedicated to Adam and Eve. Along with works known to have been translated from foreign languages, dozens of writings exist that were composed in Armenian and deal with the protoplasts.[3] Moreover, traditions about Adam and Eve, exhibiting apocryphal features, permeate much Armenian literature throughout the centuries.

In this chapter, we shall present three different Armenian Adam apocrypha and some associated texts, all of which reflect the legend of the cheirograph.

The Tale of the Expulsion
of Adam and Eve from Paradise

In 1898, S. Yovsēp'ianc' published a collection of Armenian apocryphal writings that included a number of Armenian Adam books.[4] This material was translated, first into English by J. Issaverdens,[5] and then into German by

E. Preuschen.[6] A new and much improved edition of these Adam books was published in 1990 by W. L. Lipscomb,[7] and an extensive list of Armenian Adam works was published by M. E. Stone in 1993 and updated in 1996.[8]

The Cycle of Four Works is one of the Armenian Adam books. It is composed of four parts, which are usually listed with separate titles. *The Cycle of Four Works* tells the tale of human history from the period before Creation down to the death of Adam and beyond. It seems likely that it was composed in Armenian. The best edition is that of Lipscomb.[9] In addition to publishing an improved text of the recension that Yovsēp'ianc' had published at the end of the previous century, Lipscomb edited and translated a second recension. A Georgian version of this work also exists.[10] The manuscripts known so far are predominantly of the seventeenth century.

The constituent parts of *The Cycle of Four Works* are the following:

1. *History of the Creation and Transgression of Adam*[11]
2. *History of the Expulsion of Adam from the Garden*[12]
3. *History of Abel and Cain, Sons of Adam*[13]
4. *Concerning the Good Tidings of Seth*[14]

Our attention is focused on the end of the first work, *History of the Creation and Transgression of Adam,* and the whole of the second one, *History of the Expulsion of Adam from the Garden.* In these documents, we find a fairly straightforward presentation of the legend of the cheirograph.[15] As in other parts of *The Cycle of Four Works,* the end of one work overlaps and supplements the beginning of the next. Thus, the elements present in both documents must be studied here in combination.

The second recension of *The Cycle of Four Works* is, on the whole, similar to the first recension, but it contains more medieval grammatical forms. It is difficult to know whether these show it to be later than the more classicizing forms found in Recension 1, or whether the latter's linguistic character is the result of deliberate editorial activity. Lipscomb did not clarify the relationship between the recensions, and there are certain elements of the story present in one and not in the other. For the most part, however, the two are the same. The text is older than its oldest, seventeenth-century witnesses, but it is hard to determine its date more precisely. Many of the known manuscripts are undated; other copies doubtless remain undiscovered, and no one has traced reuses of these literary traditions in other Armenian works. A remarkably early date for this work, however, does not seem very likely. Following is a reproduction of Lipscomb's translation.[16]

The word translated by Lipscomb as "promissory note" is Ճћռաղիր, that is, χειρόγραφον, "cheirograph"; we would prefer to translate it as "contract." A second, literal meaning of χειρόγραφον, "the imprint of a hand," is also present in this text. Adam put his hand on the rock, and presumably left a handprint there.[17] The basic elements of the myth are all found, except for the baptism.

Transgression

RECENSION 1

46. And they went outside to a dark and gloomy place <and> they remained there <six days> without eating, weeping inconsolably, and bemoaning themselves. 47. But after six days the Lord took pity on them, and he sent his angel to take them out of the darkness, and he guided and brought them into this bright world, and he showed them fruit-bearing trees with which to be satiated and to live. 48. And when Adam and his wife saw <the light of this world, Adam and his wife rejoiced and were glad> and they said, "Even though it is not so good, the light and fruits of this world are not equal to the light and fruit of the garden, nevertheless with this we shall neither <die> nor remain <in> darkness. 49. Thus they were cheerful.

RECENSION 2

50. And they fell into a dark and gloomy place, hungry and thirsty for six days. 51. Then the Lord again took pity on them, and he sent his angel to take Adam away from the gloomy place. And he brought <him> into the light of the world, and he showed him how to till the soil and to eat of its fruit. 52. Now when they saw the sun and the moon, they rejoiced until the evening. But they did not know that the sun sets and rises. Then, as the sun set, the earth became gloomy for them and darkness seized them, and they wept sorrowfully all night.

53. So much concerning Adam, whom the Lord God saved, <and> may he redeem you from the wicked Satan's deception and make <you> worthy of the just judgment and of the kingdom of light. Amen.

Expulsion

Recension 1

The History of the Expulsion of Adam from the Garden

1. Now when Adam <and Eve> fell from the garden into this world, they rejoiced over the sun until the evening. 2. But, towards the evening, when the sun set, they thought darkness had seized them <and> they would not see light again. Since there was always light in the garden, they thought all this world would be bright and sunny in the same way. They did not know that in this world there is night, or there is day. Therefore they were grieved when the sun set, as they thought it would not be light again <and> they wept and lamented till morning.

3. Now in the morning at daybreak, Satan came to him (Adam) in the form of an angel and said, "Why are you sad?"

4. Adam said, "We are sad because God created us and put us in the midst of the bright garden, but by the serpent's deception we tasted of the fruit and were ex- pelled from the garden, and we fell into darkness for some time. 5. Again the Lord took pity and sent his angel, <and> he took us out of

Recension 2

Concerning the Expulsion of Adam and Eve from the Garden

1. When Adam fell from the light, he rejoiced a little over the light of the sun. Even though the light of the sun was not equal to the light of the kingdom, nevertheless it was light. He did not know that the sun sets in the west. Now, when it became dark and evening arrived, likewise it seemed to them that darkness had come and there would not be light again. Since there was always light in the garden, they thought all this world would be with light. For they did not know that day follows night. Hence when the sun set and the day became dark, they thus thought there would not be light again. Therefore they wept and lamented till morning.

3. Now at daybreak Satan came in the form of an angel and he said to Adam, "Why are you sad?"

4. Adam said, "We are sad and we weep because God created us and put us in the midst of the bright garden, but by the serpent's deception we ate of the fruit and we were driven out of the garden, and we fell into this place of dark gloom. 5. Then God had double pity on us and sent his angel,

the darkness. And he brought us into the light of this world; although it was not like the light of paradise, nevertheless it was light. 6. But we do not know what we have done that the Lord became angry at us and has taken away that little light. That is why we lament and weep."

7. Satan said, "What did you give to that angel who took you away from the dark place and brought you into the light?"

8. Adam said, "Indeed nothing."

9. Satan said, "Why is that? Why did you not declare yourselves to be his servants together with all your offspring?"

10. Adam said, "Folly took hold of us and we did not think to say that."

11. Satan said, "What will you give to me if I give you the good news of light?"

12. Adam said, "If we could see light one time, we would become your servants, we and all our offspring."

13. Then Satan showed them the east and said, "Look and you will see light there."

14. When Satan said these words and withdrew a little, Adam and Eve looked towards the east, saw the sign of the dawn, rejoiced greatly and were glad.

15. When <the sun had risen

<and> he took us out of the darkness and brought us into the light of the world. 6. But we do not know that we have done any evil such that God became angry at us and darkness seized us."

7. Satan said. "Did you give something to that angel who brought you into the bright world?"

8. Adam said, "Did we have something which we could give?"

9. Satan said, "You should have become his servant and promised all your offspring to him. When you did not do this, consequently darkness seized you."

10. Adam said, "Greed seized us and we did not understand that."

11. Satan said, "What will you give to me if I give you the good news of light?"

12. Adam said, "If we could see the light again, we would become your servants, we and all our offspring."

13. Then Satan showed him the east and said, "You (will) see the light there."

14. Satan said this and withdrew a little. Then Adam and Eve looked to the east and saw that the sign of the sun's light had appeared. They rejoiced completely.

15. When it had risen a little,

completely they rejoiced. When>
the sun had risen a little higher,
the detestable Satan came to them
and said, "Did you see the good
news, that I made you rejoice?"

16. Adam said, "I am a servant
to you and your good news, for you
gave us light. All our offspring are
<your> servants."

17. Then Satan brought a stone
and set it before Adam, and he said
to Adam, "Put <your> hand upon
the stone and say thus, 'Let all my
offspring be your servants.'"

18. And if you do not say so,
I will bring deep darkness upon
you."

19. Then Adam put his hand
upon the stone and said, "Until
the unbegotten is born and the
immortal dies, we and all our
offspring will be your servants."

20. And Satan took the stone,
and he brought it and buried it in
the river Jordan.

21. This was Adam's promissory note in Satan's hand.

22. Until the evening Adam
and Eve rejoiced and were glad
<about the sun. But in the
evening, when the sun set, Adam
and Eve knew> that they had been
deceived by Satan; they wept and

Satan came to him and said, "Do
you see my good news, that I made
you rejoice?"

16. Adam said, "We are
servants to you and your good
news, for you gave us light. For
we shall serve you, we and all our
offspring."

17. Then Satan brought
a stone and set it before Adam,
and he said, "Put your hand upon
this stone and say thus, 'Until
the unbegotten is born and the
immortal dies, all my offspring
will be yours.'

18. And if you do not say so,
I will bring darkness to you again."

19. Then Adam put his hand
upon <the stone and> said, "Until
the unbegotten is born and the
immortal dies, all our offspring
will be your servants."

20. And the sign of the hands
upon the stone remained.

21. This was Adam's promissory note in Satan's hand. Now
Satan brought the stone promissory
note <and> buried it in the river
Jordan.

22. Again when the evening
came and the sun set in the west,
Adam knew that he had been
deceived; they wept and groaned
for five days, fasting and thirsty.

lamented, and they fasted for seven days and beseeched the Lord.

23. And after seven days the Lord took pity on them and sent his angel, and he brought a promissory note from God, put it in Adam's hand, and said, "Do not fear, Adam, if Satan has deceived you. He said to you, 'Until the unbegotten is born' because I am the unbegotten, whom no one bore. And <he said> 'the immortal one' of my divinity, which cannot die. Thus he took the promissory note from you deceitfully, so that you might remain a prisoner in Satan's hand, for you are my image. I will not destroy you and I will not leave you in his hand."

24. —For those seven days in which Adam fasted are called Aṙaǰawor.—

25. And when the sixth eon arrives, I will send from the light of my divinity my beloved son, who will come and take human form from your seed, from the holy and perfect virgin. For he shall be the son of your <son and (also) my son>.

26. And my son will annul your promissory note, free you

23. They beseeched God, and after five days God heard their prayers and sent his angel. And he announced to Adam about the incarnation of the Lord God and the deliverance from the hands of Satan.

24. And he gave Adam a promissory note from God and it was written thus: "Do not be sad, Adam; Satan has deceived you. He said 'Until the unbegotten is born and the immortal dies' because I am the unbegotten and immortal divinity, who in six eons will send my only-begotten son from the light of my divinity.

25. And he will take on flesh from a pure and perfect virgin who <is> from your seed; he will be my son <and> your son.

26. For the unbegotten will be born and he will annul the

from captivity to Satan, and give you your former glory."

27. When Adam heard this <good news>, he rejoiced greatly. And the six thousand <years> seemed like one hour.[18]

28. Blessed be God.

promissory note of your transgressions. And he will return (you) to your former glory."

27. When he heard this good news, he rejoiced. For he considered the six eons <to be> like one hour because of the angel's good news.

28. May Christ God pity you and us with the same pity. Amen.

This work relates a clear and engaging story, a lively narrative marked by an active dialogue. Like a number of other Armenian apocryphal writings, it includes the idea that after the expulsion Adam and Eve did not fall directly into this world, but into a dark, gloomy place.[19] There they did not eat, and they wept inconsolably for six days. Subsequently, an angel took them from that gloomy place to this world.

In *Expulsion,* after they depart from the Garden of Eden, they are hungry and pray to God. In response to their need, an angel comes. He instructs them in the art of agriculture and takes them to this world. Thus, they receive partial consolation for their pain and deprivation, and they are established in the world. Satan then initiates the second deception and the contract, as if to destabilize the relatively settled situation they have achieved. This pattern differs from the usual structure of the story, in which there is no gloomy place nor any immediate divine response to the protoplasts' prayer. The variation is doubtless due to the fact that the idea of the dark intermediate place was already present in the Armenian tradition.

The agricultural element in this story is noteworthy: the problem of food is raised, and so is the angelic instruction in agriculture. In Recension 1, it is true, the food issue is less stressed: they are said not to eat, which might be taken to be a penitential act. Recension 2 is much more explicit: they are said to be hungry and thirsty, not merely not to eat. The way Recension 2 is formulated indicates that they are not refraining from food deliberately, but cannot find food. When we compare it with the treatment of food and hunger in the primary Adam books, *Expulsion* is unique in that God is said to send an angel who (1) takes them out of the gloomy place and into this world and (2) teaches Adam agriculture and how to find food.[20]

Next it says that they rejoiced in this world, saw the luminaries, and then it became dark. They did not know about the rising and setting of the sun and the moon, and the deception of the cheirograph ensued. We noted above the extensive angelic instruction in the Slavonic version of the *Life of Adam and Eve*, which, like *Expulsion,* sets the teaching of agriculture immediately after the search for food. *Expulsion,* however, subsequently introduces the element of the light, and Satan's challenge to Adam and Eve is over light, not food.

This structure produces a different dynamic from that in *Life of Adam and Eve.* The gloomy place is really bad, with no light and no food; the world is much better and a cause for rejoicing. "Even though it is not so good, the light and fruits of this world are not equal to the light and fruit of the garden, nevertheless with this we shall neither <die> nor remain <in> darkness" (Recension 1 §48). That is to say, Adam and Eve's prayers have produced a partial result, not a restitution of Paradise, but a quite bearable intermediate state. To some extent, the balance that was disturbed by the fall and expulsion of Adam and Eve has been restored. Then Satan's cheirograph deception comes and upsets this second balance.

Thus, the fall is in two stages; similarly there are two deceptions and two acts of divine mercy. The first deception is in the Garden, and the first act of divine mercy is to take them from the gloomy place and to put them in this world. The second deception is the cheirograph, and the second act of divine mercy is the promise of the incarnation. In *Expulsion,* 1 §23, the language used of the divine mercy is just like the language used of divine mercy in *Transgression,* 1 §47 = 2 §51. It is because of this sense of parallelism that this document introduces a second cheirograph given by God to Adam and Eve, promising them redemption.

The idea that God gave Adam a letter is to be found in a number of sources.[21] In the eleventh chapter of the *Infancy Gospel* in Armenian, published in 1898, we find the idea that at the nativity of Christ, the Magi brought a document that was an epistle given to Adam by God.[22] The beginning of this passage reads as follows:

> The Magi said, "No other people knows this, neither having heard it nor having learned it, but only our people, which has this testimony in writing. For, after Adam's expulsion from Paradise, and Cain's murder of Abel, the Lord God gave to Adam Seth, a son of consolation, and this letter with him, written by the finger of God, closed and sealed. And Seth received it from his father and gave it to his sons and his sons, to their sons, and

after them, having received it, they gave it to Abraham. Abraham gave it
to the high priest Melchisedek and thence, (it was given to) our people,
to Cyrus, king of the Persians."[23]

This epistle or undertaking given by God to Adam and his descendants is
intriguing. It implies a deep, almost deterministic sense of the redemption
that inheres in the dynamic of the historical process and of the direct connection between Adam's sin and the birth and life of Christ. We think it is
likely that the complementary cheirograph given to Adam by God after
Adam gave his to Satan is a transmutation of some tradition like that cited
here. This divine undertaking is no different, except in its mythological con-
creteness, from that promise of redemption that God gives the protoplasts
in other versions of the story.

The statement that what Satan is bringing them is a gospel is struc-
turally similar to this notion. Thus, §§14–15 are particularly important.
Just as there is a cheirograph and a "counter-cheirograph," so there is Christ's
(God's) good news and Satan's.

Unlike the Slavonic *Life of Adam and Eve,* here Satan does not blackmail
Adam. Adam makes the proposal to deliver his children to Satan on his own
initiative, building on an idea planted in his mind by Satan. Thus, in §12
he says, in response to Satan's request, "If we could see light one time, we
would become your servants, we and all our offspring" (compare §§17, 19).
The offer is accepted by Satan. The language of "enslavement" and "freeing
from Satan" is very important in Armenian tradition, and in this book in
particular.[24] A particular feature of this text is that the deception has two
stages. It became dark and has become light. Adam and Eve, not understanding, bewail this. Satan comes and tells them that this is because they
did not give a reward to the angel who led them out of the gloomy place
(§7). They have nothing to give him, and Satan puts into their head the idea
that they can give him their offspring. In fact, however, in §16 the offspring
are given not to the angel but to Satan. This may in part be structured on
a real-life situation in which enslavement was a last option for a debtor.

The formulation of Adam's undertaking in the cheirograph is also a sort
of "deception." Satan gives him a condition which seems *prima facie* to guarantee the enslavement of Adam's offspring "forever." However, the reader
already knows, and eventually God reveals to Adam (Recension 1, §23; Recension 2, §24), that precisely when this "impossible" condition is fulfilled,
Satan will be destroyed. Moreover, God embodies this knowledge in an undertaking, a cheirograph that he gives to Adam.

The connection with the Aṙaj̆awor fast is extremely interesting. This is a five-day fast observed in the Armenian Church before Lent, and is traditionally associated with Adam and with St. Gregory the Illuminator, the evangelist of Armenia.[25] There is, moreover, no hint of crucifixion material in this text, and even the phrase "undying dies" is underplayed in it. This would be odd if we were dealing with exegesis of Colossians 2:14.[26] Again, here, there is an indication of the distinctness of the cheirograph tradition from the exegesis of Colossians 2:14.

Adam, Eve, and the Incarnation

Another Armenian apocryphon, titled *Adam, Eve, and the Incarnation,* presents both parts of the legend, the creation, and the eventual destruction of the cheirograph (§33–36). In fact, it relates the history of redemption from creation through Christ's death and resurrection. Consequently, in this writing we also find an incident based on Colossians 2:14.[27]

The text presented here is from three manuscripts. Two of them are in the Matenadaran in Erevan, nos. M5913 (seventeenth century) and M5571 (1657–1659). The third is in Paris, in Bibliothèque nationale de France arm. 306 (seventeenth century). Further details of the manuscripts are given in appendix I. These manuscripts provide us with a date *ante quem,* but none is older than the manuscripts of *The Cycle of Four Works,* discussed in the preceding section. That is to say, we can show that this work existed in the seventeenth century by the direct evidence of its manuscripts. Indirect earlier evidence (i.e. references to or secondary uses of this text) has not surfaced, although such may well exist. The fact that three quite distinct recensions existed by the mid-seventeenth century (and who knows what still lies unpublished in manuscripts?) means that the composition must have existed sometime prior to that date, although how long remains uncertain.

Adam, Eve, and the Incarnation deals in detail first with the story of Adam and Eve (§§1–43) and then with the life of Christ (§§44–69). These two chief narrative segments are linked by a bridging series of references to the prophets. A very similar narrative structure may be observed in BL Harl. 5459, which is, however, much longer than *Adam, Eve, and the Incarnation.*[28] Both parts of *Adam, Eve, and the Incarnation* have numerous contacts with apocryphal traditions. The theme of Adam and Eve's cheirograph with Satan, making their offspring subservient to him until "the unborn is born and the undying dies" (§34), dominates the book. This condition is fulfilled by Christ in his nativity and crucifixion. The text is thus about the Christian economy of redemption, and, within this framework, existing biblical and apocryphal traditions have been reused. *Adam, Eve, and the Incarnation* is closely related to the first two parts of *The Cycle of Four Works,* the *Transgression,* and *Expulsion,* but it is not clear in which direction the influence flowed.[29] Certain other relationships with Armenian Adam writings have been noted, but these are not distinctive enough to demonstrate dependence.

The three recensions differ, but the first two are more closely allied with each other than either is with the third recension. It seems likely that *Adam, Eve, and the Incarnation* was composed in Armenian, and this narrative about Adam, Eve, and Satan stands firmly within the genre of the Adam writings.

M5913	M5571	P306
20 So, (the angels) having expelled them, they, having gone forth from the Garden, fell into a dark place. They wept and mourned without food for five days.	20 And when Adam and Eve fell from the Garden they fell into a certain gloomy place. They wept and mourned for five days.	20 They went forth from the Garden and they fell, hungry. And they <mourned> for 40 days.
21 And God remembered them and sent his angel, and, having taken them, he brought (them) to this world and he showed them (how) to tend and work and to make their days pass.	21 And then God had mercy and sent an angel, and he taught them to tend and work the earth. And they saw the earth full of sprouts and plants.	21 After five days, God had mercy on them. He sent his angel and he brought them forth to a hollow of the land, and he taught them to tend and work (and) to live by that. And they rejoiced
22 But, when evening fell and the sun set, thus they perceived that darkness had seized them. They did not yet know that sometimes it is day and sometimes night.	22 And they saw the light of the sun and they rejoiced greatly, until the evening. But on the setting of the sun, they perceived that darkness had seized them, but that they	22 even until the evening. The sun set. Thus they perceived that darkness had seized them, but they did not see the light.

did not see light
any more. Inside
the garden there was
always light for them.
But they did not
know about this
world, that sometimes
it is daytime and
sometimes night.

23 Again they
wept and mourned
until morning. When
morning drew near,
Satan came in the
form of an angel <and
said>, "Why do you
<c>ry, Adam?"

24 And Adam
said, "Why do you
ask? When God
created us in the
midst of the Garden
and we did not keep
his commandments,
we went forth outside.

23 They wept and
mourned until
cockcrow. Then
the foul Satan came
to them in the form
of an angel and said,
"Adam, why do you
cry?"

24 And they
said, "How should
we not cry? We have
gone forth from a
Garden such as this
through eating of the
fruit. But here we do
not know what has
happened, that our
light has turned to
darkness and we have
become darkened in
darkness."

23 <They> wept
and lamented until
cockcrow. Then foul
Satan came <to them>
in the form of an
angel of God and said,
"Why were you crying
while you had it?"

24 They said,
"In the midst <of
the Garden> and in
the midst of the light
we were given mercy,
but by the deception
of the serpent we ate
of the tree. We were
put outside and we
are in darkness."

25 Again he
remembered us and
he gave us this world
and we saw light here,
and we rejoiced. Again
darkness came upon
us. We do not know
what wrong we have
done."

25 Again
the great God was
merciful to us and
sent his angel, and
he brought <us to>
this place <where>
there was light with-
out darkness. And we
rejoiced. Again, we do

not know what we did
(that) again the Lord
became angry with
us and darkened the
light. Therefore, we
were weeping and
we mourn."

26 And Satan
said, "What did you
give to that angel in
return for his labour,
who brought you
forth from the gloomy
places and brought
you to this world,
and taught you
to tend and work?"

27a And Adam
said, "I had nothing
to give." Satan said,
"Since you received
upon yourself innu-
merable benefits, you
should have given
(your) offspring as his
servants. When you
did not give (them),
on account of that
darkness came upon
you."

27b Adam said,
"Then what will be
our end?"

28 Satan said,
"If you will give

26 And Satan
said, "What did you
give to the angel who
brought you forth
<from> darkness
to light?"

27a Adam said,
"What did we have
to give to him?" And
Satan said, "You
should have given him
things. When you had
none, therefore
darkness seized you."

27b Then Adam
said, "What shall we
do now?" Satan said,
"That which I say to
you. If you listen to
me, you (will) see
the light again."

28 Adam said,
"Command me, my

26 Satan said,
"What did you give
to that angel who
brought you forth
from darkness
to light?"

27a Adam said,
"What do we have,
that we might give
to God?" Satan said,
"You owe him your
offspring. You did not
give (your offspring,
and) on account of
that he made it dark
for you."

27b Adam said,
"Then, how will you
be?" Satan said, "That
which I say to you, if
you listen to me, you
will quickly see the
teaching."

28 Adam said,
"Command (me), my

me your offspring, I (shall) give you the tidings of the coming of light."

29 Adam said, "Let my offspring be yours, if it will be thus." Satan said, "Since you have given your offspring, you (shall) quickly see the light." And Satan became unseen.

30 And the sun rose and cast light upon this earth and Adam and Eve were happy and said to one another, "The tidings of the angel were true; it was proper to give him our offspring, as we did."

31 But, at the third hour, Satan came again and said, "Adam," you have seen the light and you were happy; believe in me!"

32 And Adam said, "Lord, I serve you and your tidings; through you yourself we saw the light, and we were happy."

33 And Satan said, "What did you give me in exchange

lord." Satan said, "If you will give me your offspring, I (shall) give you the tidings of the seeing of light."

29 Adam said, "If I shall see the light again, let all our offspring be a servant for you." Satan said, "In a little while you (shall) see light." Then Satan himself became invisible.

30 And morning came, and the sun shone. Adam and Eve rejoiced; they said to one another: "The word of this angel was true. It was necessary to give him our offspring, as indeed we did."

31 But Satan came at the third hour and said with them, "You have seen the light and your hearts have rejoiced."

32 And they said, "Lord, we serve you and your tidings. We praise you since through you we saw the light and rejoiced."

33 Satan said, "What did you give me in exchange for

lord." He said, "Give me your offspring, and I (shall) give you tidings of light."

29 Adam said, "If we see the light again, all my offspring will be yours." And Satan left (and) went off.

30 When the sun shone, Adam and Eve sought and were saying to one another {and were saying}, "The word of this angel was true. It is necessary for us to give our offspring as we did."

31 But, at the third hour, Satan came { . . . } and said with them, "Now did you believe me, and were my tidings true?"

32 And they said, "My lord, we have believed in you. I serve you and your tidings. Through you we saw light."

for such tidings which you <received> through me, and you have seen (i.e., the light)?" And he said, "I have given you my offspring; I (will) give you whatever you ask."

34 And Satan set a flat stone before him and said, "Put your hand upon (it) and say, 'Until the unbegotten is born and the undying dies, my seed will be your servants.' If you do not say thus, I (will) bring darkness upon you again."

35 And Adam said, "Until the unbegotten is born and the undying dies, all my seed will be your servants."

36 And the place of the hands and the fingers remained upon the flat stone. That became Adam's cheirograph at Satan's hand, and having brought (it), he set it in the Jordan River.

these tidings?" And they said, "We have given you all of our offspring."

34 But Satan, having brought a flat stone, put it before them and said, "You say thus, 'Until the unbegotten is born and the undying dies, all our seed will be your servants.' If you do not say thus, you (will) remain again <in> darkness."

35 But they put their hand upon the stone <and said>, "Until the unbegotten is born and the undying dies, all our seed will be your servants."

36 This became Adam's cheirograph at Satan's hand, and the mark of (his) fingers remained upon the stone. But Satan took that stone, and having brought (it),

34 But Satan set a flat stone also before them, and said, "If you do not put your hand upon this stone and say, 'Until the unbegotten is born, until the undying dies, all my offspring will be yours {yours}.' If you do not say (that), <I shall bring> darkness upon you."

35 But Adam put (his) hand upon the flat rock and said, "Until the unbegotten is born, the undying die<s>, my seed will be your servants." And the { } imprint of the hands remained upon the rock.

36 This became the cheir<og>raph at Satan's hand and he brought, buried it in the Jordan River.

buried it in the Jordan River.

37 Adam and Eve were rejoicing until the evening. It seemed to them thus, that the sun would not set again.

38 When it became evening, the sun set and it became dark. Then they realized that they had been deceived. Adam and Eve wept and mourned and said, "Woe and a thousand woes upon us and upon our children, we have become captive by means of our cheirograph." For five days they fasted, hungry. This is that which is called *Aṙaǰawor.*

39 Again God had mercy and sent his angel to comfort <them> by means of a cheirograph, thus: "Do not doubt, Adam. I will not abandon you to destruction, for I am unborn and my Godhead is the undying.

38 And when it became evening, the sun set, and then they realized that they had been deceived. They wept and wailed and fasted for 5 days. This is (the fast) which is called *Aṙaǰawor.*

39 But God had mercy and sent the archangel Michael to them, and he said to them, "Thu<s> says the Lord, 'Do not be sad, Adam. Even though you were deceived, I will not abandon you in the power of Satan, because I am the unborn and the

38 When it became evening, and the sun set on them, he realized and knew that he had been deceived. They wept bitterly and mourned, and for five days <hungering> they fasted. That is (the fast) which is called *Aṙaǰawor.*

39 Again, God had mercy and sent his angel, who said to them, "Do not fear, Adam, if Satan deceived you by a cheirograph."

undying is my
Godhead.

40 In the sixth
millennium I shall be
separated from this
light of mine as
indivisible light. In
the womb of a virgin,
your seed, he shall
dwell, and she shall
bear my son and your
son. He it is who is
born, unbegotten,
by a virgin.

41 For by him
the blind are given
light, the lame walk,
the leprous are healed,
the poor are given
good tidings, the dead
are made alive. He
himself, having been
crucified, dies and
is made alive.

42 That is that
the undying dies. And
he (will) tear up your
deed of obligation and
free you and all your
seed from servitude
to Hell. And he will
renew <for> you your
former glory. And he
himself, having been
resurrected in the
body and having as-

40 In the sixth
millennium I shall be
separated from this
light of mine an
indivisible light. And,
having descended, he
shall dwell in the
womb of a pure
virgin. He will be
the one born of her as
a perfect man. He will
be my son.

41 He shall go
about upon the earth
and will do many
wonders; he will be
tortured on your
account; he will die.
Again, resurrected
in the body,

42 he will
descend into Hell
and will set you free.
And he will again give
you your former glory.
And he, having been
assumed in the body,
(will) ascend and be
made one with my
Godhead. That is
that the unborn is
born and the undying

40 "But, in the
sixth millennium, I
shall separate my
light, the indivisible
light, which having
come, will be born
from your seed from a
virgin womb. He will
be <m>y son and your
son. That is what <is
said> that an unbe-
gotten is born, and he
becomes a perfect man
witho<ut> sin.

41 He goes about
with men, he appears
human, and he does
wonders. Thus he
does many wonders
upon the earth. And
on your account he is
tortured and he dies,
and living, in the
body, he goes forth
from the tomb.

42 He descends
to Hell because of you
and sets you free and
restores (you) to your
former glory."

cended, (will) come to this Godhead of mine (and be) made one (i.e., with it)."

43 When Adam heard this, 6,000 years seemed to him as one day on account of rejoicing.

. . .

49 Again he came to the Jordan; at the hands of the Baptist he was baptized. The river turned back. He destroyed the cheirograph of Adam, the flat stone; light descended from heaven. In the form of a dove the holy spirit appeared from the heaven, with a voice it cried, "This is my beloved Son."

dies. And he will free you and destroy your cheirograph.'"

43 But when Adam and Eve heard (this) they rejoiced greatly.

. . .

49 He entered, at the age of thirty years, into the Jordan. The river turned back, light descended from heaven. As in the form of a dove the spirit descended upon him. A voice from the heavens testified, "This is my beloved Son." And the cheirograph of Adam he invalidated, he destroyed. And he crushed the head of the Dragon, . . .

43 When Adam heard, he also rejoiced. Six thousand years seemed as one hour on account of the rejoicing of (his) heart.

. . .

49 And thence he came. At thirty years of age, he came to the river Jordan and entered the river. The water turned backwards. The cheirograph, the flat stone, was uncovered, and the Dragon serpent appeared. And our Lord Christ, with his foot having trampled the Dragon, and he trampled the cheirograph of evil, the flat rock, and destroyed (it). <From> the heavens light shone whe<n> it was torn. In the form of a dove the holy spirit descended.

The legend of the cheirograph is to be found in very full form in *Adam, Eve, and the Incarnation*. Above, we have presented the text of all three published versions for the two main parts of the story. First, the deception: After they left the Garden, they entered an intermediate gloomy place, just as was related in *Transgression* and *Expulsion*. In *Transgression* § 46, they went hungry and mourned for six days. In *Adam, Eve, and the Incarnation,* they "wept and mourned without food for five days" (§20). After the deception, they also mourned for five days (§40). Intriguingly, the second period of five days without eating is called fasting, and it is connected with the Armenian ecclesiastical fast of *Aṙajawor,* as was pointed out in the discussion of *Expulsion.* This fast is traditionally associated with Adam. It is this connection that may also explain the change of the number of days of this first period of hunger to five.[30] The period of hunger in the gloomy place must have arisen from the search for food. That is why they are said to be hungry rather than to fast. However, no actual search for food is mentioned in this text; nor is it mentioned in *Transgression* §46, although it is a major motif in the Armenian and Georgian *Life of Adam and Eve,* and lies behind the present state of the Latin version of that work.[31] The angelic instruction in agriculture follows as an act of divine grace, and the words of the Paris manuscript are particularly explicit: the angel taught them "to tend and work (and) to live by that" (§21). They are expelled to the gloomy place, and the gift of this world, like the instruction in agriculture, is an expression of God's mercy toward them.

The idea of the gloomy place is represented in an Armenian miniature of the expulsion. In manuscript M4820, painted in Vaspurakan in the fourteenth century, we see the following scene.[32] Inside a frame, which delimits the Garden of Eden, Adam and Eve are observed to the left and right respectively. Adam is seated on a throne and has a halo. Eve is standing and has no halo. They are both barefooted and wearing red garments with black shirts. Between them grows a tree with leaves and flowers. Their names are written by them and by the serpent (see below); the words are inscribed "the serpent deceiving Eve." This is an unusual picture and represents the temptation of Eve before the expulsion (see figure 10).

Outside the frame, but up against it, is a winged serpent. This figure doubtless reflects two things. Apocryphal traditions exist according to which Satan entered the serpent and they "hung their feet around the wall of the Garden" (*Penitence of Adam,* 44[17]:1) For this reason, the serpent is lying along the frame, and Adam and Eve are looking at him.[33] The wings are often found in Jewish and Christian tradition: in the biblical curse Satan is told, "and on your belly you shall go" (Genesis 3:14). From that, it might be thought to follow that before the curse he did not slither on his belly, but had legs and wings. This, at least, was what ancient Jewish and Christian exegetes inferred from the biblical expression.[34] The final element of

10. Fol. 4a, Matenadaran Ms M4820, fourteenth century. The expulsion and fall of Adam and Eve.

this miniature is two small, dark figures tilted backward and half-lying down, outside the frame in the center of the lower margin. These are identified by inscriptions as "Eve" and "Adam who went forth from the garden." We venture to propose that the dark color indicates not just their loss of the paradisiacal luminosity, but the gloomy place into which they fell. This picture represents three stages of the story of the fall in one: the deception, the expulsion, and the fall into the gloomy place.[35]

The continuation of the text resembles *Transgression* and *Expulsion:* when darkness fell, they became distressed, for "they did not know that sometimes it is day and sometimes night" (§22). Satan comes in angelic form in the morning. Adam interprets the night that has just passed as another punishment from God (§§23–24). As in *Expulsion,* Satan convinces Adam and Eve that they should have given a reward to the angel who led them out of the gloomy place; because they did not do so, he implies, the darkness came. Adam has nothing to give, and Satan offers to solve the problem in exchange for the cheirograph.

Satan's deceit of the protoplasts is two-staged, just as it is in *Expulsion.* First, he says that if Adam and Eve give him their offspring, light will come.[36] Then he disappears (§29) and comes back after the sun has risen. Now he has "proved" himself trustworthy: Adam and Eve draw this conclusion (§30), and he demands their belief (§32). Adam agrees to serve him and repeats his gift of his offspring. Satan brings a flat stone and asks Adam to pronounce the conditions of the cheirograph: "until the unbegotten is born and the undying dies, my seed will be your servants." If Adam refuses, Satan says, he will bring darkness (§34). This is done, the contract is sealed, the imprint of Adam's hand remains on the stone, and Satan sets it in the Jordan (§36).

When the sun has set once more, Adam and Eve realize Satan's deception; they fast for five days, which is the *Aṙaǰawor* fast. God makes a cheirograph with them (§39), announced by the angel and promising the incarnation of Christ (§40). A brief biography of Christ's miracles ends with his death and resurrection (§41). Then he will descend to hell and tear up Adam's deed of obligation[37] and free him and his seed from servitude to Hell (§42). The language of servitude and freedom can be observed elsewhere in this text; see §§27 and 38.[38]

It is clear that this section is a promise of the descent of Christ into the underworld when he will tear up Adam's deed of obligation.[39] Moreover, the very promise, which contains the expression "deed of obligation," is itself designated "a cheirograph." It is precisely God's "anti-cheirograph." Just as Satan's words are described as "teaching" or "good tidings," that is, as his gospel, in implicit contrast with Christ's gospel,[40] so God's promise of redemption is called a cheirograph in deliberate opposition to Satan's.[41]

Because the term this passage uses for the "deed of obligation" differs from that which it uses for "cheirograph," we may conclude that here the author is introducing a tradition related to Colossians 2:14. In such a context, the use of a different term for the document that Christ will tear up in his descent into the underworld and for the cheirograph of the legend is striking indeed.[42] The destruction of that cheirograph which Adam had given Satan is described separately, in the coming part of *Adam, Eve, and the Incarnation* (see below). In his death and resurrection, Christ will restore Adam to his primal glory.

In the discussion of the Slavonic Variant C, we noted that it is one of the very few known documents fully to integrate the descent into the underworld into the legend, by making Satan's hiding of the cheirograph a two-stage process: first in the Jordan and then in Hades. Christ's decisive destruction of it will come only in Hades.[43] We also noted two iconographic combinations of these traditions. The first is a striking Russian icon of the baptism and crucifixion, side by side, with hell in the lowest register underneath both the Jordan and the cross.[44] In some baptisms, known from Gračanica in Yugoslavia and from a modern Greek icon, we observe Christ in the Jordan trampling the doors of hell, from which serpents' heads emerge. In the modern Greek icon, serpents come out of the door, just as they come out of the stone of the cheirograph.[45] The iconography of Gračanica and of the modern Greek icon is particularly striking because the serpents' heads connect the doors explicitly with certain versions of the cheirograph legend.

These images, however, like Slavonic Variant C, represent the bringing together of Colossians 2:14 and the legend of the cheirograph by integrating them in the narrative or in the iconography. What we find in *Adam, Eve, and the Incarnation* is not the same. The prophecy of the descent into hell and the tearing up of the deed of obligation is part of God's promise, his cheirograph given to Adam, and it will "free you and all your seed from servitude to Hell" and restore Adam's former glory. Yet the term "cheirograph" is not used, and the destruction of the cheirograph in the Jordan is prophesied as taking place at the time of the baptism. Strikingly, the freeing of Adam and his posterity is not mentioned in the baptism prophecy here. Thus the integration of the two traditions is done differently in *Adam, Eve, and the Incarnation,* in the Slavonic story, and in the Russian and Greek icons. *Adam, Eve, and the Incarnation* has also tried to incorporate the two traditions, but the integration is only partial. The very use of a term other than "cheirograph" indicates this. The story of the cheirograph is the major girder to which the story of the descent into the underworld and the tearing up of the deed of obligation are connected.

In the description of the baptism in *Adam, Eve, and the Incarnation,* we have all the standard elements. The water turns back, and Christ, "with his foot having trampled the Dragon, and he trampled the cheirograph of evil, the flat rock, and destroyed (it)" (§49). The statement that the water "turned backward" comes from Psalm 114:3: "the sea saw and fled, the Jordan turned backwards." In this verse from Psalms, the crossings of the Red Sea and of the Jordan are conflated, although one might argue that they represent the beginning and the end of the wilderness events.[46] As a result of the water turning back, the cheirograph was destroyed.

A remarkable miniature painting illustrates this incident. It is a painting of the baptism by Aṙakʻel Gełamacʻi, in Gospel M10805 from the village of Salajor (Karin), fol. 23v. The miniature shows Christ trampling a large serpent or dragon that is holding a white tablet in its mouth. This tablet is the cheirograph, and on it a handprint is visible.[47] This iconography seems to reflect exactly the view of the cheirograph given in *Adam, Eve, and the Incarnation.* This is a quite different visual interpretation of the incident from the one found in Slavonic, Romanian, and Greek paintings. There, Christ is standing on a rock, or sometimes on a rock with a number of serpents' heads coming out of it, which is an iconographic representation of the story in Variant C of the Slavonic *Life of Adam and Eve* or, without serpents, of the simple story of the placing of the cheirograph in the water. In the Armenian painting, we have a different interpretation, corresponding exactly with the details found in the Armenian texts *Adam, Eve, and the Incarnation* and *Expulsion.*

It is significant to observe that this Armenian iconography has no parallel in the Bulgarian, Romanian, and Russian paintings. It is an independent development of a different form of the story, which is widely attested in Armenian texts.

The Dragon mentioned in §49 is the *višap,* the term used for the "great fish" in Genesis 1:21, but originally designating the mythical dragons of old Armenia. Thus, the title of the painting in M10805 calls the serpent both Satan and *višap*. The terms come together in Psalm 74 (73):14, which talks about the smashing of the heads of the dragons in the water, and the Armenian Psalter uses the words "head of the *višap*," (զլուխ վիշապին).

In *Adam, Eve, and the Incarnation*, the cheirograph is clearly a contractual agreement between Adam and Satan. Moreover, a second meaning of the word χειρόγραφον is present. It is taken quite literally to mean "the writing of a hand"; therefore the handprint of Adam is found on the rock. The Armenian miniature painting we have described conflates both meanings of the term. Satan places the flat stone in the Jordan, and Christ will break the stone at the time of the baptism.

What is the function served by this story as we find it? It states part of its function explicitly: to explain the subjection of Adam and his descendants to Satan. Subjection to Satan and its converse, release from the Satanic bonds, is one of the languages in which the Armenian (and other Christian) cultures talked about salvation.[48] In the Armenian baptismal liturgy, the catechumens say thrice, "We renounce you, Satan, and all your deception, and your deceit, and your service, and your ways, and your angels."[49] According to this text, then, what Adam lost at the expulsion was immortality and the paradisiacal food—"instead of this *immortal* plant, thistles shall grow for you,"[50] it says. The search for food is a major theme in the primary Adam books, most notably the Armenian *Penitence of Adam,* and is expressed in *Adam, Eve, and the Incarnation* as well, as we have noted.[51]

However, in *Adam, Eve, and the Incarnation,* the fall from Eden did not serve to explain the subjection to Satan from which Christ redeemed the Christian believers. It was the story of the ձեռագիր, "cheirograph, contract," that performed that role. Just as the revelation of Christ's power and redemption was evident both in the baptism and in the crucifixion, in a two-stage process, so in the reverse order there were two deceptions. The redemption from the first deception came in the descent into Hades, thus bracketing the period from Adam's fall with Adam's release from hell. Within that overall structure, however, was an inner cycle composed of deception, cheirograph, and baptism. Redemption is to be found in the birth of the unbegotten and the death of the undying.

The order of events in §49 of *Adam, Eve, and the Incarnation* is intriguing. In line with the verse in Psalm 74(73), Christ trampled the dragon.[52] He then trampled the cheirograph, and, subsequently the Spirit descended as a dove and the divine voice pronounced his Sonship. The narrative then tells Christ's miracles, his death, resurrection, and ascension. At the very end, in §64, the constitutive nature of the legend of the cheirograph for this writing is made explicit:

> For this is how the pronouncement was fulfilled, that the unborn was born and the undying died and was revived and released us from the captivity of Satan.

In the Paris manuscript, this is followed by the further statement that "those who do not confess Christ God become captives of Satan and {are punished} in Hell" (§65).

In the form of this paragraph in M5913 we read: "And he will tear up your deed of obligation and free you and all your seed from servitude to Hell." This recension here evokes the verse in Colossians 2:13–14, which talks of Christ on the cross erasing Adam's deed of obligation and nailing it to the cross. The descent into the underworld, including the breaking down of its doors and the freeing of Adam and Eve, is not to be found in the New Testament. However, it belongs to one of the oldest levels of Christian tradition.[53] The erasing of the bill of obligation is drawn from Colossians 2:14, which reads ἐξαλείψας, "erasing." The term used for the bill of obligation is not that used for the cheirograph.[54]

Clearly then, it is the legend of the cheirograph that provides the structure around which the whole of *Adam, Eve, and the Incarnation* is organized. It is the second fall of the protoplasts rather than the first fall that drives the economy of salvation.

The Armenian Adam Story

Adam Story 1 is to be found in a *Miscellany* Erevan, Matenadaran M9100 of the year 1686. It has no obvious direct literary sources, but many affinities in the Armenian Adam literature. We give the relevant excerpt from our published edition.[55] The work bears no title in the manuscript, and the title we assigned in the edition is used here.

1 And when Adam fell <from the Gard>en to this world of beasts, then night's darkness came and put him in the dark. And doubting, he wept bitterly. And again the Confuser came, the malicious, wicked Satan.

2 In angelic form he appeared like a friend and said, "Why are you weeping inconsolably?"

3 Adam said to him—he spoke as to a friend—"Because I was deprived of

the immortal Garden and of the unending light and I fell to the thorny earth, and above all, darkness also ruled over me, and I do not know what I will do."

4 The all-wicked one said to him, "What will you give me if I give you light?"

5 Adam said to him, "And what has remained to me of my glory that <I shall> give it to you, because I am naked and confounded? But (I have) only a leaf from this fig-tree, which I made a covering for my nakedness."

6 Satan said to him, "Give me your soul and that of your descendants, and I will give you light."

7 But he who had become foolish and separated from divine knowledge did not recognize his (i.e., Satan's) dark will and cunning and his own and his descendants' destruction, but (being innocent) like suckling children he was deceived doubly and gave (Satan) the souls.

8 And it was not yet time to grow light (i.e., dawn). Satan said to Adam, "Set a condition (agreement) between us that until the uncreated comes into existence and the undying dies, your soul and your descendants' are <in> my hand, and then you shall see light."

9 And he set the unjust and deadly condition (agreement). And it became morning and he saw light.

10 And when once more evening came and again it grew dark, he wept because of the condition (agreement), and he was unable to dissolve (it), for it was impossible for men to break the condition, only for the uncreated One.

11 And the angel of God, having come, gave him a certain small comfort, some good news and said,

12 "In time the Word of God will come and will liberate you."

13 And, <having sat> opposite the Garden, with both wailing and laments he completed his life.

14 And Satan, having gone happily, built Hell, and all the souls of the progeny of Adam he put in there by means of his demons. And he made all the creatures of God worship and sacrifice to himself.

15 And he gathered in the souls for six thousand years.

A number of constitutive elements of the legend are missing from this story, but enough remain for us to see that it reflects the legend of the cheirograph. Among the most significant elements to be lacking is the very term "cheirograph." In §8 Satan says, "Set a condition between us." The condition (պայման) is, no doubt, another word for the cheirograph, but that is normally reflected by the calque ձեռագիր in Armenian.[56] The actual formulation of the "condition" is somewhat different from that found in *Expulsion* and *Adam, Eve, and the Incarnation*. The elements connected with the writing of the contract (i.e., the imprint of Adam's hand on the stone, the placing of the stone in the river Jordan, and the whole story of Christ's baptism as the reversal of the cheirograph) are all absent.

The factors we have enumerated so far relate to the end of the tale and the concomitant redemption, the freeing from Satan. However, the formulation of the initial part of the story also differs from the closely related narratives in *Transgression* and *Adam, Eve, and the Incarnation*. The incident of the gloomy place and the angelic instruction about agriculture are not to be found in *Adam Story I*. The problem that Adam encounters, therefore, is the darkness, and there is no hint at all of the search for food. Even a fast after the expulsion is not discussed. The single stage of the fall is parallel to a single stage of the deception, which can be contrasted with what is found in the preceding Armenian documents. A further intriguing point in the present document is that Eve is not mentioned at all. Adam is the sole actor.

As far as concerns the "condition," it may well be that the term, ձեռագիր, "cheirograph," was not well understood by the author-editor, and he replaced it with պայման, "condition," in an attempt to clarify its meaning. The agreement that Adam made with Satan could not be broken. This is stated explicitly (§10), and it forms a theme of the latter part of the document, which we have not reproduced. Although some righteous men tried to resist the "condition," they were not able to do so (§15). A prime example was Enoch, who prayed "on account of the protoplast and the agreement." Because of his righteousness, he was taken to heaven, because, if he had died upon the earth, his soul would have been subject to Satan.

Thus, the language of freeing from Satan (ազատեսցէ, "he will liberate," §11) is very central. The angel says to Enoch in §18, "There is no egress . . . unless you have liberated (ազատեցիր) your soul from Satan."[57] A promise of redemption occurs in §§11–12. There we have the angelic prediction, which, though it is called "a certain small comfort," is also designated "good tidings, gospel" [աւետիս], comparable with *Adam, Eve, and the Incarnation.* Here, there is no hint at Satan's "anti-gospel." Instead, a new element is introduced, or rather an element only implicit in other texts is here made explicit. In §14 it says that Satan "made all the creatures of God worship and sacrifice to himself." This has to do with Satan's aspirations to be god, which in a quite other way are behind the Lucifer story. That is to be found in the primary Adam books, in Latin, Armenian, and Georgian, at least. This idea is combined with the idea that the pagan deities were demons, which is found in ancient Jewish literature and thenceforth.[58]

The prophecy of redemption is very short, however, reading just "In time the Word of God will come and will liberate you" (§12). No further details are added, and there is no language of breaking, erasing, destroying, or annihilating the cheirograph. Many more details are given about Enoch, his righteousness, assumption, and eschatological role (§§16–20). Although the gathering in of the souls to Hell is discussed in some detail, their release from hell is not.

The question naturally arises whether the document as we have it was composed originally thus, or whether it is an excerpt from or adaptation of a larger work. If so, the reversal of the contract might have taken place in the second part of the "original" work. The integration with the detailed Enoch traditions is intriguing and shows a different sort of utilization of the legend of the cheirograph to that in, say, *Adam, Eve, and the Incarnation.* The particular Enoch tradition dominant here is also unique to a group of Armenian apocrypha.[59] It is integrated with the idea of subjection to Satan, so the righteous Enoch was assumed alive in order to prevent him suffering after death in Satan's clutches.

It should be noted that the idea of the gloomy place into which Adam and Eve fall directly after the expulsion is clearly not present, although it is to be found in other Armenian Adam writings. According to *Adam Story 1*, Adam went directly from the Garden to the dark night in the "world of beasts." The expression "this world of beasts" does not occur in *Adam, Eve, and the Incarnation* or in *Transgression* and *Expulsion.* In *Penitence of Adam* §4, the food Adam and Eve find after the Expulsion is described as կերակուր զազանաց, "food for beasts," in contrast with Adam and Eve's previous paradisiacal food. Thus, "world of beasts," as a designation for this world, is an extension of terminology originally relating to the quest for food.

It is intriguing that Satan is called by one of his frequent Armenian designations, բանսարկուն, "the Confuser, the Deceiver." This title is not unusual for Satan.[60] He also appears as a deceiver "in the form of an angel" in *Book of Adam* 17:1 and in *Penitence of Adam* in the corresponding place, and other Adam works use a similar expression. The double nature of the deception is made clear here by the emphasis in §7 both on Adam's innocence—like a baby's—and on Satan's double deception of him.

Armenian Adam Fragment 1

BIBLIOGRAPHY

This document is published in Stone, *Armenian Apocrypha Relating to Patriarchs and Prophets*, 2–11.

TRANSLATION

1 Adam lived for eight hundred and thirty years. 2 For, during a hundred years he drew pains (i.e., suffered) on account of the longings and desire for the Garden which came <to> his mind. 3 His soul did not depart. He remembered the sweetness and the delight of the Garden. 4 He was terrified on account of the bitter Hell to whom he had given his contract.

It is not certain whether the reference here is to the legend of the cheirograph specifically, or in a more general sense to Adam's indebtedness to hell/Satan in one or another way, although the former seems most likely.

CHAPTER SIX

The Story in Greek

A number of texts dealing with Adam's contract with Satan are known in Greek. The oldest is a poem by Georgios Chumnos of the early sixteenth century. The latest are folktales recorded in the early part of the twentieth century. We present here those known to us.

Poetic Retelling in Sixteenth-Century Greece: Georgios Chumnos

The Cretan poet Georgios Chumnos (ca. 1500) wrote a *Poem on Genesis and Exodus* more than 2,800 lines long.[1] It contains the legend of the cheirograph, in a form much resembling the Armenian tales we have just discussed. An English verse translation of the poem was published by F. H. Marshall together with the text in 1924.[2]

It starts after the expulsion of the protoplasts from Eden; Adam and Eve wept and bewailed their loss of Paradise. This idea is to be found in the Armenian *Repentance of Adam and Eve* §§12–24[3] and in the Romanian *Plaint of Adam.*[4] They set out, naked and barefooted. In Chumnos's poem, night is said to fall, and they did not know what it was.[5] The devil appeared and asked for a cheirograph, using the expression χειρόγραφον (line 21), in exchange for the light. They promised to give him their offspring. No limit is put on the cheirograph's validity. Night fell a second time, and they uncovered the devil's deceit.

In this poem, there is no mention of the fate of the cheirograph or of the Jordan River; nor is there promise of redemption or a story of Christ's destruction of the stone contract. The scope of the story may well be determined by the narrative structure of Chumnos's work. One wonders whether the reference to Adam and Eve being barefooted is a development of the nakedness theme.[6] In Genesis, Adam and Eve are provided with clothes by divine intervention, but nothing is said about shoes. Here there is no mention of the clothes that God made for them (Genesis 3:21).

Chumnos's sources for some of this material remain unclear, but Megas claims not quite precisely that elements of it are also reflected in various Greek liturgical compositions.[7] Marshall analyzed Chumnos's sources, and points particularly to the Greek *Palaea* and Variant B of the Slavonic *Life of Adam and Eve*.[8] The legend of the cheirograph is not found in the *Palaea,* as we have already pointed out.

Saul Lieberman deals with the story as it is found in the poem of Georgios Chumnos and in the Slavonic *Life of Adam and Eve.* He claims that the form of the story known to Chumnos (whose poem is close to the Greek *Palaea* in other respects) is based on a misunderstanding of that found in the Slavonic *Life of Adam and Eve*.[9] This conclusion seemed reasonable when considering the information available when Lieberman published his article. It is, however, controverted by the Armenian texts, which became known only after Lieberman's article was published.

In Georgios Chumnos's poem, as in the Armenian stories and various of the Greek forms of the cheirograph legend, the problem that leads Adam and Eve to make a contract with Satan is the search for light, not Satan's prohibition of plowing.

Lieberman pointed out a number of analogies between the material found in the cheirograph legend, as he knew it from Georgios Chumnos, and from the Slavonic *Life of Adam and Eve* and some Rabbinic sources. The chief points he makes are, first, that in *Aboth de Rabbi Nathan* A, p. 7 (ed. Schechter), we find the idea that Adam and Eve are afraid at the setting of the sun. Next, he raises the possibility that the idea of a cheirograph or contract here is connected with the one that Adam gave relating to seventy years of his life. According to Rabbinic legend, Adam was to live a thousand years, but he ceded seventy of them. This was done by means of a שטר מתנה, "deed of gift."[10] Note that the idea of the שטר that God gave is to be found in *Alfa-Beta de Ben Sira*.[11]

Chumnos's poem is the oldest Greek witness to the full-blown legend of the χειρόγραφον, although certain elements of it are much older.[12]

The Angel, <from the order> of the Cherubim, obstructs the doors,	1
he seals Eve and the Protoplast outside.	
They received the verdict of Adam together with Eve,	
and in front of Paradise they sat, and (there was) a lament.	
Adam, miserable, sat down and sighed deeply,	5
and groaned from his heart, uttered a harsh sound.	
"O, holiest Paradise, planted because of me,	
and because of Eve's counsel it was sealed up outside."	
They were removed, they left their country, and went away,	
barefooted, stark naked walked to the high ground.	10
They had never seen darkness before, they had ever day,	
the sun set, evening knocked them down.	
And darkness came upon them, and light became dim,	
they stood on their knees, the way got confused.	
Believing the day never will arise again for them,	15
but all being darkness, and evening will endure.	
Suddenly the thrice-cursed one approached; listen what he does!	
the jealous Devil came to deceive them.	
He said to them: "Promise me something, and I will take care of you,	
the Sun and the precious light and day would I make for you?"	20
And they, foolish people, made a contract,	
anyway they composed it, saying and mentioning:	
"Both we and the whole of our descendance will be governed by you,	
and whatever you tell us to do we shall not deviate from it."	
And that night passed, and another day came,	25
and again that passed, and came another day.	
And Adam again was deceived, a second time, with Eve,	
they beat their breasts, with an embittered lament.	

Modern Greek Tales

A number of modern Greek tales were recorded in the work *Laographia*, published in 1962.[13] They come from the Peloponnesus and other places, and one of the tellers was from Crete. Another, different tale in Modern Greek from Thrace was published by George Megas in 1928. Thus the story of the cheirograph seems to be spread throughout the Greek peninsula. One might have surmised that the occurrence of the tale in Thrace was due to Slavic influence, because of the pervasive and sustained Slavic influence in that area. However, its spread in both the Peloponnesus and Crete makes this idea doubtful, and it is difficult to infer from the distribution of the stories that their origin was Slavonic.[14] Moreover, we have shown in chapter 4 that the form reported by Megas is rather different from the Bulgarian-Romanian legends. In the Thracian tale, the word χειρόγραφον is used; in the other stories, Modern Greek and Turkish words for "contract" are found.[15]

THE CONTRACT (τὸ ὁμόλογο) OF ADAM AND EVE[16]

When the Protoplasts were thrown out of Paradise, they not only perceived their nakedness, but also started to perceive their hunger. Finally they were very hungry, and they set out on a road and did not know where they were going! There, at the place to which they had advanced, they saw the Jordan river in the distance. They stopped and were thinking that they would not be able to cross it. But, as they were pondering, they saw someone approaching them. He greets them and asks where they are going and what they want. They spoke to him of their hunger. He answered them that he was able to satisfy them about this and he would also direct them how to take care not to be hungry in the future; all they needed to do was sign a deed of contract, by means of which they agreed that they will always obey[17] him, and that they revere him as their god. The Protoplasts, forced by their hunger, agreed, and at once the devil presented them with a slab[18] of stone, upon which they agreed in writing to their blind submission. The Devil took the contract and threw it to the bottom of the Jordan river, and the slab of stone remained there.

When the Christ descended from heaven, he went and was baptized in the Jordan river at the exact depth where the slab was. The fire of his Divinity[19] burned the slab and destroyed (διέλυσε) it. In this way, the contract of debt was destroyed, the obligatory promise of the first parents' submission to the Devil.

For this reason also, one of the prayers of the Great Blessing of the Waters says: "The Jordan river turned back when it saw the Divine fire, descending in a corporeal form over it." The famous hymn of the Great Friday[20] says: "He who liberated Adam in the Jordan river." Accordingly, our Greek folk tradition agrees with the hymnology of our Holy Church.

The hunger! The terrible and abominable hunger! It not only forced Adam to give way to the lord of the world (i.e., Satan), but also forced Jacob to reject the place of (his) birth, and descend to Egypt. Hunger compelled Esau to sell his primogeniture for a plate of lentils. Our Saviour and Lord was tempted by the Devil because of hunger, but the New Adam did not obey him. And for this reason the hunger compels us to suffer all, indeed, to exile ourselves to remedy this necessity. The divine Homer also mentions this:

Let wine and bread then adde to it: they helpe the twofold part,
The soule and body in a man, both force and fortitude.
All day men cannot fight and fast, though never so indude
With minds to fight, for, that suppose, there lurks yet secretly
Thirst, hunger, in th' oppressed joynts, which no mind can supply.
They take away a marcher's knees. Men's bodyes thoroughly fed,
Their minds share with them in their strength. . . . .
(Homer, Il. 19, 160–171).[21]

This tale exhibits many points of great interest. First, it shares with Georgios Chumnos the stress on Adam and Eve's nakedness after the expulsion. Next, it seems at first blush to make the crossing of the Jordan the problem; but in the end it turns out to be hunger. Hunger is lamented in the fourth paragraph, and its baneful influence on Jacob and Esau is emphasized. Christ, this paragraph says, although tempted by Satan with hunger, successfully resisted. The parallel here being deliberately drawn with Adam is significantly highlighted by designating Christ "the New Adam." The implication is clear: the old Adam could not resist Satan when hungry, but the New Adam could.

In a number of the retellings of the cheirogragh legend we have examined so far, food has formed a central problem. Adam and Eve are hungry, and thus the provision of the proper food for them forms the problem that has made Satan's deceit possible. The teaching of agriculture is God's response to this problem. In this Modern Greek tale, hunger is the problem, but agriculture is not an issue; indeed, it is not mentioned. Neither does Satan prevent agriculture, nor, as in earlier forms of the story, did Michael teach it. It is just hunger itself that is the problem, but we are not told how Satan resolved it.

Hunger forms a prominent motif in the Armenian and Georgian primary Adam books, although agricultural teaching is also introduced there. Our story's concentration solely on hunger is quite striking. Moreover, the story lacks the element of deceit. Satan is not shown to have deceived the protoplasts; nor was he himself deceived.

The actual cheirograph story is fairly standard. Adam and Eve accept Satan's proposition: he will help them avoid hunger in the future if they and their children accept his dominance. (How he does this is not stated!) The agreement is written on a stone tablet, which is placed in the depths of the Jordan. Christ is baptized at this spot and destroys the agreement.

A further point is intriguing. The tale as we have it shows a certain sophistication and consciousness. It triumphantly shows that Greek popular tales are in accordance with the practice of the Greek Orthodox Church.[22] Moreover, it supports its discussion with citations about hunger from the Old and New Testaments and from Homer. However, these two bodies of material about Homer and the official Greek Orthodox church were, it seems to us, added to the story by the person who committed it to writing, and the original cheirograph tale does not extend beyond the end of the second paragraph.

This story is clearly part of the cheirograph traditions, but it does not seem to be directly affiliated with the folk stories from Romania and Bulgaria that we have discussed above.

ADAM AND CHRIST[23]

"The one who liberated Adam in the Jordan River, deigned to accept a slap. . . . "[24]

When God expelled Adam from Paradise, Adam did not know where to go or what to do. Then, the devil met him, who, in order to help him said that first they should make a deed of contract—an *homologo*—that they wrote upon a stone—because there was no paper then.

The devil seized this stone at once and threw it into the Jordan River, lest Adam find it if later he repented—as indeed he did repent—and destroy it.

It is this very stone that the Christ trod underfoot when he was baptized in the Jordan River by the precursor, and Adam was liberated from his contract with the devil.

This brief story shows a knowledge of the legend of the cheirograph, but without any details. We do not know what the problem was, how the devil deceived Adam, or any other such specific matters. Its main interest for us is in its very existence.[25]

Modern Greek: Megas's Text

In 1928 George Megas recorded and published a Modern Greek oral text with a German translation.[26]

This story clearly preserves the idea of the contract and also offers yet another etiological interpretation of the word "cheirograph." Satan literally writes the contract with Adam's hand, with its nail and its blood (compare the blood in the Slavonic Variant C). Moreover, an etiology of the creases in the palm of the hand is provided: they are writing on the hand. The strangeness of the word χειρόγραφον in the meaning of "contract" in Modern Greek is witnessed by its replacement by other terms in all the Modern Greek tales.

It is interesting that two elements of the story appear to be separate etiologies of χειρόγραφον. The first is the writing of the contract with the blood of Adam's hand, so that it is a writing by means of his hand. The second etiology is the writing on Adam's hand, the lines in his hand, with their mantic function. These double etiologies explain a term, "cheirograph," that has been lost from the text. They clearly come from an older layer of tradition in which the word "cheirograph" still occurred.

What is interesting about this telling of the legend is that there is no problem. The deceit of the devil is not explained at all. The point of the story is changed: it is no longer about why the devil rules the world. It explains the mount of Golgotha, which is made from a cairn that was formed on Adam's grave. With his blood, Christ rinsed clean the stone bearing the contract. In §8, in the writing of the contract, it does not say on what it was written, but the clear implication of §10 is that it was on a stone. That stone, it seems, was on Adam's tomb. These elements—the deceit, the stone, indeed the contract itself—are not explained in the story. We can understand them if we know the story from other sources. This is an extraordinary witness to the broad spread of the story. Our translation also includes sections §§3–7, which were not included in the German translation of Megas.[27]

1.   At the beginning was Adam, the protoplast. God took some dust from the four corners <of the world> with his hand and squeezed it together. The water was running down. He mixed it (the water and the dust), it resulted in mud, it became Adam, by this (i.e., God's) hand, neither from mother nor from father.

There was also a garden, a great garden, exceedingly beautiful. All the plants and fruits were there, inside.[28] (God) put Adam there, in the middle (of the garden); he also put the serpent (there); he also put the devil (there). Those three were there, in the middle (of the garden). God created neither the devil nor the serpent. They were not of good (intention),[29] they had no turn to be created. (God) had cast them there into the middle (of the garden) to test what Adam would do.

In the garden there were day and night, outside the garden there was only night.

2.   On the next day, as Adam was walking about in the garden, he was overcome by his solitude, and his heart was troubled.

In the evening Adam lay down. God came, removed one rib from Adam, blew on it, made a woman of it, called her Eve. He made her a woman and laid her beside Adam.

Adam woke up at night, looked up, there was a woman near him. Adam got up, ran away, and the woman ran away too, they did not know one another. God saw and said to Adam: "Adam," he said, "I gave you a companion for your entertainment."

They start to play together, to converse, but they do not know how to make children! "Of all of these fruits you will eat, of the fruit of the tree of figs you will not eat!" At that time they were completely hairy. Just like a bear, so were they.

3.   They ate from everything, going around and around; they harvested fruit in the middle (of the Garden). And Eve said, "Let us also eat from the fig." Adam said, "God said that we should not eat (of it)." She deceived Adam, "When we will taste it," she said, "we will also become gods." And they ate. They shucked their hair, all the pelt.

When they saw one another naked, they were ashamed. They squeezed their thighs and placed their hands on their heads from shame, they squeezed their armpits. There, at the places where they squeezed, the hair remained; the rest was shucked.

4.   God saw from above. He called to Adam: "Adam, Adam!" What could they say (to) God? How could they appear naked! They cut (leaves) from the tree with their knife and made sheets. It was a kind of grassy clothing, the first mantle, as they are called; this leaf was the first of all dresses. Adam took two mantles from it, and faced forward, so that his testicles were not visible, in order to appear before God!

"Adam, Adam," he said, "Did I not tell you not to eat from the fruit of the fig?"

And Adam said, "You gave me a woman, and she deceived me."

He contradicted God.

God said to the woman: "Why did you speak so that he ate from this very fruit?"

"Because," she said, "the demon deceived me."

He asked the demon. "Because the serpent deceived me," he said.

5.   At the time the serpent walked upright and would not have died: the snake would have eaten from every man that is fresh and completely fleshy; that it would eat. Its mouth was large as a boiler, so it had room for a man. When it is time for him (i.e., a man) to die, the serpent would come to eat him. For he was immortal, and had no illnesses.

God cursed the serpent, "You will fall on the belly," he said. He arose, killed the serpent, and threw it to the earth. It became dust and this dust became lice and fleas and those (insects) that now bite us. Many kinds of little snakes remained, and men still fear serpents because they wish to eat humans. We do not fear anything else. What will the serpent do to you? but anyway we fear it. It cannot eat you, but the very dust eats you.

6.   God cursed the Devil, "You are caught at no place,[30] neither from heavens nor from earth. You will live in the air and there you will be exhausted." And the Devil fled to the heavens and now is dropped some spheres down from the demon of the air, where he strikes one and that one suffers, making the legs crooked or the hands become demonic (hands).

7.   God cursed Adam and Eve.

He said to Adam, "You will work with efforts, you will strive day and night," he said. "You will feed your children with your sweat." Since then we have been suffering; you will sweat, you must wipe your sweat and protect your children.

God said to Eve, "You will bear your children with trouble, and day and night for two to three years you shall labour with them at your breast[31] with your sweat. This labour, which you will do during the day, to which I curse you, you will take and embrace in your arms. It will be not good for you."

8.   God cursed them and sent them out of Paradise. God expelled them, "Get out of Paradise!" he said.

The devil threw Adam out, "Out here" he says, "I make day and I make night," said the devil. "We will make a contract. I will put my seal on your forehead. Open your palm," he said, "I will make some ink." And he seized his fingernail, he made it a pen and was dipping it in the blood of Adam's palm, and made the contract. With his knife he made lines in the palm of the hand, removed some blood, dipped (the pen) in it, and made the contract. For this reason our hand is creased.[32]

9.   (Adam) went outside (i.e., the garden) and they did these things. The devil deceived him, he damned him. Adam went into torment. He died in torment and they called him "the accursed Adam." They buried Adam in a certain place. Whoever passed by there, cast a stone (saying): "the accursed Adam." Once a king passed by there with many thousands of soldiers, and they said:

"What is it?"

"Adam's tomb."

"Cast stones!" There a cairn (or: height) was made (i.e., Golgotha).

10.   After a fair number of years Christ was born. The time of the crucifixion

arrived. Jesus Christ determined that the Hebrews themselves would go high up on those rocks, where Adam was, there (too) Christ must go to shed his blood. They went here, they crucified him, they shed his blood, they pierced his sides. Jesus Christ did what he determined to do,[33] so that his blood might be shed and so that it should go (? drip) from stone to stone and to find the palm of Adam's hand. He rinsed it clean from the blood where the devil had dipped and written and established the contract, so as to rinse clean the sins of Adam. Because even Christ had Adam as his father, (indeed) the whole world has (Adam as its) father. For Adam is the first created: For God made him with his hand. . . .[34]

This story covers the events from the creation of Adam and Eve on. This story is formulated in popular terms, and, in addition to containing the cheirograph incident that has been discussed above, it contains a series of etiological elements. These include the origin of human body hair (§§2–3); and the origin of clothing, which builds with a humorous pun on the biblical story: Adam and Eve are πρωτοπλάστοι, "first created ones," while the clothes that Adam makes are πρωτομαντῆλες, "first garments" (§4). The story also introduces a fourth curse additional to the biblical curses on Adam, Eve, and the serpent; this is a curse on the devil (called demon here). The devil here is introduced between the curse on Eve and the curse on the serpent. The biblical curse that the serpent shall eat the dust has turned into an etiological tale of the origin of biting insects and snakes (§5). An additional element in this story is that the serpent is thought of as swallowing all who die. This idea may come from the common scene in paintings of Hades as a demon swallowing the dead. It is much older, of course, than the story known in Thrace seventy years ago. A further etiology is of the idea of the devil in the air, suspended between heaven and earth, which is due to his being cast down by God. This explains the spirits that infect the air, of course, and it has a remarkable parallel in the Armenian *Questions of Ezra* B 6. This element of the story also explains the deformed arms and legs that typify demons.

CHAPTER SEVEN

The Cheirograph
According to Colossians

Some Examples

As has become evident to the reader by now, the term "cheirograph" is characteristic of the legend in nearly all its forms.[1] On occasion, in the preceding chapters, we have also mentioned the only New Testament use of χειρόγραφον, in Colossians 2:14, and the Christian exegesis of this verse. Some further observations on this subject will be set forth here, because much of what has been written about the cheirograph legend is melded with the issues of the exegesis of Colossians 2:14. In Colossians, the word χειρόγραφον has usually been taken in the sense of bill of indebtedness, although a number of other interpretations are possible.[2]

From Colossians 2:14, the idea developed of a document of obligation or deed of indebtedness (χειρόγραφον), which Adam incurred by sinning and which was erased or destroyed by Christ on the cross. As we have remarked in an earlier chapter, the history of the understanding of this verse is complex and lies beyond the scope of the present book. Indeed, it has been the object of research in its own right. However, scholars frequently confuse "cheirograph," meaning Adam's contract with Satan (the legend), with "cheirograph" denoting the bill of indebtedness Adam incurred by sinning (deriving from Colossians 2:14). This study has heretofore traced the first sense of the word through a variety of texts. Now we shall give a few examples of the second usage, not attempting to be in any way exhaustive, but in order to provide a basis for the reader to compare and contrast these two quite different applications of the same terminology.

The tradition deriving from Colossians is typically associated with Christ's crucifixion, and most often also with his descent into Hades. The legend of the cheirograph that we have outlined in the preceding chapters is connected with the baptism of Christ and with the hiding of the cheirograph in the water. What is remarkable is the consistency with which these two traditions, each with its typical and distinctive meaning of χειρόγραφον, are held apart.

At the end of these preliminary remarks, we should stress once more that the word χειρόγραφον denotes different things in the two traditions. In the legend, it means "contract" and designates the contract that Adam signed with Satan. In the exegesis of Colossians 2:14, it is the deed of indebtedness that Adam incurred by sinning and which Christ will wipe out.

In ancient Christian tradition, we find, for example, Irenaeus (born between 140 and 160 and died in 202), who says in *Haer.* 5.17.3, *quemadmodum per lignum debitores facti sumus Deo, per lignum accipiamus nostri debiti remissionem,* that is, "Just as we became debtors of God through a tree, through a tree we receive remission of our debt." In this text, it is God who holds the bill of indebtedness that Adam incurred. That quickly changes, and by 200 C.E. at the latest, Satan, not God, holds the bill of indebtedness, which Christ on the cross annuls.[3] This change is probably related to the spread in Christian thought of the tradition of the descent of Christ into the underworld. It became accepted that Christ annulled Adam's debt not simply by being nailed to the cross, but by going down into Hades, repossessing the bill, destroying it, and bringing Adam and Eve out. The idea arose then that the bill of debt was held by Satan and not by God. This view, however, goes beyond what the New Testament says in Colossians, and bases itself on the ancient apocryphal tradition of Christ's descent into the underworld.

A text titled "The Cheirograph of Adam" is known in Armenian from the *Book of Questions* of Vanakan *vardapet* (1203–1272) and two seventeenth-century manuscripts.[4] This text sets out in elenchic form the idea of three bills of indebtedness: one incurred by Adam through breaking the divine commandment not to eat of the tree, one incurred by the Jews through transgressing their undertaking at Sinai, and one incurred by Christians who, although they have renounced Satan at baptism, in fact sin subsequently. The text continues (J840): "There are three cheirographs (i.e., bills of indebtedness), two the Lord rent upon the cross, that of Adam, and that of the Jews. And confession rends ours and penitence, through the mercy and blood of Christ."

The text cites verses relating to the cheirographs of Adam (Genesis 2:17) and of the Jews (Exodus 24:3, 7), which are in fact commandments and not statements of guilt or contracts. Yet, context clearly implies that the transgression of these commandments produces guilt, which in turn creates a bill of indebtedness.

This notion is very like that expressed in Homily 6 on Colossians by John Chrysostom:

> Seest thou how great His earnestness that the bond should be done away? To wit, we all were under sin and punishment. He Himself, through suffering punishment, did away with[5] both the sin and the punishment, and He was punished on the Cross. To the Cross then He affixed it; as having power, He tore it asunder. What bond? He means either that which they said to Moses, namely, "All that God hath said will we do, and be obedient" (Ex 24:3), or if not that, this, that we owe to God obedience; or if not this, he means that the devil held possession of it, the bond which God made for Adam, saying, "In the day thou eatest of the tree, thou shalt die." (Gen 2:17) This bond then the devil held in his possession. And Christ did not give it to us, but Himself tore it in two,[6] the action of one who remits joyfully.[7]

It is striking that the very verses that Chrysostom adduced to characterize the bills of Adam and of the Jews were those used in the medieval Armenian text. Here, quite unambiguously, it is Satan who holds Adam's bill of indebtedness.

This homily by Chrysostom also occurs in the old Armenian translation of his works, where the word χειρόγραφον is not translated by the Armenian calque ծեռագիր, but by a quite different word, դատակնիք. This compositum of *dat*, "law," and *knik'*, "seal," means "decree, condemnation." This teaches us that the ideas of Vanakan's text may well go back to Chrysostom, but they were not formulated using language drawn from the old Armenian version of Chrysostom's homily.

In Ephrem Syrus, *Carmina Sogyata* 1.24 (mid-fourth century), it is the devil who holds the bill of indebtedness.[8] This bill was written by Eve in Eden and inscribed by the serpent.

ܐܫܬܪܝܪ ܐܬ ܘܙܘܬܐ ܣܘ ܗܘܐ ܚܒܬ ܡܚܝܒ ܗܘܐ

ܥܘܬܐ ܠܘ܀ܬܝ ܝ̣ܘܡ̇ ܕܬܐܘܬܕܘܢ ܠܚܝ̈ܐ.

ܕܟܬܒ ܘܚܬܡ ܘܒܝܬܐ ܠܘ܀ܬ ܕܢܚܫܐ ܣܦܪܐ ܗܘܐܪ.

Eve became guilty in Eden with a great indictment (deed of obligation),
For from her children was demanded death for their generations.
For the serpent, an adversarial scribe, wrote and signed and sealed in his
 guile.

Behind this passage lies the idea of a bill of indebtedness that is created by
the sin of Eve in the Garden. Even though the language of writing is used,
it is by no means certain that here Ephrem's language moves beyond the
figurative. Underneath this literary figure certainly lies the view expressed
by Irenaeus and Chrysostom.

Ephrem's conceptions were more complex than this, as may be seen from
the following extracts from his *Carmina Nisibena*.[9] The decree of death
(*diathēkē*) is a bill of indebtedness (indictment) that Adam gave to Death
and Sin. In the end, Christ will get back all those whom Death and Sheol
have taken and imprisoned. Adam sinned, and because of his sin he is a debtor
to death, and in the course of his descent to Hades, Christ will undo and
annul the indebtedness.

Adam returned to his earth and made the testament.
He inscribed a great indebtedness to death and to sin,
In transgressing the commandment he sealed the deed,
Our Lord came and saved him and resurrected him,
Death changed (his words) and wrote, and Sheol was his guarantor,
For all which they plundered and seized will return in the Resurrection

Further in the same work 36.17 we find Death/Satan is speaking to Jesus
as follows:[10]

ܠܐܕܡ ܡܫܟܢܐ ܪܒܐ
ܕܒܗ ܗܘ ܠܡܝ̈ܬܐ ܟܠ ܛܫ̈ܝܢ
ܒܗ ܟܡܝܢ ܗܘܘ ܟܠܗܘܢ ܚ̈ܝܐ
ܦܓܪܗ ܕܐܕܡ
ܐܦܩ ܡܝ̈ܬܐ ܒܡܐܬܝܬܟ
ܐܝܟ ܒܐ̈ܝܕܝ

ܕܒܪ ܠܟ
ܐܝܟܢܐ ܕܟܕ ܩܒܠܬܗ
ܡܫܟܢܐ ܩܕܡܝܐ
ܗܘ ܡܟܝܠ ܐܫܠܡܬܟ ܠܟ ܟܠ
ܕܐܫܡܥ ܫܝܦܘܪܟ
ܘܐܡܬܝ

O Jesus, King
and with my entreaty
Adam, that great pledge
for in him all the dead are hidden
in him were concealed all living things.
(namely) Adam's body;
and when I hear your trumpet

accept my entreaty,
take for yourself a pledge,
lead away for yourself,
just as when I received him,
That first pledge I gave to you,
rise up, then, and reign over all
with my own hands I will lead
out the dead when you come.[11]

Another way in which a document is introduced at this point is in Origen, *Homily 6 on Exodus,* section 9 in discussion of Colossians 2:14. There the devil is said to have purchased men for the money of sins, and to have written *tabulas servitatis et peccati chirographa* for the slaves so purchased. The term "cheirograph" here is used and is related to the devil. Christ bought human beings back from the devil.[12]

In the *Commentary on Psalms* by Didymus the Blind of Alexandria (ca. 370), we find the following passage:

> Through his sins (each person) has sold himself and made himself a debtor. Now, then, that by means of which the enemy, King of Sheol, imprisons is said to be a cheirograph. Indeed, it is a cheirograph which each person has composed with his own hands. "He (Christ)," therefore, "set it aside" so that he (Satan) may no longer rule over us through the cheirograph and by that which we have composed, having inscribed ourselves in it.[13]

Many other texts exist in which these ideas predominate, both in the East and the West.[14] Pseudo-Macarius writes as follows:[15]

> Behold then, he (Satan), stirring up trouble with these things, approaches his attendants and brings together all the powers, and the ruler of evil presents the cheirographs and says: "See, these ones obeyed my word. See how the humans prostrated themselves to us." While God, being a righteous judge, demonstrates there also his justness and says to him: "Adam

obeyed you and you seized all of his hearts. Humanity obeyed you and what is my body doing here? It is blameless. That body of the first Adam was in debt to you, and justly you seized his cheirographs. But all bear witness in favor of me, that I did not sin, nor am I even indebted to you; and all bear witness in my favor (on behalf of me) that I am the son of God. For a voice above of the heavens bore witness over the earth, "This one is my son, the beloved one; listen to him (cf. Matthew 3:17, Mark 1:11, Luke 3:22)." John bears witness, "Behold, the lamb of God, the remover of sin of the world (John 1:29)." And again the Scriptures say: "Who did not make a sin nor was deceit found in him (cf. John 1:47)," and that: "The Ruler of this world comes and will discover nothing in me." But as for you, Satan, you bear witness to me, saying: "I know who you are, the son of God," and again, "What is for us and for you, Jesus of Nazareth? You came before the time to torment us (cf. Mark 1:24, 3:11)." These three testify on my behalf; who sends forth his voice above of the heavens, those on earth, and you yourself. I redeem, therefore, the body sold to you through the first Adam, I put an end to your (sg.) cheirographs. For I, having been crucified and descended into Hades, return the debts of Adam, and I command you, Hades, Darkness, and Death, cast out the souls of Adam which had been confined." And thus remaining, the wicked powers, trembling, pay back the imprisoned Adam.

Thus there is an initial connection of Adam's sin and Christ's crucifixion. The latter reverses the former. There is also a connection between Christ's crucifixion and the descent tradition; in the course of the descent, Christ takes Adam and Eve out of Hades, and so annuls the results of Adam's sin.[16] The cheirograph is moved from being nailed on the cross to being in Hades' or Satan's hands, and this is related to the descent tradition as we stated above.

The descent into Hades is in turn related to human baptism. This involves descent into the water (as into Hades) and arising reborn. Thus Christ's crucifixion is connected particularly to the baptism of humans, which annuls the results of Adam's sin.

This selection of texts from early patristic literature on shows clearly how Colossians 2:14 was exegeted. It is evident that these representative sources do not have any elements deriving from the ideas embodied in the cheirograph legend, and in this they do not differ from other texts of the same period. The legend of the cheirograph of Adam was only rarely drawn together with the exegesis of Colossians 2:14, and that happened much later and not in standard patristic texts.

On the Apostle's Discourse (Colossians 2:14–15)

In this context, considerable interest inheres in an insular Latin text published by Aidan Breen, "Anonymous, Liber Commenei: The Liturgical Materials in Ms Oxford, Bodleian Library, Auct. F.4/32," *Archiv für Liturgie-Wissenschaft* 34 (1992), 121–153, esp. 121–125. The text is to be found on pages 24–25. We present a translation by Steven C. Smith of the University of Virginia.

In the name of the Holy Trinity, amen.

Canceling the contract of the rule, which was against us. What the contract was which the apostle recalls here, and between whom it was made, and what the rule was which he tells of here, is made clear in this way. This is the exchange which occurred between Adam and the devil. Adam sold life for death, a long life span for a short one, incorruptibility for corruptibility.

Why did the devil do this? So that no man might enter into heaven after him; <he did it> when he heard the Lord saying to Adam: "On whatever day you eat of this tree, you will die."

Who wrote this contract? The devil.

By what hand? By the hand of the devil's wickedness.

On what page? In the memory of the devil, just as it is said of the saints, "Your names have been written in the heavens"—that is, in eternal memory. It is customary that every contract be divided into two parts, in such a way as this: one half in the memory of the devil, the other in the conscience of Adam and his race. This is the wall which was between us and God, just as it is said: "Your sins separate me and you."

What is the rule he tells of here? The threefold explanation which we gained from the devil for . . . the exchange, namely, death of the body, death of sin, death of punishment.

No one was able to cancel this contract except Christ, because it was customary among the ancients for every contract which was canceled to be raised up high on a shaft in the middle of the city before the entire people, so that each of them might know that it had been canceled; afterwards it was erased by water and burned by fire. This points to Christ, who raised up his flesh, on which were written the names of the sins and evil exchanges, high on the cross, in the middle of the city of the world, on a shaft. This contract was erased in the water of baptism and burned in the fire of the passion.

And he removed it from the middle. That is, from the middle space which was between us and the devil, and from the middle space which was between us and Christ, just as it is said: "Your sins separate you," and so forth. Christ canceled it, as the apostle tells, breaking the wall of the enclosure, and he drove the devil out of the middle—that is, of our hearts—just as it is said: "He will be cast out."[17] After we had been his own external garment, he himself was driven out, so that he might tempt us from outside. And after the devil had come unjustly to seek a dwelling-place in Christ—"The prince at this world came to me," and so forth—he was justly expelled from his own dwelling-place, the human race. And after he persuaded bands of Jews and gentiles to crucify Christ in an unjust death, the devil himself perished, just as it is said: "O death, I will be your death," and so forth. Thus Christ has the title "death of death," because Christ is the true death of the devil, leaving no portion of him, and the title "bite of hell," since a bite takes one part and leaves another.

Fastening it to the cross. That is, two crosses, the cross of the example and the cross of the triumph. The cross of the example is the visible one on which the flesh of Christ was crucified, as an example for all the sons of life, so that each might crucify his own flesh for Christ. The cross of the triumph is the invisible one on which Christ crucified the devil and the sin of Adam, so that each might crucify his own sins. These two crosses are represented in the double tree on which the king of Gai was crucified. Gai, the name of the state, is understood as the abyss (*chaos*), indicating the devil as the king of hell.

Putting off the flesh.[18] That is, in the tomb he deprived himself of the unjust garment of flesh. The devil <was deprived> of his just garment, the human race, which was part of the devil's garb until the passion of Christ.

No one at all could cancel the contract until the hope and savior of the whole world had come, just as it is said: "God, omnipotent forever, the sole hope of the world." God is deservedly called omnipotent, he who canceled the sin of the contract, who loosed the chains of our consciences, who removes from the man believing in him the foulness of his nature and adorns him with the mark of innocence, the splendor of justice, and the robe of immortality, and who, in his holy fatherhood, transfers his sons to the condition of the angels.

In what ways did <the apostle> write to them? In four ways: in a lengthy style, when he lingers over the telling; in a brief style, when he speaks briefly; in a universal style, when he speaks of the two peoples;[19] in an exclusive[20] style, when he speaks from a great height.

What sources does he use to corroborate his discussion? The law and the prophets, the words of the teacher,[21] logic, things which are of nature or opposed to it, worldly wisdom.

Under what personas does he speak? Men before the law, men under the law, men under grace, men under the peace to come.

The one who was predestined, because he was the son of God with the power of divinity in him, also watches for (?) the first son, because divinity was not in him.

CHAPTER EIGHT

Conclusion and Implications

The reader who had the patience to follow the preceding chapters this far may well wonder: Why study this legend at all? What is its importance and its interest? Does it embody and reflect ways of viewing the world, human beings, and their relationship with the divine? Or is it just a curiosity, a by-way of human imagination and speculations?

The answers to these questions are varied in character and context. For one thing, this sort of cultural detective work is both exciting and some-times extremely illuminating. Many surprises await those who search out the paths by which traditions such as the cheirograph legend spread, meta-morphosed, and spread yet further. Tracing this progress is important for those interested in cultural history: What were the geographical and cul-tural channels of transmission? Oriental Christianity is a multiform phe-nomenon, but its separate and diverse churches and traditions are often lumped together summarily in Western books on the history of Christian thought. A tradition as distinctive as the cheirograph legend serves, like a scientist's stain on a microscope slide, to highlight interconnections that would otherwise remain latent.

From another perspective, the remarkable geographical spread of the cheirograph legend is itself a very meaningful consideration. Over six cen-turies, from the fourteenth century to the twentieth, it is to be found in a large but clearly demarcated geographical area. It spread from Moscow in the north to Crete in the south, from the Caucasus in the east, through the Balkans—Yugoslavia, Bulgaria, and Romania—and south to Mount Athos and the Greek area. It is found in Thrace and as far south as the Peloponnesus and Crete. It is noteworthy that these locations can be divided into three major groupings: the Caucasus (Armenia and Georgia), the Slavonic and Balkan areas, and Thrace and the Greek world.

Where is it not found? Remarkably it is not found in Syria or Palestine, Egypt or Ethiopia; it never seems to have penetrated south of the Caucasus into the Christian Middle East.[1] It is not found in the West, either, in the Latin or European vernacular traditions and sources, in countries replete with traditions and tales about contracts made by humans with Satan, of which the story of Dr. Faust is a famous, but by no means an isolated, instance.

The legend of the cheirograph is extraordinarily popular in the Romanian-speaking area, and in Moldavia in particular. It is deeply rooted in the art, music, song, and literature of these regions. Did it originate there? This does not seem to be the case. The Romanian Orthodox Church was profoundly influenced by the Slavonic-speaking Orthodoxy that adjoined it. Yet, the geographical spread of the legend indicates that it does not seem likely to have been of Slavonic origin, either. In chapters 3 and 4, we presented material that shows that the morphology of the legend in the Balkan areas was often very distinctive, featuring the "agricultural obstacle" and sayings such as "the living are yours and the dead are mine." Indeed, that form of the legend is dominant in these countries. Yet, simultaneously, throughout this area the version of the legend connected with light also occurs, albeit usually as a minor theme.

The occurrence of the legend in a range of Greek-speaking areas, on the one hand, and in the Caucasus, on the other, suggests to us that it originated in a Greek-speaking or Byzantine area and spread from there to lands influenced by Byzantine culture. In the Greek and Caucasian areas, the agricultural obstacle scarcely occurs, and all is focused around light.

The legend's extensive occurrence among the Armenians is equally striking. Without that, one might have claimed unreservedly that it is of Greek origin and spread throughout the Orthodox churches: Greek, Slavonic, Romanian, and Georgian. Yet it is found extensively utilized in the Armenian tradition, and it is well to remember that from the fifth century on, the Armenian Apostolic Church struggled against the Byzantine and was anti-Chalcedonian in doctrine. It is regarded as heretical by the Orthodox churches and, of course, views them in the same way.[2] This is a reminder that geographical and confessional borders do not always coincide with the cultural. Again, a fascinating trail of transmission is thus made evident.

The types of cultural creations that carry the legend are also very diverse. In literature, it is notable that no trace of it has been discerned so far in the more formal works of ecclesiastical exegesis or homiletics, nor is it found in the liturgy or hymnography. In Armenia, it is to be found chiefly in apocryphal writings. This is generally true also in the Slavonic area, in Russian and Old Church Slavonic. It comes up in Romanian and Bulgarian popular songs and folktales. In Greece, we find it in epic biblical poetry and in popular stories. All through this large geographical area it appears in art, in miniature paintings, in frescoes (in the Balkan lands, Romania, Moldavia, and Mount Athos), on icons, and on liturgical objects such as crosses, book-bindings, and so forth.[3]

It appears, therefore, that we have tapped into a nonformal level of Christian culture in distinct geographical areas. Attention has been paid in recent years to the relationship between the teaching of the Church and popular belief. Stewart's book on the relationship of the two on one of the Greek islands is most intriguing in showing the interplay between them.[4] The paragraphs appended to the Modern Greek story cited above add the double seals of authority of the practice of the church and a citation from Homer to a folk tradition about the cheirograph. In that case, the tradition has been twice domesticated.

We have not been able, during our analysis of the documents and other sources containing the legend, to pinpoint one form as the original from which the others developed. The only distinctive pattern is geographical; the agricultural form of the legend seems to have been tied to the Slavonic and Balkan areas, while the form featuring light as the problem is found all over in different variants.

A second factor making the study of this legend of particular interest is that it concerns Adam and Eve. The stories of Adam and Eve became explanations of the human condition in this world both because of their intrinsic content and because of the fashion in which they were worked out in some Jewish and in Christian sources. The way that they are told, retold, and interpreted reflects and determines how people viewed the world. The Pauline understanding of Adam's fall, and particularly Augustine's interpretation of it, led the West to lay a special stress on the idea of sin. The imperfect human state—death, childbirth, agricultural labor, and the rest—is a result of Adam's disobeying the divine commandment. Human sin goes

back to Adam's sin; since then, original sin is inherent, this situation is resolved only by the crucifixion of Christ. Adam and Eve are expelled from
the Garden, human beings are cursed, sin is rampant because Adam and Eve
deliberately disobeyed a direct divine commandment. It requires the incarnation, the crucifixion, and the Passion of Christ, the New Adam, to undo
the mischief wrought by the old Adam.

The cheirograph legend deals with how humans became subject or enslaved to Satan. This language as a way of talking about the this-worldly
condition is of great significance in early Christianity, and remains so in the
eastern churches. Humans in this world and after their death are under Satan's authority, barring special divine intervention. Indeed, subjection to
the prince of this world is already a problem in the New Testament: see John
12:31, 14:30, 16:11; cf. 2 Corinthians 4:4. The legend of Adam's contract
with Satan explains how this subjection came about and how it was, eventually, annulled.

Therefore, Christian baptism was understood as the renunciation of
Satan—an abjuration repeated thrice in the course of the baptism ceremony—
and also as a guarantee of future freedom from Satan. There is a strong sense
of the devil's domination of humans, and of the efficacy of the Christian faith
in giving surcease from it. It is not by happenstance that the language of
slavery and freedom is so prominent here.

The problem that the legend is addressing, then, is not one of sin or
disobedience. The rule of Satan over this world—or, in another formulation,
over the dead—was not the result of the protoplasts' deliberate disobedience of God's command or of an original sin. That is the Western, the "Au-
gustinian," view. Instead, it was the result of not perceiving, not understanding, the situation. Satan had disguised himself, Satan had made lying
promises, and Adam and Eve did not recognize the deception or him who
spoke it. As one text puts it, "Adam was like a suckling child," completely
naïve, innocent. It is for this reason that Satan could deceive the protoplasts
so easily. So humans entered the difficulties of the this-worldly state because
of a mistake, through that deception that is so strongly stressed in the cheirograph legend. Satan succeeded in tricking them. The protoplasts did no sin,
transgressed no divine command. They were beguiled by the devil's disguise
and sold themselves and their children into slavery by mistake.

In the primary Adam books, there is also a deception, but that deception is a replay, with a variation, of the one in the Garden. Eve is deceived
by Satan's words and breaks off her penance, but Adam isn't; he sees that it

is Satan. He does better than he did in the Garden. Eve has been deceived once again into disobeying a commandment, in this case Adam's commandment not to leave the river.

In the legend, Eve and Adam were equally deceived, and together they discovered the deception. However, there is no commandment involved, and this deception carried within it the deception of the deceiver. Satan, being deceived by himself, lost the very advantage he sought to gain. His deception bore the seed of redemption.

It is as if there are two arches inside one another. The inner arch is composed of the cheirograph leading to subjection to Satan and then Christ's baptism and liberation from Satan. This arch is the stage upon which the immediate drama is played. This world, its woes and sorrows are there. Outside it, more remote and embracing the arch of the cheirograph legend, is the arch of disobedience leading to the earthly state and death or original sin, which are only atoned for by Christ's crucifixion. The outer arch starts earlier on the time line of the world than the inner one, in the Garden, and is completed later than it, in the crucifixion. The inner arch commences after the expulsion and concludes with Christ's baptism. Thus it is held within the outer one. Spatially the same contrast exists. The sin was in God's garden, and the crucifixion, taking place in this world, bridged lower space in the descent into Hades and upper space in the ascension. The mistake of the cheirograph was made in this world, and Christ's baptism and destruction of the stone contract took place in the Jordan River, though it was, of course, the first of the great events of Christ's revelation.

This means that within the overarching economy of salvation from Adam's sin to Christ's crucifixion, a more limited world was perceived. In that more limited world, understanding of the human condition was provided by the cheirograph legend. The human condition was, in this smaller perspective, due to a mistake and not to sin. Adam made a mistake; he did not disobey God's command. How different did the world feel when this idea was in the foreground?

The double structure must have led to a perception of the human state that was very different from that of the West. The sense of sin and guilt must have been less oppressive; the yearning for freedom from this-worldly subjection to the devil very acute.

Texts in the Original Languages

The Slavonic Version

In the texts published below, the punctuation and orthography of original editions are preserved.[1]

PUBLISHED MANUSCRIPTS

P   Sofia, National Library, ms 629 (433), Plovdiv, 16th century, fols. 21–30; ed. Ivanov, 1925, 211–217.

S   Sofia, National Library, Ns 299 (681), Serbian, 15th century; ed. Ivanov, 1925, 211–217 (apparatus: C).

m   Vienna, Österreichische Nationalbibliothek, ms slav 149, Serbo-Bulgarian, 16–17th century; ed. Jagič, 1893, 31–33.

t   Moscow, Monastery of the Trinity-St. Sergius, ms 794, 16th century; ed. Tikhonravov, 1863, 6–15.

pp   Moscow, State Historical Museum, ms 358, fols. 183–192; 15–16th century; ed. Pypin, 1862, 1–31; Tikhonravov, 1863, 298–304.

pp'   Moscow, State Historical Museum, ms 380, fol. 31, 17th century; ed. Pypin, 1862, 4–7.

tr   Moscow, State Historical Museum, Undolskii collection, 17th century; ed. Tikhonravov, 1863, 1–6.

pr   Kazan, Theological Academy, ms 868, fols. 36–43; 17–18th century; ed. Porfiriev, 1877, 208–216.

pr'   Kazan, Theological Academy, ms 925, fols. 1–9; 17–18th century; ed. Porfiriev, 1877, 90–96.

Fr   Collection of Fr. Theodore of Dubovets, fols. 108–116, 17th century; ed. Franko, 1896, 19–23.

Fr' Manuscript from Dragobits of 1743; ed. Franko, 1896, 23–26.

ts   Late schismatic ms; ed. Tikhonravov, 1863, vol. 1, 16–17.

BIBLIOGRAPHY

Franko, I., 1896

Апокрифы и легенды з україньских рукописив. *Apokrify i legendy z ukrainiskikh rukopisiv* (Apocrypha and Legends from Ukrainian Manuscripts), 5 vols. Lvov, 1896–1910, vol. 1, 19–26.

Ivanov, J., 1925

Богомилски книги и легенды. *Bogomilski knigi i legendy* (Bogomil Books and Legends), Sofia, 215, 218–219, 223–227.

Jagič, 1893

Slavische Beiträge zu den biblischen Apokryphen: I, Die altkirchslavischen Texte des Adambuches, Vienna, 9–10, 31–33.

Kagan, M. D., 1988

«Апокриф о Адаме и Еве .» "Apokrif o Adame i Eve" (The Apocryphal Book about Adam and Eve) ed. D. S. Likhachev. Словарь книжников и книжности древней Руси. *Slovar' knizhnikov i knizhnosti drevnei Rusi* (Dictionary of Book-Men and Book-Knowledge in Old Russia), Leningrad, vol. 2, part 1, 49–51.

Porfiriev, I. J., 1877

Апокрифические сказания о ветхозаветных лицах и событиях. *Apokrificheskie skazaniia o vetkhozavetnykh litsakh i sobytiiakh* (Legends on Old Testament Personalities and Events). *Sbornik otdeleniia russkogo iazyka i slovestnosti Imperatorskoi Akademii Nauk* 17, no. 1, St. Petersburg, 40–42, 93, 211–212.

Pypin, A. N., 1862

«Ложные и отреченные книги русской старины.» "Lozhnye i otrechennye knigi russkoi stariny" (False and Rejected Books of Russian Antiquity). Памятники старинной русской литературы, издаваемые гр. Г. Кушелевым-Безбородко. *Pamiatniki starinnoi russkoi literatury,* izdavaemye gr. G. Kushelevym-Bezborodko (Monuments of Old Russian Literature, ed. Graf Kushelev-Bezborodko), St. Petersburg, vol. 3, 1–7.

Tikhonravov, N. S., 1863

Памятники отреченной русской литературы. *Pamiatniki otrechennoi russkoi literatury* (Monuments of Russian Rejected Literature). St. Petersburg, vol. 1, 3–4, 12–13, 16–17, 298–304.

Turdeanu, E., 1981

Apocryphes slaves et roumains de l'Ancien Testament. Leiden: Brill, 75, 115.

VARIANT A

Manuscripts

P   Ivanov, 1925, 215.

S   Ivanov, 1925, 215.

m   Jagič, 1925, 31-33.

t   Tikhonravov, 1863, 12-13.

pp   Pypin, 1862, 2; Tikhonravov, 1863, 299.

pp' Pypin, 1862, 5.

tr Tikhonravov, 1863, 3–4.
pr Porfiriev, 1877, 211–212.
pr' Porfiriev, 1877, 93.
Fr Franko, 1896, 20–21.
Fr' Franko, 1896, 23.

Text

The text presented here follows that of ms. P:

1 Тако вьзжть волови и вьзѡра, да створи себѣ храна.[1] 2 Тогда диаволь приде и ста и не дас Адамоу землж работати и реч Адамоу: моꙗ ѥс земнаꙗ, а бж҃їꙗ сжт нбса и раи;[2] да аще цѥши мои бит, да работи землж, аще ли хоцѥши бж҃и бити, поди в раи. 3 Адамь реч гднѣ сжт нбса и зем`лѣ и раи[3] и вьсѣ в`селенаа. 4 Диꙗволь реч емоу: не дамь ти землж работати, аще не запишеши м'нѣ ржкописанїе свое, да си мои. Адамъ реч : кто земи г҃ь, тоговъ ес'мь азь и чжда моꙗ. Диꙗволь вьзрадува сж. 5 Адамъ бо знаꙗше, ꙗко Г҃ь снити хоцѥть на землж и ѡблещис҃хоцѥт вь чл҃вчи ѡбразь и попрати хоцѥть диꙗвола.[4] 6 И реч диꙗволь: запиши м'нѣ ржкописанїе свое.[5] И записа Адамь: кто земи г҃ь, тоговъ и азь и чжда моꙗ.[6]

---

1 да створи себѣ храна: omm. pp pp' tr pr pr'; храна: храмину t.

2 раи: om. m.

3 раи: om. t pp pp' tr pr pr' Fr Fr'; море m S

4 ѡблещис҃хоцѥт вь чл҃вчи ѡбразь и попрати хоцѥть диꙗвола: родитисꙗ ѡ Девы pp' tr pr pr' Fr Fr'.

5 + и рече ко мнѣ господь роукописание сие t; + и взꙗ плечꙗ pp pp' tr; и взꙗтъ Адамъ черніло pr Fr; і взꙗ Адамъ мочꙑ pr'.

6 + дьꙗволъ же вземь рукописанїе Адамле и держаше его pp pp' pr pr'; держаше его: держание tr Fr.

VARIANT B

Manuscript

pp Pypin, 1862, 2; Tikhonravov, 1863, vol. 1, 300–301; Jagič, 1893, 9–10.

Text

1 А инде писано во ст҃мъ писаньи, 2 Адамъ бѣше в раю славꙗ Бога со архангелы и ангелы во свѣ҃т не мерчаюци[м]; 3 изгоніомоу҃ж ему бывшю из раꙗ за преступленїе его, и не вѣдаша того Адамъ, е҃ж ноць и день пре҃ж его Богомъ сотворена бы[с], и сѣде прꙗмо раю и плакашеся по раиско[м] жи[т]и. 4 И при[д] ноць и бы[с] т'ма и въскрича Адамъ глаголꙗ: горе мне, престоупившомоу божию заповѣдь, изгнану изъ свѣтлаго раискаго житьꙗ, пресвѣтлаго немерчающаго свѣта.

Ѡ свѣ҃т мои пресвѣтлыи, - плачасꙗ и рыдаꙗ глаголаше, - 5 оуже не оузрю сиꙗнїꙗ твоего и не мерчающаго свѣ҃т ни красоты раискїꙗ ни вижю; Г҃и, помилоуи м[ꙗ] па[д]шаго[с]. 6 Приде же кнемоу дїаво[л] глаголꙗ емоу: чт҃о сꙗ стонеши и рыдаеши? 7 Адамь҃ж рече: свѣ҃т ра[д] пресвѣтлаго сокрывшагоса мене ра^д .- 8 Дїаво^л рече емоу: азъ ти дамъ свѣтъ, запиши^с ми рукоисанїе^м и рⳘдъ свои и ча^д. 9 Адамъ же свѣта ради дастъ емоу роукописанїе и написа тако: чии е^с свѣ^т, того азъ и чада мои, - и приде день и свѣтъ восїа по всеи вселеннеи; 10 дьяволъ же вземъ роукописанїе адамле, сокры и (въ їорда^н пⳙ^д камене^м, где Хрто^с кр^стлса).[1]

---

1 Bracketed words crossed out.

VARIANT C

Manuscripts

ts   Tikhonravov, 1863, vol. 1, 16–17.

1 Святый апостолъ Варфаломей вопроси святаго апостола Андрея Первозваннаго, како и кіимъ образомъ праотецъ нашъ Каин родися икако (рукописаніе) праотецъ нашъ Адамъ даде діяволу рукописаніе. 2 Праотецъ наш Каинъ сквернавъ родися, глава на немъ яко и на протчихъ человѣцехъ, на персѣхъ и на челѣ дванадесѣть главъ зміиныхъ, 3 еже егдаже Евва сосцы своими питаше, тогда зміевы главы чрево ея терзающе а отъ того терзанія и лютаго мученія прабаба наша Евва окрастовила. 4 И видѣ Адамъ жену свою страждущу вельми, скорбяше о неи. И пріиде къ нему діяволъ во образе человѣка и глагола ему: Что мнѣ даси, исцѣлю сына твоего Каина и жену твою Евву отъ такова мучительства свобожду? 5 И глагола Адамъ ему: Да что ти дамъ?. И рече діяволъ: Даси на ся рукописание. И рече ему Адамъ: Каковое дамъ ти рукописание? 6 И глагола діяволъ: Заколи козлища и знаменуи на камени, еже дамъ ти, и рече сице: жівыи Богу, а мертвыя тебѣ. 7 И сотвори Адамъ тако, якоже повелѣ ему діяволъ и принесе ему плиту велію каменную, и закла Адамъ козлища, и источи кровь въ сосудъ, и омочи оби руцѣ свои въ крови той, 8 и положи руцѣ свои на плиту бѣлаго камня и вообразися руцѣ адамовы на плитѣ той. 9 И пріиде діяволъ къ Каину и оборва дванадесять главъ зміиныхъ, положи ихъ на камень и на рукопгсаніе то и вверзе оную еже во Іордане рѣку и заповѣда діяволъ главамъ зміевымъ стрещи то рукописаніе 10 и бѣ хранима тѣми главамі зміевыми до пришествія Господа нашего Іисуса Христа. И егда пріиде на Іорданъ ко Іоанну креститися нашего ради спасенія, тогда зміевы главы сташа въ струяхъ іорданскихъ противу Господа и сокруши зміевы главы въ водѣ. 11 И відѣ діяволъ зміевы главы сокрушены, тоюда взя діяволъ и останокъ того рукописанія и внесе во адъ, иже бы заключены быша святіи. 12 Егда Господь нашъ Іисусъ Христосъ воскресе изъ мертвыхъ, тогда и останокъ того рукопгсанія адамова растерза и загляди и діявола связа, а души изъ ада свободи и въ первую породу, въ рай, введе къ своему ⳙтцу и къ своему хотѣнію. 13 *Изъ древнихъ рукописменныхъ страстей хргстовыхъ римскихъ харатейныхъ.*

The Armenian Expulsion of Adam from the Garden

BIBLIOGRAPHY

S. Yovsēpʻiancʻ, *Անկանոն Գիրք Հին Կտակարանաց* [*Uncanonical Books of the Old Testament*] (Venice: Mechitarist Press, 1898), 312–314; J. Issaverdens, *The Uncanonical Writings of the Old Testament Found in the Armenian Mss. of the Library of St. Lazarus* (Venice: Mechitarist Press, 1901), 47–51; E. Preuschen, "Die apokryphen gnostischen Adamschriften, aus dem Armenischen übersetzt und untersucht," in *Festgruss B. Stade* (Giessen: Ricker, 1900 and *separatim*), 31–33; W. L. Lipscomb, *The Armenian Apocryphal Adam Literature*, (University of Pennsylvania Armenian Texts and Studies, 8) (Atlanta: Scholars Press, 1990), Recension 1, 128–141; Recension 2, text 246–248, translation 267–269.

MANUSCRIPTS AND RECENSIONS OF THE CYCLE OF FOUR WORKS

Lipscomb uses the following witnesses to Recension 1:

Y   Venice: Mechitarist, Old no. 729, undated.[2] Lipscomb did not have a photographic copy of the manuscript, and he used the printed text.

A   Erevan: Matenadaran, no. 682, fols. 96v–101r, undated. The manuscript contains three of the four parts of *The Cycle of Four Works,* omitting only the first of them.

B   New York, H. P. Kraus Rare Books and Manuscripts, MS VT915, fols. 4v–23v, dated 1662.

C   Erevan: Matenadaran, no. 2126, fols. 81r–83r dating from 1697. This manuscript contains the final four–fifths of *History of Abel and Cain.* Collations of this manuscript were also published separately by Stone.[3]

D   London: British Library, Ms Harl. Or. 5459, fols. 2v–12v, dated 1698.

Lipscomb also knew of a further witness to Recension 1, which was not available to him, viz.:

F   Venice: Mechitarist, no. 262, fols. 163v–167v.

Lipscomb also published an edition and a first translation of Recension 2 of *The Cycle of Four Works.* The text he drew from the following source:

Z   *Սկիզբն Գրոց որ կոչի ժողովածու.* Constantinople, 1717, fols. 1–42.[4]

He also knew of one manuscript of this recension, but did not have access to it, viz.:

T   Tiflis: Kekelidze Institute of Manuscripts, no. 47, fols. 7r ff.

Recension 1

ՊԱՏՈՒԹԻՒՆ ՍՏԵՂԾՄԱՆ ԵՒ ՅԱՆՁՄԱՆՆ ԱԴԱՄԱՅ

46 Եւ եղեալ արտաքս ի տեղի մումն եւ խաստր, <վեց օր> անդ մնացին, առանց ուտելոյ, անմխիթար լային եւ կոծէին դանձինս իւրեանց

47 Իսկ <Հետ վեց աւուրն> ողորմեցաւ նոցա Տէր, եւ առաքեաց դղբեշտակ իւր Հանել դնոսա ի խաստրէն, եւ առաչնորդեալ եբեր դնոսա ի լոյս աշխարՆս, եւ եցոյց նոցա դպտղաբերս այնով լիանալ եւ ապրիլ։

48 Իսկ իբրեւ տեսին Ադամ եւ կին իւր <դլոյս աշխարՆիս ուրախացաւն եւ խնդացին Ադամ եւ կինն իւր>, ասացին. Թէպետ չէ բարունիմն, եւ աշխարՆիս լոյս եւ պտուղ չեն Հաաաար լուսոյ եւ պտղոյ դարխտին. բայց ոչ սովաւ մաՆ <լինիմք> եւ կամ <խաստրի> մնամք։

49 Այսպէս ուրախ կացին։

○ ՊԱՏՈՒԹԻՒՆ ԵԼԱՆԵԼՈՅՆ ԱԴԱՄԱՅ Ի ԴՐԱԽՏԷՆ

1 Իսկ երբ անկաւ Ադամ ի դրախտէն յաշխարՆս, ուրախութեամբ կացին ի վերայ արեգական եւ լուսնին մինչեւ յերեկոյին։

2 Իսկ երեկուն, երբ որ արեգական մտաւ, նոքա գիտացին թէ խաստր կալաւ դնոսա, այլ ոչ տեսանեն դլոյս. քանզի դրախտին Հանապազ լոյս էր, նոյնպէս գիտացին թէ աշխարՆս ամենայն լուսաւոր եղիցի. դայն ոչ գիտէին թէ յաշխարՆս գիշեր լինի, կամ ցերեկ կայ. վասն այն տրտմեցան իբրեւ մտաւ արեգական, Հանց գիտացին թէ այլ ոչ լուսանայ, լացին եւ կոծեցան մինչեւ ցառաւուտն։

3 Իսկ առաւուտին Հաաախօսին, եկն առ նա Սաաանայ ի կերպ Հրեշտակի, եւ ասէ. Ընդէ՞ր տրտում էք։

4 Ասէ Ադամ. վասն այն տրտմիմք, քանզի ստեղծեալ էր դմեզ Աստուած եւ եղեալ ի մէջ լուսեղէն դրախտին, եւ պատրանօք օձին Ճաշակեցաք ի պտղոյն եւ ելաք ի դրախտէն, եւ անկանք ի խաստր ժամանակս ինչ։

5 Դարձեալ ողորմեցաւ Տէր եւ առաքեաց դղբեշտակ իւր, <եւ> եՆան դմեզ ի խաստրէն. եւ բերեալ ի լոյս աշխարՆս, թէպետ չէր Հաաար լուսոյ արքայութեան, բայց լոյս էր։

6 Իսկ ոչ գիտեմք թէ դի՞նչ գործեցաք, որ բարկացաւ ի վերայ մեր Տէրն եւ խափանեաց դայս սակաւ լոյսս. վասն այն կոծամք եւ լամք։

7 Ասէ Սաաանայ. դի՞նչ եատուք այն Հրեշտակին, որ դձեզ եՆան ի մութ տեղւոջէն եւ եբեր ի լոյս։

8 Ասէ Ադամ. եւ ո՞չ ինչ։

9 Ասէ Սաաանայ. Չի է, ընդէ՞ր ոչ ասացիք դձեզ ծառայ նմա ամենայն ծնունդով ձերով՞ք։

10 Ասէ Ադամ. Յիմարութիւն կալաւ դմեզ եւ դայդ ոչ իմացաք ասել։

11 Ասէ Սաաանայ. Չի՞նչ <տայք> ինձ <թէ> տամ ձեզ աւետիք լուսոյ։

12 Ասէ Ադամ. եթէ մի անգամ լոյս տեսանիցեմք, քեզ ծառայ լինիմք մեք
եւ ամենայն ծնունդքն մեր:

13 Իսկ Սատանայ ցուցանէր նոցա յարեւելից <կողմն>, եւ ասաց.
Հայեցարուք եւ անդ տեսանիցէք լոյս:

14 Իբրեւ ասաց Սատանայ պայս բանս, եւ ինքն սակաւ մի Հեռացաւ. եւ
Հայէին Ադամ եւ Եւայ դէպ յարեւելից կողմն, տեսանէին գնչաս լուսանալոյս.
յոյժ ուրախացան եւ խնդացին:

15 Իբրեւ <ծագեաց արեգակն կատարելապէս խնդացին իբրեւ> սակաւ մի
բարձրացաւ արեգակն, եկն առ նոսա պիղծն Սատանայ, ասէ. Տեսա՞ք
զաւետիսն զի ուրախացոյց զձեզ:

16 Ասէ Ադամ. ծառայ եմ քեզ եւ աւետեաց քոց, զի դու լուսաւորեցեր զմեզ.
ամենայն ծնունդքն մեր ծառայ եմք:

17 Իսկ Սատանայ բերեալ քար մի եւ եդ առաջի Ադամայ, եւ ասաց Ադամայ.
Դիր զձեռդ ի վերայ քարիս եւ ասայ այսպէս. Ամենայն ծնունդքն իմ ծառայ քո
եղիցին:

18 Եւ թէ ոչ ասես այսպէս, խոր խաւար բերեմ ի վերայ քո:

19 Իսկ Ադամ եդեալ ձեռն ի վերայ քարին, եւ ասաց. Մ՛ինչեւ անձինն ծնանի
եւ անձառն մեռանի, մեք եւ ամենայն ծնունդքն մեր ծառայ եղիցի քեզ:

20 Եւ առեալ Սատանայ զքարն, եւ տարեալ թաղեաց ի զետոն Յորդանան:

21 Այս եղեւ ձեռագիր Ադամայ ի ձեռն Սատանայի:

22 Մ՛ինչեւ յերեկոյն ուրախացան եւ խնդացին Ադամ եւ Եւայ <ի վերայ
արեգական. իսկ յերեկոյն արեգական իբրեւ մտաւ գիտացին Ադամ եւ Եւայ> որ
խաբեցան ի Սատանայէ, լացին եւ ողբացին, մ՛ինչեւ եօթն օրն անօթի կացին
եւ զՏէրն աղաչեցին:

23 Եւ յետ եօթն աւուրն ողորմեցաւ նոցա Տէրն, եւ առաքեաց զՀրեշտակ
իւր, եւ բերեալ ձեռնագիր յԱստուծոյ եւ ի ձեռն Ադամայ, եւ ասէ. Մի երկնչիր
Ադամ թէ խաբեաց զքեզ Սատանայ. վասն այն ասաց քեզ թէ մ՛ինչեւ անձինն
ծնանի, զի անձին ես եմ որ ոչոք ծնաւ. անձառն իմ աստուածութեան <ասէ>,
որ ոչ ունի զմահ. վասն այն այսպէս խաբեցութեամբ էառ զձեռնագիրն ի քէն,
որ մնաս դու զերի ի ձեռն Սատանայի. բայց ոչ թողում զքեզ զերի զի ի ձեռն
Սատանայի. զի դու պատկեր իմ ես. ոչ կորուսից զքեզ եւ ոչ թողից ի ձեռն նորա:

24 — Զի այն եօթն օրն որ պաՀեաց Ադամ, այն ասի առաջաւոր —:

25 Եւ ի մտանել վեց դարուն, առաքեցից ի լուոյ աստուածութեան իմոյ
զորդի իմ սիրելի. որ եկեալ մարմնանայ ի զաւակէ քումմէ, ի սուրբ եւ
յանարատ կուսէն. զի նայ եղիցի որդի որդւոյ <քո եւ որդի իմ>:

26 Եւ որդին իմ շնչեացց զձեռագիր քո, եւ ազատեցէ զքեզ ի զերութենէ
Սատանայի եւ տացէ քեզ զանացին վասն քո:

27 Իբրեւ զայս <աւետիս> լուաւ Ադամ, ուրախացաւ յոյժ. վեց Հազար
<տարին> իբրեւ ժամ մի երեւեցաւ:

28 ՕրՀնեալ է Աստուած:

Recension 2

o ՊԱՏՈՒԹԻՒՆ ԵՒ ՃԱՌ. ՎԱՍՆ ՍՏԵՂԾՄԱՆՆ ԱԴԱՄԱՅ ԵՒ
ՄԱՐԴԱՆԱԼՈՅՆ ՔՐԻՍՏՈՍԻ ԱՍՏՈՒԾՈՑ ՄԵՐՈՑ

50 Եւ անկան ի տեղի մթին եւ աղջամղջին քաղցած եւ ծարաւած մինչեւ
վեց օր։

51 Ապա դարձեալ ողորմեցաւ Տէրն ի վերայ նոցա եւ առաքեաց զՀրեշտակն
Հանել զԱդամ ի խաւարային տեղեաց. եւ բերել ի լոյս աշխարՀ. եւ եցոյց նմա
գործել գերկիր, եւ ի պտղոյ նորա կերակրիլ։

52 Իսկ նոքա իբրեւ տեսին գարեգակն եւ զլուսին, ուրախացան մինչեւ
յերեկոյն եւ ոչ գիտէին թէ արեգակն մտանէ եւ եյանէ. ապա Հանց որ մտաւ
արեգակն եւ մթացաւ երկիր նոցա եւ խատար կալաւ զնոսա, տրտմութեամբ լացին
զգիշերն ամենայն։

53 Այսքան առ այս վասն Ադամայ։

54 Զոր Տէր Աստուած փրկեալ ապատեցէ զձեզ ի խաբէութենէ չարին
Սատանայի. եւ արժանի արասցէ արդար դատաստանին. եւ արքայութեան
լուսոյն ամէն։

o ՎԱՍՆ ԵԼԱՆԵԼՈՅՆ ԱԴԱՄԱՅ ԵՒ ԵՒԱՅԻ Ի ԴՐԱԽՏԷՆ

1 Յորժամ Ադամ անկաւ ի լուսոյն, սակաւ մի ուրախացաւ ի վերայ լուսոյ
արեգականնն թէպէտ չէր Հաստատար արեգական լոյսն արքայութեան լուսոյն. բայց
լոյս էր. նա ոչ գիտէր թէ ի մայրն մտանէր արեգակն։

2 Իսկ որ մթացաւ եւ երեկոյ եղեւ, այնպէս թուեցաւ նոցա թէ մոլմ եղեւ եւ
այլ ոչ լուսանայ. քանզի դրախտն Հանապազ լոյս էր. եւ նոյնպէս գիտէին թէ
աշխարՀս ամենայն լուսով լինի. զի ոչ գիտէին թէ ցերեկն գիշեր կու փոխի.
վասն որոյ իբրեւ մտաւ արեգակն, եւ մթացաւ օդն, նա այնպէս իմացան թէ այլ
չի լուսանայր. վասն որոյ լացին եւ կոծեցին մինչեւ ցառաւօտն։

3 Իսկ ի Հատախոսին եկեալ Սատանայ ի կերպս Հրեշտակի եւ ասէ ցԱդամ.
ընդէ՞ր տրտմիք։

4 Ասէ Ադամ. վասն այն տրտմիմք եւ լամք զի ստեղծեալ էր զմեզ Աստուած,
եւ եղեալ ի մէջ դրախտին լուսեղէն. եւ պատրանօք օձին կերաք ի պտղոյն. եւ
արտաքսեցաք ի դրախտէն. եւ անկաք ի տեղիս այս խատար մթին։

5 Ապա կրկին ողորմեցաւ մեզ Աստուած. եւ առաքեաց զՀրեշտակ իւր
Հանեալ զմեզ ի խաւարէս եբեր ի լոյս աշխարՀ։

6 Այլ ոչ գիտեմք թէ ինչ չար գործեցաք որ բարկացաւ Աստուած ի վերայ
մեր եւ խատար կալաւ զմեզ։

7 Ասէ Սատանայ. Ի՞նչ տուիք այն Հրեշտակին որ եբեր զձեզ ի լոյս
աշխարՀ։

8 Ասէ Ադամ. Ի՞նչ ունէաք որ տայաք։

9 Այլ Սատանայ պարտ էր ձեզ ծառայ լինիլ նմա եւ զամենայն ծնունդս ձեր խոստանայ նմա. երբ զայդ ոչ արարիք վասն այն խստար կալաս զձեզ:

10 Այլ Ադամ. յապշութին կալաւ զմեզ եւ զայդ ոչ իմացաք:

11 Այլ Սատանայ. զի՞նչ տաջք ինձ թէ տամ ձեզ զալետրիքն լուոյ:

12 Այլ Ադամ. եթէ միասանգամ լոյս տեսանիցեմք ծառայ լինիմք քեզ մեք եւ ամենայն ծնունդն մեր:

13 Իսկ Սատանայ ցոյց եւ նոցա յարեւելս եւ ասաց. անտի տեսանէք զլոյս:

14 Զայս ասաց Սատանայ եւ սակաւ մի Հերացաւ. իսկ Ադամ եւ եւայ Հայեին ընդ արեւելս եւ տեսանէին զի նշան լուոյ երեւէր արեգականն. կատարեալ խնդացին:

15 Իբրեւ սակաւ մի բարձրացաւ, եկն առ նա Սատանայ եւ ասէ. տեսանէք զալետրիսն իմ որ ուրախացուցի զձեզ:

16 Այլ Ադամ. ծառայ եմք քեզ եւ աւետեաց քոց. զի դու լուսատրեցեր զմեզ. զի ծառայեմք քեզ մեք եւ ամենայն ծնունդն մեր:

17 Իսկ Սատանայ բերեալ քար մի եւ եդ առաջի Ադամայ եւ ասէ. դիր զձեռն քո ի վերայ քարիդ եւ ասա այսպէս. մինչեւ անձինն ծնանի, եւ անմահն մեռանի ամենայն ծնունդն իմ քեզ եղիցի:

18 Եւ եթէ ոչ ասէք այսպէս. դարձեալ խստար բերեմ առ ձեզ:

19 Իսկ Ադամ զձեռն ի վերայ եղեալ ասաց թէ մինչեւ անձինն ծնանի եւ անմահն մեռանի ամենայն ծնունդն մեր ծառայ քո եղիցի:

20 Եւ մնաց նշան ձեռացն ի վերայ քարին:

21 Այն եղեւ ձեռագիր Ադամայ ի ձեռն Սատանայի. իսկ Սատանայ տարեալ զձեռագիր քարն թաղեաց ի դեռն Ցորդանանու:

22 Դարձեալ իբրեւ երեկոյ եղեւ մտաւ արեգակն ի մայրն. գիտաց Ադամ որ խաբեցաւ, լացին եւ ողբացին մինչեւ Հինգ օր անօթի եւ ծարաւ:

23 Աղաչեցին զԱստուած եւ յետ Հինգ աւուրցն լուաւ Աստուած աղօթից նոցա եւ առաքեաց զՀրեշտակ իւր. եւ աւետեաց Ադամայ վասն մարդանալույն Տեառն Աստուծոյ եւ ազատին ի ձեռաց Սատանայի:

24 Եւ եստուր Ադամայ զձեռագիրն Աստուծոյ. եւ էր գրեալ այսպէս. մի տրտմիր Ադամ. խաբեաց զքեզ Սատանայ. վասն այն որ ասաց թէ մինչեւ անձինն ծնանի. եւ անմահն մեռանի. զի անձինն եւ եմ. եւ անմահ աստուածութիւն. որդ ի վեզ դարուն առաքեցից զմիածինն որդին իմ ի լուոյ աստուածութեան իմոյ:

25 Եւ մարմին առցէ ի սուրբ եւ յանարատ կուսէ. զոր ի զատակէն քումմէ եղիցի որդին իմ, որդի քո:

26 Զի անձինն ծնանի եւ չնչէ զձեռագիր յանցանաց քոց. եւ դարձուցէ զքեզ յառաջին փառս քո:

27 Իբրեւ զայս աւետիս լուաւ ուրախ եղեւ. զի վեց դարն իբրեւ ժամ մի
Համարէր վասն աւետեացն Հրեշտակին:

28 Որ նոյն ողորմութեամբն ողորմեցի Քրիստոս Աստուած ձեզ եւ մե. ԱՄԷՆ:

Adam, Eve, and the Incarnation

The three manuscripts of the following work are all published by Stone.[5] Two
of them are in the Matenadaran in Erevan, nos. 5913 (seventeenth century) and 5571
(copied in 1657–1659 in Smyrna and in Surat' [India]). The third is in Paris, Bibliothèque nationale de France, arm. 306 (seventeenth century). The work cannot
be dated exactly, but it is undoubtedly medieval.

M5913	M5571	P306

20 Իսկ Հանեալ
գնաստ. եւ նորայ եղեալ
ի դրախտէն.
անկան{ի}. ի տեղի
խաղարային լացին եւ
սգացին անարատ
աւուրս Հինգ.

20 Ե<ւ> յորժամ
անկան ի դրախտէն
Արամ եւ եւայ. անկան
ի տեղի մի միժային.
լացին եւ սգացին
աւուրս Ե.

20 Եյան նորայ ի
դրախտէն եւ անկան.
աննոտ լացին եւ
<ա>զեցին մինչեւ խ
աւր.

21 եւ յիշեաց
գնաստ Աստուած եւ
առաքեաց գՀրեշտակ
իւր եւ առեալ գնաստ
բերեալ ի յաշխարս
եւ եգուց նոցա վարել
եւ վաստակել. եւ անցու-
ցանել գաւուրս իրեանց

21 եւ ապա
ողորմեցաւ Աստուած.
եւ առաքեաց
գՀրեշտակ եւ ուոց
նոցա աշխարՀս վարել
եւ վաստակել. եւ
տեսեալ նոցա աշխարՀ.
լի բուսօք եւ տնկօք:

21 եւ ե աւր
{յետ} ողորմեցո նոցա
Աստուած առագաց
գՀրրշտակ իւր. եւ
Հանել գնաստայ ի սա
աշխարիս եւ ուոց
նոցա վարել եւ վաս-
տակել այնով ապրել.
եւ նորա ուրախացան:

22 Իսկ յորժամ
եղեւ երեկոյ. եւ ի
մտանել արեգակնին.
նորայ այպպէս իմացան
թէ խաստր կալաւ
գնաստ դեռ չգիտէին
թէ երբեան տիւ լինի.
եւ երբեան գիշեր:

22 եւ տեսին
գլուս արեգականն
եւ ուրախացան յոյժ.
մինչեւ ցերեկոյն: Իսկ
մտանել արեգականն
նոքա իմացան թէ
խատար կալաւ գնաստ.
այլ ոչ եւս տեսանեն
գլոյս. ի մէջ դրախտին
Հանապազ լոյս էր
նոցա. իսկ ոչ գիտէին
այս աշխարՀս թէ
երբեան ցերեկ լինի
երբեան գիշեր.

22 եւ մինչեւ
յերեկոյն արեգակն
մտաւ. նորայ այպէս
յիմացան. թէ խատար
կալաւ գնաստ այլ ոչ
տեսան գլոյսն.

23 Դարձեալ լացին

23 լացին նորայ եւ

23 լաց<ին> եւ

եւ ապացին մինչեւ
ցառաւօտն. ի մատա-
նել առաւօտույն
եկեալ Սատանայ զի
կերպարանս Հրեշտակի
<եւ ասէ>. զի <ի>աս
Արամ.

24 եւ ասէ Արամ
զի Հարցանես յերբ
Աստուած ստեղծ զմեզ
ի մէջ դրախտին. եւ
մեք ոչ պահեցաք
զպատուիրանս նորա
արտաքս ելաք:

25 Դարձեալ
լիշեաց զմեզ եւ ետ
մեզ աշխարՀս եւ
տեսաք աստ լույս. եւ
ուրախացաք. դարձեալ
խաւար եկն ի վերա
մեր ոչ գիտեմք թէ
զինչ վրնաս գործեցաք:

26 եւ ասէ
Սատանայ զինչ տրւիր
այն Հրեշտակին վո-
խանակ աշխատաց.
որ էՀան զքեզ ի մուֆն
տեղացն. եւ եթեր զքեզ
ի յաշխարՀս. եւ ուտաց
քեզ վարել. եւ
վատակել:
27 ա եւ ասէ Արամ
ոչինչ ունէի որ տայի.
ասէ Սատանա յերբ որ
անչաի երախտիք
ունէիր ի վերա քո

ապացին մինչեւ
Հաախիոսն: Իսկ պիրծն
Սատանայ եկն առ
նոսա ի կերպս
Հրեշտակի. եւ ասէ.
Արամ. զիարդ լաս.

24 եւ նորա ասեն.
ինչպես չյամք.
այսպիսի դրախտէն
եյանք ի պադղույ
ճաշակելով. իսկ աստի
ոչ գիտեմք թէ զինչ
գործեցաք որ խատա-
րեցաւ լոյս մեր եւ
մֆացաք ի խաւարի:

26 եւ ասէ
Սատանայ. զինչ տուաք
Հրեշտակին որ զձեզ
<ի> խատէ ի լոյս
եՀան:

27 ա Ասէ Արամ.
Զինչ ունէաք որ տամք
ի նա. եւ Սատանայ
ասէ. Պարտ էր ձեզ
տալ նմա ինչս. յերբ

ոքպացին նոքայ մինչեւ
Հոալխոսն. իսկ պեղծ
Սատանայ {երկնո}
նոսա. ի կերպս
<րանս> Հրեշտակի.
եւ ասէ {յնոյսյ}. վլի
լայք <զ>ինչ եղեւ ձեզ:

24 նոքայ ասեն.
թէ ի մէջ <դրախտին>
եւ ի մէջ լուսոյն
մխիթարէաք. իսկ
խամբմամբ օծին
կերայք ի պտղոյն. ար-
տայքսեցայք եւ խոսոր
անկանք:

25 Դարձեալ
ողորմեցո մե<զ>
Աստուած եւ առագաց
զՀրշտակ իւր. եւ էՀան
զմեզ ի խաւոր տեղոշէն.
եւ էՀան տեղիս էր լոյ
առանց խոսորի. եւ
ուրախացանք դարձեալ
ոչ գիտեմք թէ զինչ
գործեցայք. դարձեալ
բարկացո Տէր ի վերայ
մեր. եւ խոսրեցոյց
զլույսն վասն այն լայք
եւ ռիապանք:

26 Ասէ Սատանայ.
զինչ եռոյք այն
Հրշ<տ>ակին. որ զձեզ
խոսրէն ի լոյս խանեց.

27ա Ասէ Արամ.
զինչ ունիաք որ
տայինք Աստուծոյ: Ասէ
Սատանայ. պարտ է
ձեզ նմայ գծնունդ ձեր.

պարտ էր քեզ ծրնունդն
տալ իւրն ծառատութիւն.
յերբ չունիր վասն այն
խասար եկն ի վերա քո։
27ր Ասէ Արամ.
ապաք գինչ լինի
կատարած մեր։

28 Ասէ Սատանա
թէ ինձ տացես գծնունդ
քո տամ քեզ աւետիք
լուանալոյ։

29 Ասէ Արամ քեզ
լիցի ծնունդն իմ թէ
այրոպէս իցէ։ Ասէ
Սատանա յերբ որ
տուիր գծնունդ քո
փոտով տեսանես
գլուան. եւ Սատանայ
անյայտ եղեւ։

30 Եւ ելեալ
արեգականն եւ
լուսաւորեաց գաշխար-
Հս եւ ուրախ եղեւ
Արամ եւ եւս եւ ասէին
ընդ միմիանս թէ
րստուգ եղեւ աւետիք
Հրեշտակին. արժան էր
տամ նմայ գծնունդն
մեր որպէս տուաք։
31 Իսկ Դ ժամուն
դարձեալ եկն Սատա-
նայ եւ ասէ Արամ
տեսեր գլուան եւ ուրախ
եղեր Հաատացիր ինձ։

32 Ասէ Արամ {ի
քէն} ծառայ եմ քեզ եւ
քո աւետացն. ի քէնէ

չուտաք. վասն այն
կալաւ րզձեզ խասար։

27ր Իսկ Արամ
ասէ. Զինչ արասցուք
այժմ։ Ասէ Սատանայ.
Զինչ որ ասեմ ձեզ. թէ
լսէք ինձ դարձեալ
տեսանէք րզլոյս։
28 Ասէ Արամ.
Հրամայեա ինձ տէր
իմ։ Ասէ Սատանայ. թէ
տացես ինձ գծնունդն
քո, տամ քեզ աւետիք
լոյս տեսանելոյ։
29 Ասէ Արամ. Թէ
տեսից միսս անգամ
զլոյս, ամենայն ծնունդ
մեր ծառա լիցի քեզ։
Ասէ Սատանայ. Սակաւ
մի ժամս տեսանես
րզլոյս. իսկ ինքն
Սատանայ եղեւ
աններեւոյթ
30 Եւ եղեւ առաւոտ
եւ ծագեաց արեւ.
ուրախացան Արամ եւ
եւայ. ասեն ընդ
միմիանս. Ստուգ եղեւ
բան Հրեշտակին.
պարտ էր նմա տալ
գծնունդրն մեր, որպէս
եւ տուաք։

31 Իսկ Սատանայ
Դ ժամուն եկն եւ ասէ
ընդ նոսա. տեսաք
րզլոյս եւ ուրախացան
սիրտ ձեր։

32 Եւ ասեն. Տէր
ծառա եմք քեզ. եւ քո
աւետացդ. գոՀեմք

չեւորւ վասն այն
խատարեցոց գձեզ։

27ր Ասէ Արամ.
Ապայ ինչպէս լինիք։
Ասէ Սատանայ. թէ գոր
ինչ ասեմ. թէ լսէք ինձ
փուտով տեսանւք
գուտամ։
28 Ասէ Արամ.
Հրամայաց տէր իմ։
Ասէ. տուք ինձ
գծնու<ն>դն ձեր. եւ եւ
տամ ձեզ. օեետիկ լուտոյ։
29 Ասէ Արամ. թէ
միւս անգամ
տեսանեմք գլու.
ծնունդն իմ ամենայն
քո եղէցի. եւ եթող
գնաց Սատանայ։

30 Եբրեւ արեգակն
ծագեաց խնդրեցին
Արամ եւ եւայ։ եւ
ասէին ընդ միմեանս
{եւ ասէին}. թէ ստուգ
եղեւ բանն Հրշշտակիս.
պարտ է տալ ծնունդ
մեր որպէս տուաք։

31 Իսկ Դ ժամոյն,
եկն {առնոյս} Սատա-
նայ եւ ասէ. ընդ նոսայ.
այժմ Հաատացաք
ինձ. եւ ստուք եղեւ
աւետիք իմ։
32 Եւ նոքայ ասեն.
տէր իմ. Հայ{տ}ցաք ի
քեզ. ծառայ եմ քեզ եւ

տեսաք զլոյս եւ ուրախ
եղաք:

33 Եւ ասէ
Սատանայ զինչ տուիր
ինձ փոխանակ այդ-
պիսի աւետացդ որ {ըն-
կար} չհնէն եւ տեսար:
Եւ նայ ասէ եառու`քեզ
րդձրնունդ իմ տամ քեզ
գոր ինչ խնդրես:

34 Եւ եառ Սատա-
նայ, սալ քար մի
առաջի նորա. եւ ասէ
դիր գձերն քո ի վերա.
եւ ասէ մինչեւ անծինն
ծնանի եւ անմարՇն
մեռանի զաւակ իմ
ծառա քո եղեցի: Թէ ոչ
ասես այդպէս դարձեալ
խաւար բերեմ ի վերայ
քո:

35 Եւ ասէ Արամ
մինչեւ անծինն ծնանի.
եւ անմարՇն մեռանի
զամենայն ծնունդրդ իմ
ծառա քո եղիցի.

36 Եւ մնաց գտեղի
{տ}եռացն եւ մատանն-
ցըն ի վերայ սալ
քարին. այն եղեւ
ծեռայզիր Արամայ ի
ծերն Սատանայի: եւ
տարեալ եառ ի զերն
Յորդանանու:

37 Ուրախանային
Արամ եւ Եւայ մինչեւ
ցերեկոյն. նոցա

զքէն որ ի քէն տեսաք
զլոյս եւ ուրախացաք:
33 Ասէ Սատանայ.
Չինչ եառուք ինձ
փոխանակ այդ
աւետացդ: Եւ նոքա
ասեն. զամենայն
ծնունդն մեր տտաւք
քեզ:

34 Իսկ Սատանայ
բերեալ սալ քար մի եւ
եղ առաջի նոցա եւ
ասէ. Թէ այապէս ասէք,
թէ մինչեւ անծինն
ծնանի. եւ անմարՇն
մեռանի. ամենայն
զաւակն մեր ծառայ քո
եղիցին. Թէ ոչ ասէք
այապէս դարձեալ
խաւարի մնաք:

35 Իսկ նոքա ձեռն
եդին ի վերայ սալին
թէ. մինչեւ անծինն
ծնանի եւ անմարՇն
մեռանի, ամենայն
զաւակ մեր ծառայ քո
եղիցին.

36 Այն եղեւ
ծեռագիրն Արամայ ի
ծերն Սատանայի եւ
նշան մատանեացն ի
վերայ սալին մնաց:
Իսկ Սատանայ առեալ
զայն քարն, տարեալ
թաղեաց ի Յորդանան
զերն.

քո աւետացն. ի քէն
տեսանք զլոյս:

34 Իսկ Սատանայ
եւ սալ քար մի եւ
առաջի նորա. եւ ասաց
եթէ ոչ դնէք գձերն ի
վերայ քարիդ. եւ
ասէք թէ մինչեւ անծին
ծնանի մինչեւ անմարՇն
մեռանի. ամենայն
ծնունդդ իմ քեզ {քեզ}
եղեցի. Թէ ոչ ասէք
խոար {բերանիմ} ի
վերայ ձեզ:

35 Իսկ Արամ եղ
գձերն ի վերայ սալ
քարին եւ ասաց. Թէ
մինչեւ անծին ծնանի
անմարՇ մեռան<ի>
զաւակ իմ քո ծառայ
եղէցի. եւ մնաց {ի}
Շետ ծեռացն ի վերայ
քարին.

36 Այն եղեւ
ծեռ<ագ>իր Արամայ ի
ծերն Սատանայի. եւ
տարաւ թաղաց ի
Յորդանան գետն:

այպէս թրւեցաւ թէ
այլ ոչ մնանէ
արեզակնն:

38 Իրրեւ երեկու
եղեւ մտաւ արեզակին եւ
մշացալ ապա իմացան
որ խաբեցան. լացին եւ
ըսգացին Արամ եւ Եւայ
եւ աւէին վայ եւ .Ռ.
վայ մեզ եւ մեր գաա-
կացն. որ մեր ձե-
րայզրումն զերի եղաք.
Ե. աւր անւրաադ
պանՀեցին այն է որ
առաջաւոր ասեն:

39 Դարձեալ
ողորմեցաւ Աստուած եւ
առաքեաց գՀրեշտակ
իւր մխիթարել զն<ո-
սա> ձեռնագրով
այպէս. Թէ մի
երկմտեր Արամ ոչ
թողից ըզքեզ ի
կորուստ զի անձին եւ
եմ եւ անձմաՀն իմ
աստուածութիւնա.

40 Ի վեց դարոն
բաժանեցյաց ի լատդն
իմ. լրա անբաժանելի ի
յարգանդ կուսի գաակի
քո բնակեցցէ եւ ձնցէ
որդի. իմ եւ որդի քո
այն է որ անձինն
ձնանի կուսէ.

41 զի նովաւ
կուրքն. լուսաւորին
կաղքն գնան. բորրոտք
սրբին աղքատոք. աւ-
եւտարանին. մեռեալք
կենդանանան ինքն
խաչեալ մեռանի. եւ
կենդանանայ.

38 Եւ իրրեւ երեկոյ
եղեւ մտաւ արեզակին եւ
ապա իմացան որ
խաբեցան. լացին եւ
կոծացին եւ նուադ
պանՀեցին գաուրա Ե.
այս է որ յատաջատոր
ասեն:

39 Իսկ ողորմեցաւ
Աստուած եւ առաքեաց
առ նոսա Հրեշտակա-
պետն Միքայէլ. եւ ասէ
ցնոսա. Այապէ<ս> ասէ
Տէր. մի տրտմիք
Արամ. թէպէտ խաբե-
ցաք. ոչ թողից գձեզ ի
ձերն Սատանայի.
քանզի անձինն եւ եմ,
եւ անձմաՀն իմ
աստուածութին.

40 ի վեց դարուն
բաժանեցյաց ի լոյսոյ
իմոյ լոյս անբաժանելի.
եւ իջեալ բնակեցից ի
յարգանդ մաքուր
կուսի. Մ՛ա եղեցի
ձնեալն ի նմանէ մարդ
կատարեալ. եղիցի իմ
որդի.

41 շողեցի ի
վերայ երկրի եւ բագում
սքանչելիս արասցէ.
չարչարեցից վասն քո
մեղցի. դարձեալ կեն-
դանացեալ մարմնով

38 Եւրեւ երեկոյ
եղեւ եւ մտաւ արեզակին
նոցայ. լիմացալ եւ
ձանսաւ որ խաբեցաւ.
լացին դառնայպէս եւ
սգեցին եւ Ե օր
անատադ պանՀեցին,
այն է որ յատաջատոր
ասեն:

39 Դարձեալ
ողորմեցո Աստուած եւ
առագաց գՀրրշտակ
իւր որ աւէ նոցա. մի
երկնչիր Արամ. Թէ
խաբաց գքեզ Սատա-
նաս ձերայզրով:

40 Իսկ ի ԶՈւ
տարուն բայժայնեցյաց
ի լատոյ իմոյ գլուան
անբաժանել<ի> որ
եկեալ ձնցի ի գոաւկի
քումէ ի կու յարգան-
դէ. եղցի որդի <ի>մ
եւ որդի քո. այն է որ
անձին ձնանի. եւ լինի
մարդ կատարեալ
առան<գ> մեղադ.

41 շողի ընդ
մարդկան երեւի
մարդայպէս. եւ
սքանչելիս առնէ
Աստուածայ{ա}յպէս.
բագում սքանչելիս
առնէ ի վերայ
աշխարՀի եւ վասն քո

չարչարի եւ մեռանի. եւ
կենդանի մայմնով
ելանի ի գերեզմանէ.

42 այն է որ
անմահն մեռանի. եւ
պատառէ զգիր
պարտեաց քոց եւ
ազատէ զքեզ եւ
զամենայն զաւակ քո ի
ծառայութենէ դժոխոց.
եւ նորոգեցէ զքեզ
առաջին փառան քո. եւ
ինքն կենդանացեալ
մարմնով վերացեալ
դայ առ Աստուա-
ծութիւնս իմ միւտորի:

42 իշզէ ի դժոխս
եւ ազատեցէ զքեզ. եւ
դարձեալ տացէ քեզ
առաջին փառն քո. եւ
ինքն Համբարձեալ
մարմնով վերանա. եւ
{ի} միանալ առ աս-
տուածութիւս իմ. այն
է որ անծինն ծնանի եւ
անմահն մեռանի. եւ
ազատէ զքեզ եւ շնչէ
զձեռագիրն քո:

42 եւ իջանէ ի
դժոխս վասն քո եւ քեզ
ազատէ եւ ի քո
յառաջին փառն
դարձուցանէ:

43 Իբրեւ լուաւ
դայս Ադամ նմայ
ապապէս թրււեցաւ թէ
Չ՞Ր տարին իբրեւ աւր
մի է վասն ուրա-
խութեան.

43 Իսկ յորժամ
լուան Ադամ եւ եւալ,
խնդացին յոյժ.

43 Եբրեւ լուաւ
Ադամ եւ ուրախացաւ.
Զ՞Ր տարին իբրեւ գմի
ժամ Համարէր, վասն
ուրախութեան սրտին:

. . .

49 Դարձեալ եկն ի
Ցորդանան. ձեռեամբ
մկրոչին մկրտեցաւ.
զեռն դապի յետ
դարձաւ Ադամա ձեռա-
գիր սալ քարն
շրնչեցաւ. լյան ի
յերկնից իջաւ. ապանա-
կերպ սուրբ Հոգին
երեւեցաւ յերկնից
ձայնի գոշեաց թէ դայ
է որդի իմ սիրելի:

. . .

49 երեսնամեալ ի
յորդանան գետն դէմ
յետ դարձաւ լույան ի
յերկնից իջաւ
ապաւակերպ որպէս
Հոգին ի վերայ նորա
իջաւ ձայն ի յերկնից
վկայեաց. թէ դայ է
որդի իմ սիրելի:. եւ
ձեռագիրն Ադամայ
ըստուկ փոխեաց
ընշեաց. եւ ի դլուս
վիշապին
քախշախեաց.

. . .

49 եւ անդի եկաւ
երեսնամայ եկ գետն
յորդանան եւ մտաւ ի
գետն. ցուրն դէմն ի
Հետ դարցաւ ձեռագիր
սալ քարն. բացո եւ
ալց. վիշապան երեւեցո:
Եւ տէր մեր Քրիստոս
ունիւ կոփեալ զգի-
շապն. եւ չաղեաց
կոխաց զձեռագիր սալ
քարն եւ շնչեաց: երկ-
նից լոս ծագեաց
եր<ք> պատառեցո
ադաւ<ն>այկերպ սուրբ
Հոգին եջո Հայրական
ձայն վկայեցաւ թէ դայ
է որդի իմ սիրելի.
դմայ լուարուք ցուրն ի
գնալ Հրամայաց
ձեռամբ մկրոչին
մկրտեաց: եւ ել:

Adam Story I

Erevan: Matenadaran, M9100, is a Miscellany (*ժողովածու*) written in 1686 C.E. by Markos *erēcʿ*.[6] The text presented here starts at the top of fol. 32v and is followed on fol. 35r by an unpublished text titled *Վասն Տապանակիս Աստուծոյ* Concerning the Ark of God.

1 Եւ իբրեւ անկանէ <Ադամ>ի դրախտէն լայխարՐս այս գագանաց. նա եկն գիշերային խաւարն եւ խատրեցոյց զնա. եւ տարակուեալ լայր դառնապէս։ Եւ եկեալ միա անգամ խոռվեռցուցիչ բանասարկռն չար Սատանա.

2 Հրեշտակակերպ տեսեամբ երեւեցաւ որպէս բարեկամ. եւ ասէ րնդէ՞ր լաս անմխիթար։

3 Ասէ ցնա Ադամ որպէս բարեկամի խոսի. վասն զի գրկեցայ անմարՐակական դրախտէն եւ յանանց լուտյն. եւ անկայ երկիր փշեղէն. եւ ի վերայ ամենայնի խատր եաս տիրեռց իմձ եւ ոչ գիտեմ զինչ արարից։

4 Ասէ ցնա ամենաչարն. զինչ տացես ինձ եթէ տացից քեզ զլոյս։

5 Ասէ ցնա Ադամ. եւ զինչ մնաց ինձ ի փատացն իմռգն զի տաց քեզ. վասն զի մերկ եւ անտառակ եմ. բայց միայն ի տերեւ թենոյս գոր արարի ծածկոյթ մերկութեանս։

6 Ասէ ցնա Սատանայ. Տուր ինձ գՐոգիդ քո. եւ գծունրոց քոյ եւ ես տացից քեզ լոյս.

7 Իսկ լիմարեալն եւ աստուածային գիտութենէն որոշեալն ոչ ծանեաւ գխասարային

նռրա կաման եւ գխորագիտութիւնն. եւ գիր եւ գծունրոցն իւրո կորուստ. այլ գօրէն կաթնասուն տղայոց. խաբեցաւ կրկին. եւ եոտ գողիսն.

8 Եւ դեռ չեր ժամ լուսանալոյ. Ասէ Սատանա ցԱդամ. Դիր պայման ի միջի մերռւմ. զի մինչեւ անեղն եղանի. եւ անմարՐն մեռանի. Հողիստ քո եւ ծունրոց քոյ իմ ձեռս լինի. եւ ապայ տեսանես լոյս.

9 Եւ եղիր գանիրաւ եւ գմաՐացուցիչ պայման. եւ եղեւ առաւոտ եւ եռես գլոյս.

10 Եւ իբրեւ դարձեալ եղեւ երեկոյ. եւ մթացաւ դարձեալ. եկաց վասն պայմանին. եւ ոչ կարաց գերծանիլ զի անՐնարին էր արաց ի թակել գպայմանն. բայց ի անեղէն։

11 Եւ եկեալ Հրեշտակ Աստուծոյ եոտ նմա փորք մի մխիթարութին աւետիս եւ ասէ։

12 Եթէ ի ժամանակի եկեսցէ Բանն Աստուծոյ. եւ ագատեսցէ գքեզ.

13 Եւ {աներալ} յանդիման դրախտին եւ Ցառաչանօք եւ Ցեծեծանօք վՑարեռց գկեանս իւր.

14 եւ երթեալ Սատանայի որպ֊սպիսութեամբ շինեաց դժոխս եւ զամենայն ֊դժոխս յառաջ եկելոց Արմատայ անդ մոտանէր դժորն իրրոււբ. եւ զամենայն Ասպիածոյ սոտեծոտւոծֆս իւր երկրպագո եւ դոՀամատոյց արար.

15 եւ զդժոխս ժողովեաց վեց Հատար սարի.

16 եւ յումանս ծագեաց շառաւիղ Ասստուածգքխոսութեան. եւ ԾզնեԾսան եւ ոչ կարացին օզնել ինչ. վասն զի { } սատաչին դարութն. Եւովք գտեալ ընտրեալ եւ ԾՀարց զպատուՁռ ան՟ւարին ցուցցն.

17 եւ իրրեւ յուաս շինեաց ասման ինչ երկաթի եւ եդ ի զլուխ իւր եւ սստեալ ի զլուխ լերինն. եւ կ ամ ոչ Եւոեւ զերկիին այլ լայլով առոթԾեր վասն ՚Ծաիւսստոտեծֆն եւ պյսմանին.

18 եւ Եկեալ Հրեշտակ Ասստուծոյ եւ ասԾ ցՁսա. եթԾ ոչ որ եւ լինի Համր անՀարին ցուցցն. բայց մխայ֊ն զդժոխս քն ապատեցեր ի ՍատանայԾ.

19 եւ եթԾ վախԽանիս ասո ոչ եթԾ թույ սսայոյ Հոդոյ քն. վասն արդարոււթեան քն. այլ ՀրամանաԾ Ասստուծոյ սարայց զբեզ ընդ կենդանոյն երկԾոն.

20 եւ կացցես ի տեղի արդարորցն կենդանԾ մխնՁեւ յորն վերքֆն. յայնժամ աԾԾելուց մարդարԾուԹՁււ֊ սպատՁն. եւ գիզք. զի ինչես եւ յասնֆխՁսանեցես դորդֆն կորրստեան եւ բարոեցես զբշՁմարֆւֆն Ասստուած: եւ Քրիստոսի վասր լասխսԾութան ամԾ֊ն:

Armenian Adam Fragment I

The text has been edited by Stone from Erevan: Matenadaran, M2126, p. 234, dated 1660.[7]

4 ՁարֆՀուրֆֆ եւ երկնԾֆ ի դասն դժոխոց. որ ծեռույֆֆ Ծր սսՁեալ։

Georgios Chumnos

The following text is cited from Marshall's edition of British Library Add 40724, to which he added Cod. Marc. gr. IX.17. He knew of a third copy in Vienna. It has been noted previously that a fourth copy exists, in the Library of St. Catherine's Monastery at Mount Sinai.[8]

Ἄγγελος, τάγμα Χερουβίμ, 'ς τὲς πόρτες ἐμποδίζει,
    τὴν Εὔαν καὶ πρωτόπλαστον ἀπόξω τοὺς σφαλίζει.
Ἐπῆραν τὴν ἀπόφασιν Ἀδάμος μὲ τὴν Εὔα,
    καὶ ἐνάντιον τῆς παράδεισος ἐκάτζασιν καὶ κλαῖγα.
Καθίζει Ἀδὰμ ὁ θλιβερὸς καὶ βαραναστενάζει,
    καὶ ἀπὸ ψυχῆς ὠδύρετο, δριμειὰν φωνὴν φωνάζει.
Παράδεισε ἁγιώτατε, διὰ μέναν φυτεμένος,
    καὶ διὰ τῆς Εὔας τὴν βουλὴν ἀπόξω σφαλισμένος.
Σηκώνουνται, μισεύγουσιν, παγαίνουν τὴν ὁδόν τως,

5

ξυπόλυτοι καὶ ὁλόγδυμνοι περιπατοῦν 'ς τὸ γόν τως (sic)   10
Σκότος δὲν εἴδασιν ποτέ, εἴχασιν πάντα μέρα,
    ὁ ἥλιος ἐβασίλευσεν, πλακώνει τους ἑσπέρα.
Καὶ φθάνουν τους τὰ σκοτεινά, θαμπώνεται τὸ φῶς τως·
    κοντεύγουνται τὰ γόνατα, χάνεται ἡ ὁδός τως.
Πιστεύοντας ποτὲ 'ς αὐτοὺς νὰ μὴ ἀνατέλλῃ ἡμέρα,   15
    μὰ νά 'ναι πάντα σκοτεινὰ καὶ νὰ κρατῇ ἑσπέρα.
Κ' εἰς μιὸν ὁ τρισκατάρατος, ἄκου τὸ τί τῶν κάμνει,
    ὁ διάβολος ὁ φθονερὸς εἰς πλάνος πῶς τοὺς βάνει.
Λέγει τως τί μου τάσσετε, κ' ἐγὼ νὰ σᾶς ξεδράμω,
    ἥλιον καὶ φῶς ὡραιότατον καὶ μέραν νὰ σᾶς κάμω;   20
Καὶ αὐτοὶ ὠλιγοψυχήσασιν, χειρόγραφον τοῦ κάμνουν,
    (εἴ)τια λογῆς τοῦ τάξασιν, λέγουν καὶ ἀναθιβάνουν.
Ἡμεῖς καὶ ὅλα τὰ τέκνα μας μὲ σέναν νὰ κρατοῦμεν,
    κ' εἰς εἴ τι μᾶς εἰ θὲς εἰπεῖν, οὐδὲ ποσῶς νὰ βγοῦμεν.
Κ' ἡ νύκτα κείνη ἐπέρασεν, κ' ἦλθεν ἡ ἄλλη μέρα,   25
    καὶ πάλιν κείνη ἐπέρασεν, κ' ἦλθεν ἡ ἄλλη ἑσπέρα.
Καὶ Ἀδὰμ πάλιν γελάστηκεν δεύτερον μὲ τὴν Εὔα,
    τὸ στῆθος τως ἐδέρνασιν, φαρμακεμένα κλαῖγα.

Modern Greek Tales

1. τὸ ὁμόλογο τοῦ Ἀδὰμ καὶ Εὔας

    Ἐκ τῆς Ἐφημ. «Μορέας τῆς Τριπόλεως» τῆς 6ης Ἰανουαρίου 1929.
    Ἐπειδὴ κατ' αὐτὰς ἔρχονται τὰ Ἅγια Θεοφάνεια ἀπεφάσισα ὅπως
ἀποστείλω πρὸς δημοσίευσιν τὴν ἑξῆς λαϊκὴν περὶ τὸν Πρωτοπλάστων
παράδοσιν.
    Ὅταν οἱ Πρωτόπλαστοι ἐξεβλήθησαν τοῦ Παραδείσου, δὲν
ᾐσθάνθησαν μόνον ὅτι ἦσαν γυμνοί, ἀλλ' ἤρχισαν νὰ αἰσθάνωνται καὶ τὴν
πεῖναν. Τέλος ἐπείνασαν πολὺ καὶ ἔλαβον ἕνα δρόμο χωρὶς καὶ ἐκεῖνοι νὰ
γνωρίζωσι ποῦ πηγαίνουν! Ἐκεῖ ποὺ ἐπροχώρουν βλέπουν ἔξαφνα ἀπὸ
μακρὰν τὸν ποταμὸν Ἰορδάνην. Ἐσταμάτησαν καὶ ἐσκέπτοντο ὅτι δὲν θὰ
κατορθώσουν νὰ τὸν διαβοῦν. Ἀλλ' ἐν" ἐσκέπτοντο, βλέπουσι νὰ ἔρχεται
ἕνας πρὸς αὐτούς. Τοὺς χαιρετᾷ καὶ ἐρωτᾷ ποῦ πηγαίνουν καὶ τί θέλουν.
Ἐκεῖνοι τοῦ ὁμιλοῦν περὶ τῆς πείνας των. Αὐτὸς δὲ τοὺς ἀποκρίνεται ὅτι
δύναται νὰ ἱκανοποιήσῃ αὐτοὺς περὶ τούτου καὶ νὰ τοὺς ὁδηγήσῃ ὅπως
φροντίσωσι καὶ εἰς τὸ μέλλον νὰ μὴ πεινῶσιν, ἀρκεῖ ὅμως νὰ ὑπογράψωσιν
ὁμόλογον, δι' οὗ νὰ ὁμολογῶσιν ὅτι θὰ ἀκολουθῶσι πάντοτε αὐτὸν καὶ θὰ
τὸν ἔχωσιν ὡς θεόν των. Οἱ Πρωτόπλαστοι ἀναγκασθέντες ἐκ τῆς πείνης των
ὑπεσχέθησαν τοῦτο, καὶ ἀμέσως τοὺς παρουσιάζει μίαν πλάκα καὶ ὁμολ-
ογοῦσιν ἐπὶ ταύτης διὰ γραφῆς τὴν τυφλὴν των ὑποταγήν. Ὁ δὲ διάβολος
ἔλαβε τὸ ὁμόλογον, καὶ ἔρριψεν αὐτὸ εἰς ἕνα βρύλιαγκα[9] τοῦ Ἰορδάνου
ποταμοῦ, καὶ ἔμεινεν ἡ πλάκα ἐκεῖ. Ὁ δὲ Χριστὸς καταβὰς ἐκ τοῦ Οὐρανοῦ
ἐπῆγε καὶ ἐβαπτίσθη εἰς τὸν Ἰορδάνην καὶ εἰς τὸν βυθὸν ἀκριβῶς ἐκεῖ ὅπου
ἦτο ἡ πλάκα, τὸ δὲ πῦρ τῆς Θεότητος κατεύκασε τὴν πλάκα καὶ τὴν διέλυσε
καὶ οὕτω ἐλύθη καὶ ἡ χρεωστικὴ ὁμολογία τῶν προπατόρων τῆς ὑποσχέσεως

καὶ τῆς ὑποταγῆς αὐτῶν εἰς τὸν διάβολον. Διὰ τοῦτο καὶ μία εὐχὴ τοῦ Μεγάλου Ἁγιασμοῦ λέγει· «Ὁ Ἰορδάνης ἐστράφη εἰς τὰ ὀπίσω θεασάμενος τὸ πῦρ τῆς θεότητος, σωματικῶς κατερχόμενον ἐπ᾽ αὐτόν». Τὸ δὲ περιλάλητον τροπάριον τῆς Μεγάλης Παρασκευῆς λέγει· «Ὁ ἐν Ἰορδάνῃ ἐλευθερώσας τὸν Ἀδάμ». Ὥστε ἡ λαϊκή μας Ἑλληνικὴ παράδοσις συνᾴδει μὲ τὰς ὑμνῳδίας τῆς Ἱερᾶς μας Ἐκκλησίας.

Ἡ πεῖνα! ἡ φοβερὰ καὶ ἀποτρόπαιος πεῖνα! Ὄχι μόνον τὸν Ἀδὰμ ἐξηνάγκασε νὰ ὑποκύψῃ εἰς τὸν κοσμοκράτορα, ἀλλὰ καὶ τὸν Ἰακὼβ ἠνάγκασε νὰ ἀρνηθῇ τὸν τόπον τῆς γεννήσεώς του καὶ νὰ ὑπάγῃ εἰς Αἴγυπτον. Τὸν Ἡσαῦ νὰ πωλήσῃ τὰ πρωτοτόκιά του ἀντὶ πινακίου φακῆς. Ὁ δὲ Σωτήρ μας καὶ Κύριός μας ἕνεκα τῆς πείνης ἐπειράχθη ὑπὸ τοῦ διαβόλου, ἀλλ᾽ ὁ νέος Ἀδὰμ δὲν ὑπήκουσεν εἰς αὐτόν. Καὶ ἔκτοτε πάντας ἡ πεῖνα ἐξαναγκάζει νὰ ὑφιστάμεθα ὅλα καὶ μάλιστα νὰ ἐκπατριζώμεθα διὰ νὰ θεραπεύσωμεν τὴν ἀνάγκην ταύτης. Τοῦτο ἀναφέρει καὶ ὁ θεῖος Ὅμηρος Ἰλ. Τ 160-171.

Σίτου καὶ οἴνοιο· τὸ γὰρ μένος ἐστὶ καὶ ἀλκή.
Οὐ γὰρ ἀνὴρ πρόπαν ἦμαρ ἐς ἠέλιον καταδύντα
ἄκμηνος σίτοιο δυνήσεται ἄντα μάχεσθαι...
δίψα τε καὶ λιμός, βλάβεται δέ τε γούνατ᾽ ἰόντι...
ἀλλ᾽ ἄγε λαὸν μὲν σκέδασον, καὶ δεῖπνον ἄνωχθι.

Ν. ΛΑΣΚΑΡΙΣ (Λασταῖος)

ADAM AND CHRIST

2. In addition, in *Laographia* in 1962, the following tale was published. The following details are given of the storyteller. The story was recorded by Antonios Michalakeas, a teacher, in 1960. He heard it from a man, Ch. Laskaris, seventy-five to eighty years old, who had died twenty years before. He lived in Kalamata and hailed from Bassara in the Peloponnese.

«Ράπισμα κατεδέξατο ὁ ἐν Ἰορδάνῃ ἐλευθερώσας τὸν Ἀδάμ...»
Στίχος ἐκ τοῦ ΙΕ΄ Ἀντιφώνου τῆς Μεγ. Πέμπτης.

Ὅταν ὁ Θεὸς ἔδιωξε τὸν Ἀδὰμ ἀπὸ τὸν Παράδεισο, ὁ Ἀδὰμ δὲν ἤξερε ποῦ νὰ πάῃ καὶ τί νὰ κάνῃ. Τότε τὸν συνάντησε ὁ διάβολος ποὺ γιὰ νὰ τὸν βοηθήσῃ τοῦ εἶπε νὰ κάνουνε πρῶτα ἕνα συμφωνητικὸ —ὁμόλογο— ποὺ τὸ γράψανε —δὲν εἶχε χαρτὶ τότε— πάνω σὲ μία πέτρα.

Τὴν πῆρε τότε ἀμέσως τὴν πέτρα ὁ διάβολος καὶ τὴν ἔρριξε στὸ(ν) Ἰορδάνη ποταμό, μήπως καὶ τὴ βρῇ ὁ Ἀδὰμ σὰν μετανοιώσῃ ἀργότερα — ὅπως καὶ μετάνοιωσε— καὶ τὴ χαλάσῃ.

Πάνω σ᾽ αὐτὴ τὴν πέτρα πάτησε ὁ Χριστός, ὅταν βαφτίστηκε στὸν Ἰορδάνη ἀπὸ τὸν Πρόδρομο, καὶ ἔτσι λευτερώθηκε ὁ Ἀδὰμ ἀπὸ τὴ συμφωνία του μὲ τὸ διάβολο.

(Ὅπως τὸ ἄκουσα ἀπὸ τὸ Χρῖστο Λάσκαρι, γέροντα ἐτῶν 75-80, συνταξιοῦχο τεχνίτη τοῦ μηχανοστασίου Σ.Π.Α.Π. τῆς Καλαμάτας, καταγόμενον ἀπὸ τὸν Βασαρᾶ τῆς Λακεδαίμονος· ἀπέθανε πρὸ 20 ἐτίας).

1960　　　　　ΑΝΤΩΝΙΟΣ ΜΙΧΑΛΑΚΕΑΣ
　　　　　　　Μετεκπαιδευόμενος δημοδιδάσκαλος

Megas's Tale

A rather long and very interesting version of the cheirograph story was recorded by George Megas in Thrace in the 1920s. The text of his transcription is given here. B. Moncó has added some notes on the terminology of the text, and her notes are marked by (BM) at their end. The dialect is quite distinct. We have abided by Megas's division of the text into sections.

1.   Ὁ Ἀδάμς ἔμπροστα κ' ἔμπροστα πρωτόπλαστος. Πῆρεν ὁ Θεὸς πὸ τέσσερις κόχες γῆς μὲ τὸ χέρι τ', τό σφιξε, ἔτρεξε τὸ νερὸ κάτ'· τ' ἄφσε, ἀπόμνε χῶμα, γίνκεν Ἀδάμ· πὸ τοιοῦτο χέρι, νὲ πὸ μάννα, νὲ πὸ μπαμπᾶ.

Εἶχε κ' ἕναν κῆπο,[10] ἕναν μπαχτσιὰ τρανό, ὡραιότατο. Ἐκεῖ μέσα ἦταν ὅλα τά φυτὰ κ' οἱ καρποί. Ἔδωσε καὶ τὸν Ἀδὰμ κεῖ μέσα, ἔδωσε καὶ τὸν ὄφιο, ἔδωσε καὶ τὸν διάβολο. Κεῖνοι τρεῖς ἦταν μέσα κεῖ. Τὸν διάβολο καὶ τὸν ὄφιο δὲν τοὺς ἔφκιασεν ὁ Θεός· κεῖνοι δὲν ἦταν τῆς προκοπῆς, δὲν ἦταν ἀράδα νὰ τοὺς φκιάσῃ. Τοὺς ἔβαλε κεῖ μέσα νὰ δοκιμάσῃ τὸν Ἀδὰμ τί θὰ κάμῃ.

Μέσα 'ς τέκεῖνο τὸ μπαχτσιὰ ἦταν μέρα καὶ νύχτα, ὄξω ἀπ' τὸ μπαχτσιὰ ἦταν ὅλο νύχτα.

2.   Μιὰ μέρα ἀπάνω κάτ' Ἀδάμς διάερε μέσ' 'ς τὸ μπαχτσιὰ μαναχός τ', σεκιλντίτσκ' ἡ καρδία τ'.[11]

Τὸ βράδυ ἔπεσεν Ἀδάμς. Πάει ὁ Θεὸς, ἀπ' τὸν Ἀδὰμ ἔβγαλεν ἕνα πλευρό, τὸ φύσηξε, τὸ καμε γυναῖκα, τὴν ὠνόμασε Γεύα.[12] Τὴν ἔκαμε γυναῖκα, πλάγιασε κοντὰ 'ς τὸν Ἀδάμ.[13]

Ξύπνησεν Ἀδάμς τὴ νύχτα, κοιτάζει, μιὰ γυναῖκα κοντά του. Σηκώνεται Ἀδάμς φεύγ', κ' ἡ γυναῖκα φεύγ'· δὲ ξέρουνται αὐτοί. Βλέπ' ὁ Θεὸς, τὸν λέει τὸν Ἀδάμ· «Ἀδάμ, λέει, σ' ἔδωκα ἕνα σύντροφο νὰ ἠγλεντᾶς».

Χίρσαν κοντὰ νὰ πααίνουν, νὰ κουνουστίζουν[14] μὰ δὲν ξέρουν νὰ κάμουν παιδιά! Ἀπ' ὅλ' τς καρποὶ νὰ φᾶς, ἀπ' τς συκομουριᾶς τὸ ξύλο νὰ μὴ φᾶς σῦκο. Κι αὐτοὶ ἦταν τότε μαλλιαροί· ἀρκοῦδα ὅπως εἶναι, ἔτσ' ἦταν.

3.   Αὐτοὶ γυρνοῦντας γυρνοῦντας ἔτρωγαν ἀπ' ὅλα, ἔβοσκαν[15] κεῖ μέσα. Ἡ Γεύα εἶπε· Νὰ φᾶμε κι ἀπ' τὸ σῦκο. Εἶπεν ὁ Ἀδάμς· Θεὸς εἶπε νὰ μὴ φᾶμε. Τὸν γέλασε τὸν Ἀδάμ[16]· «Ἅμα φᾶμε, λέει, θὰ γίνουμε κ' ἐμεῖς Θεοί», κ' ἔφαγαν. Τίναξαν τὴν τρίχα τς, τὸ μάλλι ὅλο.[17]

Ἅμα δγιήθκαν γκολιόμπαρ'[18] ἕνας ἀπ' τὸν ἄλλον ἀντράπκαν· ἔσφιξαν τὰ μπούτια τς καὶ τὰ χέρια τά βάλαν 'ς τὸ κεφάλ' ἀπ' τὴν ἀντροπή τους καὶ τὶς ἀμασκάλες τὶς ἔσφιξαν. Κεῖ ποὺ ἔσφιξαν, κεῖ πόνμε[19] μαλλί, τᾶλλο τνάχκε.[20]

4.   Ὁ Θεὸς εἶδγε ἀπὸ πάνω, τὸν φώναξε τὸν Ἀδάμ· «Ἀδάμ, Ἀδάμ.» Τί νὰ ποῦν 'ς τὸ Θεό, πῶς νὰ βγοῦν γκολιόμπαρ'! Ἔπιασαν μὲ τὸ τσακί τς,[21] ἔφκιασαν τσιβούδια ἀπὸ τὸ ξύλο[22] καὶ εἶναι κάτι χορτάρια, πρωτομαντῆλες τὶς λέν. Κεῖνο τὸ φύλλο εἶναι ἀπ' ὅλα πρῶτο, καὶ πῆραν δυὸ μαντῆλες ἀπὸ κεῖνες κ' ἔβαλαν μπροστὰ καὶ πίσω νὰ μὴ φαῖνται τὰ καλαμπαλικία τς·[23] θὰ βγοῦν 'ς τὸ Θεό!

«Ἀδάμ, Ἀδάμ, τὸν λέει, δὲ σ' εἶπα νὰ μὴ φᾶς αὐτὸ τὸ σῦκο τὸν καρπό;»
Κι ὁ Ἀδὰμ εἶπε·
«Μ' ἔδωκες μιὰ γυναῖκα κι αὐτὴ μὲ γέλασε» — Εἶπε τὸ Θεὸ λόγια
καρσί.[24]—Λέει τῇ γυναῖκα ὁ Θεός·
«Γιατὶ εἶπες κ' ἔφαγεν ἀπ' αὐτὸν τὸν καρπό;»
«Μένα, λέει, μὲ γέλασεν ὁ δαίμονας». Λέει τὸ δαίμονα,
«Μένα μὲ γέλασεν ὁ ὄφιος,» λέει.

5.   Τότε τὸ φίδι πάαινεν ὀρθὸ καὶ δὲν θὰ ἦταν πεθαμός· θὰ νὰ τρώῃ ὁ ὄφιος
πὸ ἕναν πὸ ἕναν τς ἀνθρῶπ', μπιντιβοί, ὁλόκεροι θὰ νὰ τς τρώῃ.
—Ἦταν τὸ στόμα τ' τρανὸ σὰν καζάνι καὶ τὸν γιούντιζε[25] τὸν ἄνθρωπο
—Ἦρθε καιρὸς νὰ πεθάνῃ, θὰ πααίνῃ νὰ τὸν τρώῃ ὄφιος· κεῖνος ἦταν
πεθαμός, ἀρρώστιες δὲν εἶχε. Τό δωσε ντουβὰ[26] ὁ Θεός·
«Νὰ πέσῃς τῆς κοιλιᾶς», λέει. Ἔγειρε, σκοτῶθκε τὸ φίδι κι ἀνέλυσε 'ς
τῇ γῆς[27]· γίνκε τόζι[28] καὶ κεῖνο τὸ τόζι γίνκε ψεῖρες καὶ ψύλλοι καὶ κεῖνα
μᾶς τρῶν τώρα. Ἀπόμναν καὶ τέτοια τέτοια φιδούδια κι ἀκόμα ἄνθρωπος
φοβᾶται ἀπὸ τὸ φίδι, γιατὶ ἤθελε τὸν τρώει τὸν ἄνθρωπο. Τίποτα ἄλλο δὲ
φοβόμαστε. Τὸ φίδι τί θὰ σὲ κάμῃ; μὰ κεῖνο φοβόμαστε. Δὲ μπορεῖ νὰ σὲ φάῃ,
μὰ σὲ τρῶν τὰ τόζια.

6.   Τὸν διάβολο τὸν καταρίσκε Θεός·
«Νὰ μὴν πχιάνεσαι πουθενά· νὲ ἀπ' τὸν οὐρανὸ νὲ ἀπ' τῇ γῆς. Νὰ ζᾶς
'ς τὸν ἀγέρα κ' ἐκεῖ ἀπάν' νάι λειώσ'ς.» Κι ὁ διάβολος ἔφκι[29] 'ς τὰ οὐράνια
καὶ τώρα γέρ' καμιὰ βολὰ ἀπ' τὸ δαιμόνιο ἀγέρας κάτ' καὶ πατάει καένας
καὶ παθαίν', στραβών' τὸ ποδάρ' ἢ τὸ χέρ' κ' εἶναι δαιμονικὰ κεῖνα.

7.   Καταρίσκε καὶ τὸν Ἀδὰμ καὶ τῇ Γεύα Θεός. Λέει τὸν Ἀδάμ·
«Νὰ δουλεύῃς, νὰ πολεμᾶς,[30] λέει, μέρα νύχτα, μὲ τὸ γίδρο νὰ ταΐζ'ς τὰ
παιδιὰ σ'.»—Πέκει γανιάζμε[31] τώρα· νὰ γιδρών'ς, νὰ σφουγγίζ'ς τὸ γίδρο
σ' καὶ νὰ φυλάγ'ς τὰ τέκνα σ'—
Τῇ Γεύα τὴν εἶπε·
«Νὰ γεννᾶς τὰ παιδιὰ σ' μὲ τὸ ζόρι[32] καὶ μέρα νύχτα δυὸ-τρία χρόνια
ἀπ' τὰ στῆθι σ' καὶ νὰ δουλεύῃς μὲ τὸ γίδρο σ' καὶ τῇ δουλία, ποὺ θὰ κάμῃς
τὴν ἡμέρα, θὰ ναι καταραμέν', νὰ τὴν παίρ'ς νὰ τὴν βάζ'ς τὴν ἀμάσκαλη
σ'· δὲν ἐχ' προκοπή».

8.   Τοὺς καταρίσκε Θεός, τοὺς ἔβγαλε ἀπ' τὸν Παράδσον ὄξω. Τοὺς ἔδιωξε
Θεός· «Φεῦγα, λέει, ἀπ' τὸν Παράδσο».
Τὸν ἔβγαλε δαίμονας τὸν Ἀδάμ. «Ἔβγα, ὄξω, λέει. Γώ, λέει, ὄξα φκιάνω καὶ μέρα, λέει διάβολος, φκιάνω καὶ νύχτα. Θὰ φκιάσουμε ἕνα σενέτ,[33]
θ ὰ σὲ βαρέσω καὶ σφραγίδα 'ς τὸ τσακάλ'.[34] Ἄνοιξε τὴν ἀπαλάμη σ', λέει,
θὰ κάμω μελάνη», κ' ἔπιασε τὸ νύχι τ', τὸ καμε πέννα καὶ βουτοῦσε 'ς τὸ
γαῖμα ἀπ' τὸν Ἀδὰμ τῇ χούφτα κ' ἔκαμε τὸ σενέτ. — Μὲ τὸ τσακί τ' τὸν ἔκαμε
γραμμὲς 'ς τὴν ἀπαλάμη κ' ἔβγαλε γαῖμα καὶ βουτοῦσε κ' ἔκαμε τὸ σένετ.
Γιὰ ταῦτο εἶναι τὸ χέρι μας κομμένο.

9.   Βγῆκεν ὄξω αὐτός, τὰ καμαν ἐκεῖνα. Τὸν γέλασε, τὸν κόλασε. Πάει 'ς
τὴν κόλαση, πέθανε 'ς τὴν κόλαση Ἀδάμς καὶ τὸν ἤλεγαν «Καταραμένος

Άδάμς». Τὸν παράχωσαν σ' ἕνα μέρος τὸν Ἀδάμ. Ὅποιος περνοῦσεν ἀπ' ἐκεῖ, ὅλοι ἀπὸ μιὰ πέτρα ἔρρηχναν· «Καταραμένος Ἀδάμς»! Περνάει κ' ἕνας βασιλιᾶς μὲ ἀσκέρια³⁵ χιλιάδες πολλοὶ κ' εἶπαν·

«Τί ναι αὐτό;

—Ἀδὰμ τάφος.

—Ρῆξτε πέτρες». Γίνκεν ἕνας καλὲς ἐκεῖ (πύργος, ὕψωμα).

10. Πὸ κάμποσα χρόνια γεννῆθκε Χριστός. Ἦρθε καιρὸς νὰ σταυρωθῆ. Αὐτοὶ τς Ὁβραῖγ' τς ἔκαμε τῆ γνώμη Ἰσοῦ Χριστὸς νὰ πᾶν' ἐκεῖ ψηλὰ 'ς τὶς πέτρες, πού ταν Ἀδάμς, ἐκεῖ νὰ πάῃ Χριστὸς νὰ χύσῃ τὸ γαῖμα τ'. Πᾶν' ἐκεῖ, τὸν σταύρωσαν, τὸν ἔχυσαν τὸ γαῖμα τ', τὸν τρύπησαν τὶς ἀμασκάλες τ'. Ἰσοῦ Χριστὸς ἔκαμε τῆ γνώμη τς, γιὰ νὰ χυθῆ τὸ γαῖμα τ', νὰ πάῃ ἀπὸ πέτρα σὲ πέτρα σιακάτ' νὰ βρῇ τ' Ἀδὰμ τὴν ἀπαλάμη, νὰ τὴν ξεπλύν' ἀπ' τὸ γαῖμα, ποὺ βουτοῦσε ὁ δαίμονας κ' ἔγραφε κ' ἔκαμε τὸ σενέτ, γιὰ νὰ ξεπλύνη τὶς ἀμαρτίες τ' Ἀδάμ, γιατὶ κι ὁ Χριστὸς τὸν εἶχε μπαμπᾶ τὸν Ἀδὰμ, γῆς οἰκουμέν'³⁶ τὸν εἶχε μπαμπᾶ· Πρωτόπλαστος· ὁ Θεὸς τὸν ἔκαμε μὲ χέρ' ...

11. Ἄντρας θέλ' ὅλο 'ς τῆ γῆς νὰ κοιτάζ'· εἶναι πὸ τῆ γῆς φκιαγμένος. Γυναῖκα εἶναι πὸ τάντροῦ· δὲ εἶναι πὸ χῶμα. Γυναῖκα εἶναι τρόπος νὰ κοιτάζῃ τὸν ἄντρα, γιατί ναι πὸ τὸν ἄντρα φκιαγμένη κι ὁ ἄντρας νὰ κοιτάζῃ τῆ γῆς. Ἄντρας ἔχ' εὐκή· ὅπου νὰ πάῃ, μὲ τ' ἀμάξι θὰ φέρῃ. Γυναῖκα ὅ τ' δουλειὰ νὰ κάμῃ, θὰ τὸ βάλῃ 'ς τὴν ἀμασκάλη τς ἀπκάτου. Γιὰ ταῦτο λένε «τῆς γυναίκας ἡ δουλειὰ δὲν πιάνει τόπο». Κ' ἕνα πλευρὸ νὰ μετρήσῃς τῆ γυναῖκα, τάντροῦ ἕνα ξύκ'κο³⁷ εἶναι. Κ' ἔχ' δίκαιο ἄντρας, ἅμα γυναῖκα δὲν κάμ' καλά, τὸ πλευρὸ κεῖνο, πού ναι τάντροῦ, νὰ τὸ τσακίσῃ· ἔχ' δίκαιο· αὐτὴ θὰ πονέσῃ. Κι ἂν σοῦ πῇ τίποτα, νὰ τς πῇς «Ἀμ' ἐγὼ τὸ δίκο μ' τὸ πλευρὸ βάρεσα». Ἀλλοῦ νὰ μὴ τὴν κροῦς· 'ς τὸ πλευρό, 'ς τὸ δικό σ' τὸ πλευρό.

An Ethiopic Text Close to the Legend

Ethiopic Conflict of Adam and Eve with Satan
(Malan 1.16)[1]

This Christian writing deals with, among other subjects, a series of conflicts between the protoplasts and Satan. It was translated from Arabic into Ethiopic after the seventh century; beyond that, little can be said about its date. The Ethiopic text was published in the nineteenth century and was translated into English, French, and German; the Arabic text was recently edited by Battista and Bagatti, based upon nine manuscripts.[2] The material cited from this work contains the idea of the protoplasts' search for light, but does not have the legend of the cheirograph in it. The collocation of themes in chapters 11–16, of which excerpts are given here, is quite notable, and these chapters may have been written in deliberate tension with the Satanic form of the cheirograph myth.

Turdeanu considers that the Ethiopic *Conflict of Adam and Eve* contains elements constitutive of the legend of the cheirograph. This is also the view of F. M. Marshall, who says, "The germ of this legend occurs in the Ethiopic version of the *Book of Adam and Eve* (ed. S. C. Malan, p. 15)."[3] There are indeed some notable similarities between this apocryphon and the legend, but they certainly do not justify Turdeanu's assertion that the legend's "connections avec un apocryphe éthiopien . . . indiquent son origin orientale." The following common points may be observed in book 1 of *Conflict of Adam and Eve with Satan,* chapters 11–16: (1) the problem of light and darkness; (2) Satan as deceiver; (3) the divine promise to free the protoplasts "from the hand of Satan"; and (4) the promise of the incarnation and the ensuing redemption. However, the narrative found in this work does not contain the element of the cheirograph. There is, as far as we know, no evidence for the existence of the full cheirograph legend within the Ethiopic tradition.

11. . . . Both Adam and Eve . . . came and entered the Cave of Treasures.

But [when in it] Adam could not see Eve; he only heard the noise she made. Neither could she see Adam, but heard the noise he made. . . .

He then said to her, "Remember the bright nature in which we lived, while we abode in the garden! . . . Think, oh think of that garden in which was no darkness while we dwelled therein.

12. And Adam beat himself, and threw himself on the ground in the cave, from bitter grief, and because of the darkness, and lay there as dead. . . . But the merciful Lord looked upon the death of Adam, and on Eve's silence from fear of the darkness. . . .

13. Then, when God . . . heard Adam's voice, He said to him:—

'O Adam, so long as the good angel was obedient to Me, a bright light rested on him and on his hosts.

But when he transgressed My commandment, I deprived him of that bright nature, and he became dark.

But he transgressed, and I made him fall from heaven upon the earth; and it was this darkness that came upon him.

And on thee, O Adam, while in My garden and obedient to Me, did that bright light rest also.

But when I heard of thy transgression, I deprived thee of that bright light. Yet, of My mercy, I did not turn thee into darkness, but I made thee thy body of flesh, over which I spread this skin, in order that it may bear cold and heat. . . .

Thus, O Adam, as this night deceived thee. It is not to last forever; but is only of twelve hours; when it is over, daylight will return. . . .

For I made thee of the light; and I willed to bring out children of light from thee, and like unto thee. . . .

Yet I knew that Satan, who deceived himself, would also deceive thee. . . .'

But God the Lord said to Adam, 'Verily I say unto thee, this darkness will pass from thee, every day I have determined for thee, until the fulfillment of My covenant; when I will save thee and bring thee back again into the garden, into the abode of light thou longest for, wherein there is no darkness. I will bring thee to it—in the kingdom of heaven.'

Again said God unto Adam, 'All this misery that thou hast been made to take upon thee because of thy transgression, will not free thee from the hand of Satan, and will not save thee.'

'But I will. When I shall come down from heaven, and shall become flesh of thy seed, and take upon me the infirmity from which thou sufferest, then the darkness that came upon thee in this cave shall come upon Me in the grave, when I am in the flesh of thy seed.

'And I, who am without years, shall be subject to the reckoning of years, of times, of months, and of days, and I shall be reckoned as one of the sons of men, in order to save thee.'

14. After this Adam and Eve ceased not to stand in the cave, praying and weeping, until the morning dawned upon them.

And when they saw the light returned to them, they restrained from fear, and strengthened their hearts.

Then Adam began to come out of the cave. And when he came to the mouth of it, and stood and turned his face towards the east, and saw the sun rise in glowing rays, and felt the heat thereof on his body, he was afraid of it, and thought in his heart that this flame came forth to plague him.

He wept then, and smote upon his breast, and fell upon the earth on his face, and made his request, saying:—

'O Lord, plague me not, neither consume me, nor yet take away my life from the earth,' For he thought that the sun was God.

Inasmuch as while he was in the garden and heard the voice of God, and the sound He made in the garden, and feared Him, Adam never saw the brilliant light of the sun, neither did the flaming heat thereof touch his body.

Therefore was he afraid of the sun when flaming rays of it reached him. He thought God meant to plague him therewith all the days He had decreed for him.

For Adam also said in his thoughts, As God did not plague us with darkness, behold, He has caused [this sun] to rise and plague us with burning heat.

But while he was thinking in his heart, the Word of God came [unto him and said]:—

'O Adam, arise and stand up. This sun is not God; but it has been created to give light by day, of which I spake unto thee in the cave [saying]: that the dawn would break forth, and there would be light by day.'

'But I am God who comforted thee in the night.'

And God ceased to commune with Adam.

APPENDIX THREE The Term χειρόγραφον in the Papyri

BEATRIZ MONCÓ

This investigation took its beginning from the echo of a tale and from shadows on a fresco. Michael Stone was pursuing the traces of a previously unknown legend. He knew how to put the pieces of an exciting puzzle together. The reader of this book has followed its footprints through virgin territory that Michael Stone explored for him. A single piece was lacking: the precise meaning of the word χειρόγραφον.

The Compound Word χειρόγραφον

The word "cheirograph" does not appear in the Modern Greek texts transmitting the legend, but only in the poem by Georgios Chumnos. The modern text recorded by Megas has a Turkish word for contract: *senét*. In any case, this text teaches us that whatever, if any, Greek word was used previously it was understood as "contract." The additional witnesses that contain the word translated as "cheirograph" are the Armenian and the Old Slavonic.

The Armenian word is ձեռագիր, from ձեռ, "hand," and գիր, "writing, book." The Slavonic word is рѫкопычю, which is also a compound of руко, "hand," and a second element, путю, related to the verb пұатю, "to write." Both the Armenian and the Slavonic terms appear to be normal compound words in their respective systems according to the rules of both Armenian and Slavonic noun formation.[1]

The Greek word presumably reflected by the Armenian and the Slavonic is χειρόγραφον, as Stone suggests. The word χειρόγραφον is not an ordinary Greek composition. Nouns whose first element is nominal and whose second is verbal are ordinarily agentive nouns. Examples of such composite nouns are, for instance, κρεόφαγος, "carnivorous"; γηροβοσκός; "who supports his parents"; οἰκοδόμος, "architect."[2] The type of *composita* represented by χειρόγραφον, which designates objects in neuter gender, is not frequent until the Hellenistic age.[3] There are just a few examples of it: our familiar (τὸ) χειρόγραφον, "note by hand" (first occurrence in the papyri, second century B.C.E.), and (τὸ) χειρόμυλον, "hand-mill" (Cassius Felix, fourth century C.E.). The latter word derives from a previous one, (ἡ) χειρομύλη, of feminine gender. The retarded position of the accent in χειρόμυλον and χειρόγραφον accords with the accentual rules of composition.[4]

In modern times, the Greek term χειρόγραφον designates a manuscript book. It corresponds to the medieval Latin *manuscriptum*, or *manu scriptum*, "written by hand."[5] This word for manuscript book (or manuscript document) does not appear until 1039, and is completely absent from Classical Latin. It derives from the expression *liber manu scriptum*, or *codex manu scriptum*, "book written by hand." In Romance languages, it does not appear before the Renaissance, and then probably because of the need to differentiate between a book written by hand and a printed one.[6] The first witness to *manuscript* in French is dated 1594.[7] In Italian, *manoscritto* is not well attested until 1601,[8] and the Spanish *manuscrito* not before 1650.[9] These words derive directly from Medieval Latin *manu scriptum*, which was adopted in Romance languages. They are not vernacular words, nor inner creations of the Romance languages. Germanic languages use the same compositional technique as the Greek, Latin, Armenian, and Slavonic languages. In German, the first attestation is the late Middle High German form *hantschrift*. The specific meaning of "document" continues in German until the eighteenth century. Since then, *Handschrift* has referred almost exclusively to "manuscript book."

In Semitic languages, a similar compound exists for "manuscript," but the order of the elements is reversed. For example, in post-biblical Hebrew we find the term כתב יד, where the element "writing" precedes the element "hand."[10] In Tosefta Baba Qama VII, 4, it appears with the meaning of "handwriting." The "modern" meaning "manuscript" does not appear until modern or Israeli Hebrew.

In short, the procedure of noun formation, in respect of this word, differs in Semitic and Indo-European languages. The similarity between Armenian, Slavonic, Greek, and Latin may be due to compositional techniques in word formation. Medieval Latin *manuscriptum* is not a calque of Greek χειρόγραφον, because *scriptum* is not equivalent to -γραφον. Moreover, the loan word *chirographum* is found in Latin from the late Republic on and designates a specific type of document (see below, p. 146). A question arises here: Are Armenian ձեռագիր and Slavonic рькопучю calques of the Greek judicial term χειρόγραφον, like Latin *chirographum*,[11] or are they inner-Armenian and inner-Slavonic developments, like Latin *manuscriptum?* If this second possibility is correct, and I think it is, does it reflect the juridical meaning of χειρόγραφον in Byzantine times? And which jurisprudence does it reflect?

The Juridical Term (χειρόγραφον)

As we have seen, the meaning "manuscript book" is the usual one in modern times, and has been so since the Renaissance, when the word appears in Romance and Germanic languages. But other meanings precede it in ancient languages. The basic one is that of handwriting. For instance, in Hebrew it appears with the meaning "signature" in the Mishnah, Kethuboth II, 3ff. In Greek something similar happens.

The word χειρόγραφον occurs in the papyri at least 308 times in the nominative-accusative singular form (χειρόγραφον).[12] According to Liddell-Scott-Jones, its main meaning is "manuscript note," and a secondary one is "note of hand, bond," attested among others in P. Rein 7.22 and Plutarch 2.829a, both of the second century C.E.[13]

The denominative verb χειρογραφέω means (a) "report in writing," (b) "give a guarantee by note of hand," (c) "make an attested declaration."[14] According to Moulton and Milligan, χειρόγραφον, properly "written with the hand," "a signature," is very common in the sense of a "written agreement," or more technically "a certificate of debt, a bond."[15] Various definitions of the word χειρόγραφον are offered by different authors in particular editions of papyri.

The word χειρόγραφον is a technical judicial term that designates a private document for a private affair.[16] It appears to be used at the end of the third century B.C.E. in Egypt and becomes frequent by the second century. Youtie and Winter defined the word χειρόγραφον as "an acknowledgment of obligation in epistolary form, written without the intervention of a public notary."[17] Epistolary formulae determine the character of the document. Indeed, fixed formulae are so important for the understanding of a document such as a χειρόγραφον that some authors even talk about cheirographon as a "literary style."[18] Some of these fixed formulae are the salutation ἔρρωσο before the date, at the end of the letter, or the beginning ὁ δεῖνα τῷ δεῖνι χαίρειν.[19] Partly because of its formal character, Friedrich Preisigke proposed the specific meanings of "Schuldsein" (IOU) and "Privaturkunde" (private document). Preisigke opposes private and notarial documents.[20]

The lexicon of Lampe offers the meaning of "written record of a debt, bond" in the first place. This is, in fact, the specialized but ordinary meaning of χειρόγραφον in late Hellenistic and Greco-Roman Greek. Χειρόγραφον is a technical word for the private contract written for an amicable loan, or εὐχρηστία, "without the intervention of a public notary." Loans between friends were common, and there was a fixed written formula for them. The legal formulation of an amicable loan or εὐχρηστία is εὐχρεστεῖν κατὰ χειρόγραφον καὶ διαγραφήν, "to make an amicable loan according to the *cheirograph* (certificate of debt) and the *diagraphe* (certificate of payment)." An illustrative example is P. Oxy VIII. 1132 (162 C.E.): τὸ δὲ κεφάλαιον δανεισθέν σοι ὑπ᾽ ἐμοῦ κατὰ χειρόγραφον, "the capital sum lent to you by me in accordance with the cheirograph."

A cheirograph is a special "certificate of debt," which does not need the authentication of a notary in order to be valid. As Preisigke noted, an amicable loan can be effected through a private document (i.e., χειρόγραφον) or simply orally (ἀγράφως). The written way is the preferred in Egypt, while in Greece the agreement can be made orally.[21]

Among the examples that Lampe assembles, one must point out the quasi-definition offered by John Chrysostom, *Homily 2.4 in Col.:* χειρόγραφον γάρ ἐστιν, ὅταν τις ὀφλήματων ὑπεύθυνος κατέχεται, "There is a χειρόγραφον when one becomes liable for his debts."[22] The χειρόγραφον is written by the debtor and, as Youtie and Winter pointed out, in epistolary form.[23] It starts with the date, and both parties to the agreement are introduced. Next the debtor admits his debt and undertakes to pay it in a determined span of time. Then he specifies the fine he will pay in case he will not return the loan at the accorded date.

During the second century C.E., the cheirograph may lose its similarity to a formal letter, that is, the heading and the final salutation.[24]

In Roman times, the word χειρόγραφον is found as a technical term in a letter written by Cicero in the year 53 B.C.E. (*Epp. ad Familiares* VII, xviii. 12).[25] The word is borrowed directly from Greek and is not translated into Latin: *Itaque quoniam vestrae cautiones infirmae sunt, Graeculam tibi misi cautionem chirographi mei.* "Then, since your stipulations are invalid, I sent to you a guarantee in the Greek manner as cheirographs."[26] This sentence is obscure to the commentators. Among others, Shackleton Bailey, in the commentary to his edition, does not give a satisfactory explanation of the term *Graeculam cautionem:* "Certainly not a *syngrapha,* but a note in Greek, perhaps containing some admonitions." F. Frost Abbot is more accurate when pointing out that the adjective *Graeculam* is very obscure, but is the key to understanding the text. He explains the text as follows: "The guaranty-bonds drawn up by your lawyers for your clients are so poor that I am afraid your position will not be a stable one if you depend upon your own support. This letter, therefore, is a guaranty, with a Greek coloring to it, to be sure, of my support."[27]

The adjective *Graeculam* is frequently used by this author with the intention of ridiculing. Among the Romans, Greeks had the bad reputation of being touchy. It means that the practice of writing χειρόγραφα for amicable loans was already known to Cicero and was ridiculed because it was considered unnecessary.[28]

The term *chirographum* is found in other Latin sources and is attested at Pompei and Herculaneum.[29] In spite of the fact that the Latin word is a calque of the Greek term, Roman jurisprudence gives it new formal aspects. For instance, the date is written at the end of the document (i.e., P. Turner 17, 69 C.E., or P. Rendel Harris 66, 155 C.E.).[30] The most important difference, however, is the double writing of the document. See, for instance, BGU I.300[12] (148 C.E.): τ[ὸ] χειρόγραφον τοῦτο δισσὸν γραφὲν ὑπ᾽ ἐμοῦ κύρι[ο]ν ἔστω, "let this *chirographum* written by me in duplicate be valid." In contrast with other types of private documents, such as the συγγραφή, at first cheirographs were not written in duplicate,[31] and no official copy was preserved in any public archive. Later on, in Roman times, a copy was deposited in the δεμόσιος χρηματισμός, or Central Archive.[32] An example of that is to be found in P. Oxy IV 719[30] (193 C.E.): βου[λόμενος οὖν] ἐν δημοσίῳ γενέσθαι τὸ αὐθεντικὸν χειρόγραφον, "being therefore desirous that the original cheirograph should be registered at the Archive." Further examples are P. Rendel Harris 66 (155 C.E.), P. Rendel Harris 146 (184 C.E.), P. Oxy. 1715 (292 C.E.), and so on.

Another new formal aspect in the Roman period is that, despite the etymology of *cheirograph,* sometimes the debtor does not write it, but another person, the debtor being illiterate. The identity of the scribe is given in the subscription (ὑπογραφή), using a fixed formula. Some examples of this are P. Merton 25 1.30 (214 C.E.)[33]: Ὡρίωνος ἔγραψα ὑπὲρ αὐτοῦ μὴ εἰδότος γρ(άμματα), "Orion wrote for him (i.e., the debtor), being illiterate"; P. Oxy 2350 iii 1.30–33 (223–224 C.E.)[34]: Αὐρήλιος Διογένης ὁ καὶ Πείσων Καλλινείκου ἔγραψα ὑπὲρ αὐτοῦ μὴ εἰδότος γράμματα. "Aurelios Diogenes alias Peison wrote for him, who is illiterate"; P. Merton 36 (360 c.e): Καττᾶς Ἐυσταθίο(υ) | ἔγραψα ὑ(πὲρ) αὐτο(ῦ) γρ(άμματα) μὴ εἰδ(ότος), "Kattas son of Eustathios wrote for him being illiterate."

In order to be valid, a cheirograph had to be complete, and without erasure or addition. See, for example, P. R. Harris 83 (212 c.e.): τὸ χειρόγραφον τοῦτο ἁπλοῦν γραφὲν χωρὶς | (15) ἀλίφαδος καὶ ἐπιγραφῆς κύριον ἔστω παν|ταχῆ καὶ παντὶ τῷ ἐπιφέροντι ὡς ἐν δημο|σίῳ κατακεχωρισμένων, "And this *cheirograph,* in a single copy, without erasure or addition, shall be valid everywhere, as if registered in the archives."

Papyrus sheets were made from the stem of the papyrus plant. It was cut into strips, which were laid vertically and then horizontally, fastened together, and pressed to form a single sheet or κόλλημα. The preferred side for writing was that of the horizontal fibers (the so-called *recto*), but often the back, called the *verso,* was also used. There were two ways of canceling a document: either to cross it out (χιά-ζομαι, χιασθῆναι), or simply to erase the writing or to wash it out (ἐξαλείφω).[35] If this second method was used, the same sheet of papyrus could be reused to write a new document. A new document written on an erased one is a palimpsest. A document modified by any of these two methods was considered invalid: BGU III.717[24] (149 c.e.): χειρόγρα[φον] . . . χωρὶς ἀλίφατος καὶ ἐπιγραφῆς, "a decree neither washed out nor written over." Milligan mentions Colossians 2:14, ἐξαλείψας τὸ κατ' ἡμῶν χειρόγραφον, in connection with this document.[36] BGU I.179, from the time of Antoninus Pius, and BGU I.272 (138–139 c.e.) were both crossed out and canceled.

The cheirograph in the legend that M. Stone studied is a written bond. The devil gives Adam and Eve either food or light, and because that cannot be repaid, they give him their souls and the souls of their children. Thus, a loan is converted into an exchange. In the various examples of the legend in which the written cheirograph exists, it lacks formal characteristics that would permit us to assign it to one or another period in the history of Hellenistic and Byzantine Greek law. There is no date, because the cheirograph was signed during the first night of the world, and thus calendars did not exist. It is written by Adam, who is the debtor, but is not addressed to the devil, because he did not want to identify himself. One can argue that it was written in a single copy, but there was no archive to register the duplicate.

It is clear enough that the cheirograph of the legend refers to a document called *chirographum.* This document changes its formal characteristics through time, and was the written record of an amicable loan. It will be destroyed, according to Colossians 2:14, by the common method of invalidating it.

The Armenian and Slavonic versions of the legend ultimately derive from a Greek Byzantine version or versions of the legend. These Greek Byzantine texts must have originated at a time when the legal meaning of cheirograph was still understood, that is, not much after the first half of the sixth century, when the last cheirographs are found.[37]

Notes

INTRODUCTION

1. R. H. Charles, ed., *The Apocrypha and Pseudepigrapha of the Old Testament* (Oxford: Oxford University Press, 1913), 1.x.

2. L. S. A. Wells. "The Books of Adam and Eve," in Charles, *Apocrypha and Pseudepigrapha,* 2.123–154. He provided a translation of only the first chapters of the Slavonic version.

3. Ibid., 2.130. He signals various passages in the Pauline epistles, particularly Romans 5:12–14, where he discerns similarity to verses from *Apocalypse of Moses.*

4. See p. xii. In view of the very fragmentary nature of the Coptic text, we shall refer only to five versions in the following discussion.

5. G. A. Anderson and M. E. Stone, *A Synopsis of the Books of Adam and Eve: Second Revised Edition,* Early Jewish Literature, 17 (Atlanta: Scholars, 1999), gives the texts of these works in parallel columns in the original languages and in English translation. The first edition of the synopsis was published in 1994.

6. See M. de Jonge and J. Tromp, *The Life of Adam and Eve and Related Literature* (Sheffield: Sheffield Academic Press, 1997), 66–67. For a full discussion of the scholarly literature, see M. E. Stone, *A History of the Literature of Adam and Eve,* Early Judaism and Its Literature, 3, (Atlanta: Scholars Press, 1992), where the debate surrounding the date, original language, and textual relations is discussed in detail. The preceding two paragraphs are based largely on material in that work. See also Hans Martin von Erffa, *Ikonologie der Genesis: Die christlichen Bildthemen aus dem Alten Testament und Ihre Quellen* (Munich: Deutscher Kunstverlag, 1989), who has a survey of the Adam books and of their main iconographic themes on pp. 268–340; he also deals with Adam's contract with the devil on pp. 340–342 and includes an extensive bibliography.

7. Paul's use of Adam traditions is summarized by Levison, who also gives a detailed study of Adam in various ancient Jewish writings; see John R. Levison, *Portraits of Adam in Early Judaism: From Sirach to 2 Baruch,* Journal for the Study of the Pseudepigrapha Supplement Series, 1 (Sheffield: JSOT Press, 1988).

8. The terms "primary" and "secondary" were first applied to the Adam literature by Stone, *History of the Literature of Adam and Eve,* 3–5.

1. THE LEGEND OF ADAM AND EVE

1. For an introduction to the chief ancient Jewish apocryphal books, see M. E. Stone, ed., *Jewish Writings of the Second Temple Period,* Compendia Rerum Iudaicarum ad Novum Testamentum, 2.2 (Philadelphia and Assen: Fortress and van Gorcum, 1984). Recent collections of mainly ancient texts are James H. Charlesworth, ed., *The Old Testament Pseudepigrapha,* 2 vols. (Garden City, N.Y.: Doubleday, 1983, 1985), and H. D. F. Sparks, ed., *The Apocryphal Old Testament* (Oxford: Oxford University Press, 1984). Much work has also been done recently on the extensive apocryphal literature of the New Testament. The standard collections are Montague Rhodes James, *The Apocryphal New Testament* (Oxford: Clarendon, 1924), and E. Hennecke and W. Schneemelcher, *The New Testament Apocrypha* (Cambridge and Louisville: J. Clarke & Co. and Westminster/John Knox Press, 1991–92). James's classical collection has recently been re-edited by J. K. Elliott, *The Apocryphal New Testament* (Oxford: Clarendon Press, 1993). The efforts of the *Association pour l'étude de la litterature apocryphe chrétienne,* and the corresponding series of works being published by Brepols, are enriching, and almost certainly will revolutionize, our knowledge of the Christian apocryphal literature.

2. We use the term "apocryphal" to designate all of these expansions of biblical tales and documents, a usage that is convenient, but not always consistent. This practice should be distinguished from that of students of ancient Judaism who use the term "Apocrypha" for a distinct collection of works, those included in the pre-Tridentine Vulgate, that are not to be found in the Hebrew Bible.

3. The primary Adam books are the *Apocalypse of Moses* (Greek) and the parallel Latin, Armenian, Georgian, Slavonic, and fragmentary Coptic works. The most recent survey of a large range of Adam books is to be found in Stone, *History of the Literature of Adam and Eve.* G. A. Anderson and M. E. Stone published synoptic texts of these Adam books in *A Synopsis of the Books of Adam and Eve: Second Revised Edition.* Bibliography on the *Cave of Treasures* is given in Stone, *History of the Literature of Adam and Eve,* 90–95. A good deal of information about the Adam books may be found on an Internet site developed by G. A. Anderson and M. E. Stone at <http://jefferson.village.virginia.edu:80/anderson/archive.html.>

4. E. C. Quinn, *The Quest of Seth for the Oil of Life* (Chicago: University of Chicago Press, 1962).

5. W. W. Heist, *The Fifteen Signs before Doomsday* (East Lansing: Michigan State College, 1952); M. E. Stone, *Signs of the Judgment, Onomastica Sacra and the Generations from Adam,* University of Pennsylvania Armenian Texts and Studies, 3 (Chico: Scholars Press, 1981).

6. Ruth Mellinkoff, *The Horned Moses in Medieval Art and Thought,* California Studies in the History of Art, 14 (Berkeley: University of California Press, 1970).

7. Steven D. Fraade, *Enosh and His Generation: Pre-Israelite Hero and History in*

Postbiblical Interpretation, Society of Biblical Literature Monograph Series, 30 (Chico: Scholars Press, 1984).

8. Further examples are to be found in M. E. Stone and T. A. Bergren, *Biblical Figures outside the Bible* (Philadelphia: Trinity Press International, 1999).

9. Brian O. Murdoch, *The Irish Adam and Eve Story from Saltair na Rann,* vol. 2: *Commentary* (Dublin: Dublin Institute for Advanced Studies, 1976).

10. See, for example, Brian O. Murdoch, *The Fall of Man in the Early Middle High German Biblical Epic: The "Wiener Genesis," the "Vorauer Genesis," and the "Anegenge,"* Göppinger Arbeiten zur Germanistik, 58 (Göppinger: Kümmerle, 1972): idem, "Eve's Anger: Literary Secularization in Lutwin's Adam und Eva,'" *Archiv* 215 (1978), 256–271; idem, "Sethites and Cainites: The Narrative Problem of Adam's Progeny in the Early Middle High German Genesis Poems," in *German Narrative Literature of the Twelfth and Thirteenth Centuries: Studies Presented to Roy Wisbey on His Sixty-fifth Birthday,* ed. Martin H. Jones, Volker Honemann, Adrian Stevens, and David Wells (Tübingen: Max Niemeyer, 1994), 83–97. See also idem, *Adam's Grace: Fall and Redemption in Medieval Literature* (Cambridge: D. S. Brewer, 2000).

11. J. M. Evans, *Paradise Lost and the Genesis Traditions* (Oxford: Clarendon Press, 1968).

12. Other approaches to the same material are evident in works dealing with biblical figures: M. E. Stone and J. Strugnell, *The Books of Elijah, Parts 1 and 2,* Texts and Translations, 5 (Missoula: Scholars Press, 1979); M. E. Stone, D. Satran, and B. G. Wright, *The Apocryphal Ezekiel,* SBL Early Judaism and Its Literature, 18 (Atlanta: Scholars Press, 2000), and the essays collected in Stone and Bergren, eds., *Biblical Figures outside the Bible.* We could easily expand the bibliography dealing with these topics and the spelling out of their detailed character.

13. Stone, *History of the Literature;* M. J. Kister, "Adam: A Study of Some Legends in *Tafsīr* and *Ḥadīṯ* Literature," *Israel Oriental Studies* 13 (1993), 113–174; Jane I. Smith and Yvonne Y. Haddad, "Eve: Islamic Image of Women," *Women's Studies International Forum* 2 (1982), 135–144; Levison, *Portraits of Adam;* Peter Schäfer, "Adam II. Im Frühjudentum," in *Theologische Realenzyklopädie* (Berlin: de Gruyter, 1977), 1: 424–427; Peter Schäfer, "Adam in jüdischen Überlieferung," in *Vom alten zum neuen Adam: Urzeitmythos und Heilsgeschichte,* ed. W. Strolz (Freiburg, Basel, and Vienna: Herder, 1986), 69–93.

14. See the remarks of B. Moncó on p. 146.

15. The published information on Greek sources is assembled in chapter 6. The Bulgarian and Romanian material is discussed in chapter 4. Bulgarian texts were published by J. Ivanov, *Livres et Légendes Bogomiles (Aux Sources du Catharisme)* (Paris: Maisonneuve et Larose, 1976), 311–313. This is a French translation of a Bulgarian text originally published in 1925; see also Emile Turdeanu, *Apocryphes slaves et roumains de l'Ancien Testament,* SVTP, 5 (Leiden: Brill, 1981), 116. The Romanian, and particularly the Moldavian, witnesses to this story are described by Turdeanu, *Apocryphes slaves,* 117. Popular songs reflecting the legend are discussed in ibid., 127–141. We have been informed orally that to this day, folk songs in Romania take up the themes of the cheirograph legend.

16. The positive and negative valences of light and dark are well known. The mixture of light and dark in the daily cycle is seen here as an indication of the imperfection of this world.

17. There are different formulations of this theme. Thus, e.g., the modern Greek

telling of the story recorded by George Megas says, Μέσα τέκεῖνο τὸ μπαχτσιὰ ἦταν μέρα καὶ νύχτα, ὄξω ἀπ᾽ τὸ μπαχτσιὰ ἦταν ὅλο νύχτα, "in that Garden there was day and night; outside the Garden there was only night" (§ 1): see chapter 6 and G. Megas, "Das Χειρόγραφον Adams. Ein Beitrag zu Col 2: 13–15," *ZNW* 27 (1928), 308.

18. Perhaps Adam signed by his handprint because writing had not yet been invented (B. Moncó).

19. See appendix 3, p. 145.

20. The theme of the deception is partly analyzed by Turdeanu, *Apocryphes slaves,* 119. In some forms of the story, moreover, in making the contract Satan does not just ask for subjection, but also pronounces his "Gospel." See chapter 5, p. 72.

21. The placing of the stone in the Jordan River is surely related to Joshua 4:9–10. Joshua 3:16 and 4:7 say that the waters of the Jordan stopped flowing when the priests carrying the sacred ark entered the water. In Psalm 114:3, the crossing of the Red Sea and of the Jordan are drawn together as one salvific event. The waters turn back at the theophany (Psalm 114:5–8), "The sea looked and fled, Jordan turned back. (v. 3) . . . Tremble, O earth, at the presence of the Lord, at the presence of the God of Jacob. (v. 7) . . . " In Joshua 4:12, the Israelites, one per tribe, gather stones and set them up in the Jordan as a covenant-renewal ceremony. In the cheirograph legend, Satan takes the stone contract and sets it in the Jordan. This is almost an inversion of the incident in Joshua. The Armenian text titled *Cheirograph of Adam,* discussed in chapter 7, pp. 104–105, talks of a cheirograph of Adam and a cheirograph of the Jews, but the latter is the covenant at Sinai, and the Jordan crossing is not evoked in this context.

22. This is discussed in detail below in the section titled "Dragon Heads in the Jordan" on p. 22.

23. See ibid.

24. The different versions of the *Life of Adam and Eve,* including the Slavonic, are presented in detail below.

25. *Slavonic Life of Adam and Eve,* §§33–34: see chapter 3, below. The form of the story found in the Slavonic *Life of Adam and Eve* is taken up in Romanian poems, "On the Plaint of Adam": see Turdeanu, *Apocryphes slaves,* 128–141, and below, chapter 4. The Romanian text seems to date from the eighteenth century. The same version of the legend is also to be found in the sixteenth-century Moldavian fresco that is discussed in chapter 4. Moreover, there exist reworkings of the Slavonic *Life of Adam*'s narrative in later Slavonic compositions.

26. Note also the later Romanian scenes signaled in chapter 4.

27. See right-hand side of the cathedral's nave, upper level. There are many other artistic representations of this sequence.

28. See Latin, Armenian, and Georgian *Life of Adam and Eve,* chaps. 2–8. Compare G. A. Anderson, "The Penitence Narrative in the *Life of Adam and Eve,*" *HUCA* 63 (1993), 5–20. This problem is resolved in verse 20:1a in the Armenian and Georgian versions. Of course, the biblical curse itself provides the underpinning of the story in the *Life of Adam and Eve* as well, but there it has been developed in a complex way. See M. E. Stone, *The Penitence of Adam,* CSCO, 430 (Leuven: Peeters, 1981), xiii–xiv.

29. The scene is reminiscent of the beginning of the *Testament of Abraham,* where an angel encounters Abraham plowing a field. The contexts are quite different, how-

ever, though the description of Abraham as a farmer is somewhat unusual, but cf. *Jubilees* 11:18–22. Adam plowing is also to be seen in the Moldavian frescoes, discussed in chapter 4.

30. See Latin, Armenian, and Georgian, chaps. 2–8. Compare Anderson, "The Penitence Narrative," 1–38 and note 28, above.

2. CONTRACT, PENANCE, AND REDEMPTION

1. H. G. Liddell and R. Scott et al., *A Greek-English Lexicon,* rev. H. S. Jones (Oxford, 1961), s.v. Note also in Liddell-Scott-Jones: 1. the verb χειρογραφέω, "report in writing" (papyrus second century B.C.E); "give guarantee or note of hand" (second century B.C.E.); "make attested declaration" (third century B.C.E.); 2. the cognate noun χειρογραφία, "report in writing," "written testimony." Not much can be added to this from other dictionaries. The issues are well summarized in G. Kittel and G. Friedrich, eds., *Theological Dictionary of the New Testament,* tr. G. W. Bromiley (1974), s.v. χειρόγραφον.

2. The complex issues related to the interpretation of this verse are well summarized in Kittel and Friedrich, *Theological Dictionary of the New Testament,* s.v. χειρόγραφον. Some examples of ancient exegesis are presented below in chapter 7.

3. See, for example, E. C. Best, *An Historical Study of the Exegesis of Colossians 2.14* (Rome: Pontifica Universitas Gregoriana, 1956).

4. Irenaeus, *haer.* 5.17.3. The same sort of language is to be found in Origen, e.g., *Homily on Genesis* 13: ἕκαστος δὲ ἡμῶν ὀφειλέτης ἐστὶ ταῖς ἁμαρτίαις καὶ ὀφειλέτης ἐστὶ ἔχων "χειρόγραφον". μετὰ τὸ ἐξαλειφθῆναι· (Colossians 2:14). "For each of us is a debtor through sins, and a debtor is the one who has a cheirograph. After he [i.e. Christ] erased . . . " (Colossians 2:14). The verb ἐξαλειφθῆναι, "erased," drawn from Colossians 2:14, has the meaning "to annul a contract." A similar interpretation is to be found in Ephrem, e.g., *carmina Nisibena* 48.9 in E. Beck, ed., *Des Heiligen Ephrems des Syrers Carmina Nisibena,* CSCO, 240 (Leuven: Peeters, 1963), in which he speaks of the decree (ܪܘܕܙ) of death that is a great bill of indebtedness and sin (ܚܕ ܕܘ ܠܐ ܘ ܠܐܝ) or a ܪܚܕܬܐ, "pledge"; he also uses other terms elsewhere. The similarity in the views of these three writers is striking, particularly between the latter two. The early Western medieval lexicography of the word is reviewed by B. Bischoff, "Zur Frügeschichte des mittelalterlichen Chirographum," in *Mittelalterliche Studien* (Stuttgart: Huersmann, 1966), 3. 118–121. He deals chiefly with Latin sources.

5. See chapter 7.

6. The antiquity of this legend is discussed by J.-D. Kaestli, "Témoignages anciens sur la croyance en la descente du Christ aux enfers," in *L'évangile de Barthélemy d'après deux écrits apocryphes,* ed. J.-D. Kaestli and P. Cherix (Turnhout: Brepols, 1993), 135–142.

7. One or two cases in which this did happen, including a Russian icon and a Greek folktale, will emerge in the course of our discussion.

8. In an Armenian work discussed below, *Adam, Eve, and the Incarnation,* although Adam alone is mentioned by name in the crucial section, the verbs are all plural. Eve has a role, then, but Adam's is more prominent.

9. Eve is reproached by Adam for disobeying his command, according to the pri-

mary Adam books: see Latin, Armenian, and Georgian versions 10:3. She has disobeyed Adam's command, not God's.

10. The question remains open whether, in the primary Adam books, the prophesied baptism is the reversal of the deception of Eve in the river; see M. E. Stone, "The Fall of Satan and Adam's Penance: Three Notes on *The Books of Adam and Eve,*" *Journal of Theological Studies* 44 (1993), 143–156, especially 148–153.

11. See Stone, *The Penitence of Adam,* xiii–xiv. This theme is analyzed at length by Anderson, "The Penitence Narrative." The Latin version turns the search for food into a search for forgiveness, but there are many reasons to prefer the form of the story found in the Armenian and Georgian texts.

12. This pericope is very problematic within the primary Adam books. It may be a Christian insertion; see Stone, "Fall of Satan"; M. E. Stone, "The Angelic Prediction in the Primary Adam Books," in *Literature on Adam and Eve: Collected Essays,* ed. G. Anderson, M. Stone, and J. Tromp, SVTP, 15 (Leiden: Brill, 2000), 111–131.

13. ἀναστάσεως πάλιν γενομένης, ἀναστήσω σε καὶ δοθήσεταί σοι ἐκ τοῦ ξύλου τῆς ζωῆς καὶ ἀθάνατος ἔσει εἰς τὸν αἰῶνα.

14. The families or recensions of manuscripts are those referred to by W. Meyer, "Vita Adae et Evae," *Abhandlungen der königlich bayerischen Akademie der Wissenschaften, Philosophische-philologische Klasse* 14.3 (1878), 185–250. See also Stone, *History of the Literature of Adam and Eve,* 14–30. M. E. B. Halford, "The Apocryphal Vita Adae et Evae: Some Comments on the Manuscript Tradition," *Neuphilologische Mitteilungen* 82 (1981), 417–427, especially 418–419, and her further note, "The Apocryphal Vita Adae et Evae: Some Comments on the Manuscript Tradition—A Correction," *Neuphilologische Mitteilungen* 83 (1982), 222. Compare the comments of J. H. Mozley, "The Vitae Adae," *JTS* 30 (1929), 121–149, and idem, "A New Text of the Story of the Cross," *JTS* 31 (1930), 113–127. The literature on the Rood Tree legend is quite extensive, and that cited is only indicative. See also A. S. Napier, *History of the Holy Rood Tree* (London: Kegan Paul, 1894). According to Andrew Breeze, "Master John of St. Davids, Adam and Eve, and the Rose among the Thorns," *Studia Celtica* 29 (1995), 230, "The wood of the cross is first linked with Seth's journey to Paradise and the burial of Adam in an interpolation in *Imago Mundi* by Honorius Augustodunensis in Munich Bayerische Staatsbibliothek, cod. lat. 2555, written at Windberg between 1154 and 1159." This is also the view of Moshé Lazar, "La Légende de l'Arbre de Paradis ou Bois de la Croix," *Zeitschrift für Romanische Philologie* 76 (1960), 37. [In two very important articles published after the manuscript of this book was finished, J.-P. Pettorelli made a major contribution to the study of the Latin work. He discovered and identified new manuscripts, which show that there did exist in Latin a version of the primary Adam book which had many features in common with the Armenian and Georgian versions. See J.-P. Pettorelli, "La Vie latine d'Adam et Ève," *Archivum Latinitatis Medii Aevi* 61 (1998), 5–104; idem, "La vie latine d'Adam et Eve: Analyse de la tradition manuscrite," *Apocrypha* 10 (1999), 195–296. These new texts do not influence the conclusions drawn in the present work, but will be very important for the study of the relationship between the *Apocalypse of Moses* and the Latin *Life of Adam and Eve.*]

15. Armenian *Words of Adam to Seth* 9–14:

> 9 And Seth, taking that branch, brought [it] to his father Adam and said, "Father, this from your dwelling." 10 And Adam, taking that branch, placed [it] upon [his] eyes, and his eyes were opened. 11 And looking, he saw the branch, that it was [from] that tree, of which he had eaten death. 12 And he said to his son, "My son, Seth. This is from that tree from which God commanded us not to eat." 13 And Seth said to his father, "Father, know that just as it is mortal, so it has become life-giving and bright."

In Armenian *Adam Fragment* 2 we read:

> 8 And taking this branch of [whose] fruit Adam had eaten, they brought it to Adam's grave and planted [it] above the head of Adam's tomb. It became a great tree. 9 The Doctors say that Christ was crucified on the wood of this tree, he who carried out salvation and mercy for Adam and for all his offspring . . . .

See M. E. Stone, *Armenian Apocrypha Relating to Patriarchs and Prophets* (Jerusalem: Israel Academy of Sciences, 1982), 11.

16. Armenian is less clear, reading "because you were created on the sixth day [of those upon] which he created his works." But, of course, that was true of Adam as well.

17. In *Adam Story* 2 §2 (M. E. Stone, *Armenian Apocrypha: Relating to Adam and Eve*, SVTP, 14 [Leiden: Brill, 1996], 111), we read, "And in the third hour on the very same day [on which Adam was created, M. E. S.], on Friday, Eve was taken from Adam's ribs by the hand of God, and a woman was created."

18. This is the dominant tradition. The number varies in the Latin and Slavonic versions, as is discussed in the present section.

19. This is the reading of Armenian and Georgian; no number of days is given by Latin.

20. J. M. Rosenstiehl gives much information on the tradition of Satan's fall in "La chute de l'Ange, Origines et développement d'une légende, ses attestations dans la littérature copte," *Journée d'études coptes, Strasbourg 28 mai 1982,* Cahiers de la Bibliothèque copte 1 (Louvain, 1983), 44–47; J.-D. Kaestli, "Le mythe de la chute de Satan: est-il d'origine juive?" (unpublished draft).

21. In the Armenian and Georgian versions, Eve, who was three months pregnant, went to the west; when the time of her labor arrived, she called Adam. "Then Adam, in the river Jordan . . . " (20:1a). This makes no sense at all, for it apparently implies that Adam spent nine months in the river. In 20:2a, Latin, Armenian, and Georgian have Adam seeking Eve on foot.

22. Greek varies somewhat, and Georgian has eight years, not eighteen.

23. Does this suggest that the number of thirty-six days, given in some Latin manuscripts, might be correct for Eve's penance? If so, Satan tested her exactly halfway through her penance. However, we hesitate to build too much on this textual basis, and the reading of thirty-four days seems to be well established in a number of versions and is backed by the connection with the six days of creation.

24. Exodus 34:28.

25. Apocryphal texts also take up the period of forty days' fast, see Ezra (*4 Ezra* 14:23), Baruch (*2 Apocalypse of Baruch* 76:2–4), and Abraham (*Apocalypse of Abraham* 12:1–3). It is striking that the tradents of the primary Adam books do not explicitly relate the forty-day fast of the old Adam to the new Adam's forty-day temptation.

26. Greek *Apocalypse of Moses* 7–8 and parallels (Adam's tale): Greek *Apocalypse of Moses* 16–20 (Eve's tale).

27. Latin 6:1 and parallels, but not in the main manuscripts of the Greek version. In many of the sources we will discuss, the cheirograph legend is also found in this same position in the narrative structure, immediately after the expulsion from the Garden, but before Adam and Eve are properly established in this world.

28. Anderson, "The Penitence Narrative," 1–38, has written an extensive study on this pericope in the primary Adam books. The primary Adam books are cited throughout from Anderson and Stone, *Synopsis of the Books of Adam and Eve: Revised Edition.*

29. The text, in fact, never puts in God's mouth a statement that if the penance is successful he will give them back the paradisical food; this is surmised by Adam and Eve.

30. In two Greek manuscripts, a summary of the penance story is found in the same place as in the Slavonic version. The text in these two manuscripts is clearly secondary within the Greek tradition, as an analysis of the results of the penance clearly shows. The argument demonstrating the secondary nature of these two Greek manuscripts (R and M) is summarized in de Jonge and Tromp, *The Life of Adam and Eve,* 32–33. See also note 32.

31. This variant of the story is discussed fully in chapter 3.

32. In the analysis of this version in the next chapter, we will show why the Slavonic has moved the penitence incident to chapter 29. This is also the situation in the two Greek manuscripts that contain it. In them, however, there is no cheirograph tradition, and so there is no deception. Clearly, therefore, in them the penance is secondary; regardless, the Greek has no deception at the beginning.

33. Intriguingly, Greek manuscripts R and M, which have the penance story at chapter 29, like the Slavonic *Life of Adam and Eve,* do not annul the deception. They read, "and when he said these things, the enemy deceived me a second time. And I came out of the water" (29:13). Thus, we might argue that the story's transposition to chapter 29 preceded the introduction of the cheirograph legend, and only subsequently was Satan's attempt to deceive Eve in the river said to fail. Observe, however, that the text in R and M is secondary in comparison with Armenian, Georgian, and Latin.

34. This is true except in the Slavonic version. The issue of culpability is discussed by K. E. Kvam, L. S. Schearing, and V. H. Ziegler eds., *Eve and Adam: Jewish, Christian and Muslim Readings on Genesis and Gender* (Bloomington and Indianapolis: Indiana University Press, 1999), 33–34.

35. See J. R. Levison, "The Exoneration of Eve in the *Apocalypse of Moses* 15–30," *JSJ* 20 (1989), 135–150; A. M. Sweet, "A Religio-Historical Study of the Greek *Life of Adam and Eve*" (Ph.D. thesis, Notre Dame, 1992).

36. On Satan in the Bible, see the remarks of T. Gaster, *Interpreter's Dictionary of the Bible* (New York: Abingdon Press, 1976), s.v.

37. Greek here has the word σκεῦος. The image of the musical instrument is also encountered in patristic writing on the topic. B. Moncó observes that, although just a metaphor in the text, this language is reminiscent of the Cainite Jubal, "who is the father of all those who play the lyre and pipe" (Genesis 5:21). This association of music, and particularly of the lyre, with the Cainite descendants almost certainly lies in the background of the choice of the lyre image. In Bogomil legends, the serpent is possessed of Satan's spirit: see Y. Stoyanov, *The Hidden Tradition in Europe* (London: Arkana-Penguin, 1994), 214–215; D. Oblensky, *The Bogomils: A Study in Balkan Neo-Manicheanism* (Twickenham: Hall, 1972), 208.

38. According to the Bogomil development of these themes, Satan lost his glory on his fall. See Stoyanov, *The Hidden Tradition,* 215, and Oblensky, *The Bogomils,* 227.

39. Is the odd name of Cain in certain Greek manuscripts, Diaphotos, "luminous," related to Satan's coloring? Other Greek manuscripts have a privative form, Adiaphotos, "non-luminous." We should recall that in the Latin *Life of Adam and Eve* 21:3a, Cain is said to be *lucidus,* "brilliantly shining" or of "the color of stars." Certain texts might hint that Cain was the offspring of a union of Eve and Satan, e.g., Babylonian Talmud Yebamot 103b. Is the envy sexual envy? Note also that the name Cain can be explained from the Hebrew *qn',* meaning "envy." Later, the Bogomils refer to Satan's intercourse with Eve; see Stoyanov, *The Hidden Tradition,* 216.

40. See Greek *Apocalypse of Moses,* 29:12a σχῆμα ἀγγέλου.

41. In another variant on this theme, in the *Life of Adam and Eve,* a beast—according to some versions a serpent—attacks Eve and Seth as they travel to Paradise to pray for Adam's healing. There is a lively exchange between Eve and the beast. The beast says to Eve, "On this account [her eating the fruit] our nature also has been transformed" (*Apocalypse of Moses* 11:2). Seth, however, who is called "man of God" (13b), says to the beast, "stand off from the image of God until the day of Judgment." Then the beast disappears. Here the beast plays Satan's role, but again, when challenged, it disappears, even from before a post-paradisiacal Eve and Seth.

42. See the Greek, Armenian, and Slavonic texts of 20:1 and 44.20:1 Compare the discussion of the protoplasts' glory in Stone, *Armenian Apocrypha Relating to Adam and Eve,* 20, 112, 113. There are numerous sources in Jewish and Christian literature, many of which are adduced in M. E. Stone, *Commentary on 4 Ezra,* Hermeneia (Minneapolis: Augsberg-Fortress, 1990), 245, see also Index, s.v. "glory." This is exegetically grounded in Gen. 2:24 and 3:7. See further G. A. Anderson, "The Punishment of Adam and Eve in the *Life of Adam and Eve,*" in *Literature on Adam and Eve: Collected Essays,* ed. G. Anderson, M. Stone, and J. Tromp, SVTP, 14 (Leiden: Brill, 2000), 57–81.

43. It is also possible that the special period of mourning until the end of the second day (i.e, the start of the third day) after death in ancient Jewish custom is based on the same idea. See *4 Ezra* 10:2, cf. Stone, *Fourth Ezra,* 314.

44. See above, p. 32. The European developments of this tradition are discussed by F. Ohly, *Der Verfluchte und der Erwählte: Vom Leben mit der Schuld* (Opladen: Westdeutscher Verlag, 1976). On pp. 43–56 there is a discussion of the development of this theme in medieval European literature.

45. While highlighting this symmetry, we are still loath to talk about any literary relationship between the various documents.

46. *Life of Adam and Eve* 8:3; cf. Exodus 14:29, 15:19, Joshua 3:17, 4:18, 22, Psalm 106:9, Hebrews 11:29, Wisdom 19:7.

47. One might be tempted to think that the unique reading of Latin reflects the cheirograph legend, yet that legend is unknown in the West.

48. *Apud* Turdeanu *Apocryphes slaves,* 120.

49. W. Christ and M. Paranikas, *Anthologia Graeca Carminum Christianorum* (Leipzig: Teubner, 1871), 169.

50. See R. Stichel, *Die Geburt Christi in der russischen Ikonenmalerei* (Stuttgart: Franz Steiner Verlag, 1990). 115 and plate 69.

51. See G. Millet, *Recherches sur l'Iconographie de l'Evangile aux XIVe, XVe et XVIe siècles d'après les monuments de Mistra, de la Macédoine et du Mont-Athos* (Paris: E. de Boccard, 1916), 198 and fig. 172. The book was reprinted, unchanged, in 1960.

52. I am indebted to Nira Stone for this observation.

53. The fresco is mentioned by J. Lafontaine-Dosogne, "La tradition byzantine des bapistères et de leur décor, et les fonts de Saint-Barthélemy à Liège," *Cashiers archéologiques* 36 (1988), 53–56 and note 63. See Sr. Petkovi, "Slikarstvo Spolašne Priprate Gračanice" [Painting of the Exo-Narthex of Gračanice], in *Bizantiyska Umetnost Počerkom XIV veka* [Byzantine Art from Its Inception Down to the Fourteenth Century], *Symposium Gračanica 1973* (Belgrade, 1987), 212 and fig. 6. Dr. Nira Stone is preparing a detailed study of this feature.

54. G. Cavarnos, *Guide to Byzantine Iconography* (Boston: Holy Transfiguration Monastery, 1993), 148. I am deeply indebted to Dr. N. Constas of Harvard University, whose letter of 14 May 1997 I have cited. He also provided me with a copy of Vamboulis's icon and directed my attention to Cavarnos's book. Photios Kontoglu, Ἔκφρασις τῆς ὀρθόδοξου εἰκονόγραφιας (Athens: Aster, 1960), vol. 1, 165, speaks of Christ on a single stone slab (εἰς μίαν πλάκαν) with serpents' heads. He gives illustrations of both types, the crossed slabs or doors of Hades and the single stone, both with serpents emerging from below them.

55. See chapter 4.

3. ADAM PLOWS AND SATAN FORBIDS

1. See chapter 1, 4–5; also chapter 7.

2. See the Introduction for bibliographical indications on these works.

3. See particularly Stone, *History of the Literature of Adam and Eve;* de Jonge and Tromp, *The Life of Adam and Eve and Related Literature;* Anderson and Stone, *Synopsis of the Books of Adam and Eve: Second Revised Edition.*

4. The Bogomil movement, which had spread as far as western Europe by the eleventh century, eventually withdrew to the Balkans, where it died out by the fifteenth century. The Bogomils cultivated many apocryphal texts; see Ivanov, *Livres et Légendes Bogomiles.* See also "Bogomils" in F. L. Cross and E. A. Livingstone, *The Oxford Dictionary of the Christian Church* (Oxford: Oxford University Press, 1990), 184, and further bibliography there. On the Bogomils, see Oblensky, *The Bogomils,* and Stoyanov, *The Hidden Tradition.*

5. Turdeanu, *Apocryphes slaves,* comments that many scholars believe that "les Bo-

gomiles . . . ont joué un rôle assez considérable dans la création, la traduction et la diffusion des légendes apocryphes." He notes, in particular, the number of works included by Jordan Ivanov in his work *Livres et Légendes Bogomiles.* Turdeanu, however, casts considerable doubt on Ivanov's inclusiveness in this regard (ibid 2), and on the Bogomil connections attributed to many apocrypha. This is, indeed, the main thrust of his long essay in *Apocryphes slaves,* 1–74. The case for Bogomil authorship was made by V. Jagič, "Slavische Beiträge zu den biblischen Apocryphen, I, Die altkirchenslavischen Texte des Adamsbuche," in *Denkschr. kais. Akademie der Wissenchaften, philos.-hist. Classe* 42 (Vienna, 1893), 42–43, and supported by Ivanov, *Livres et Légendes Bogomiles,* 208–210. This is discussed in Stone, *History of the Literature of Adam and Eve,* 34–35, and further references are given there. Turdeanu, *Apocryphes slaves,* 116, considers the Slavonic form of the legend of the contract (by which he means "Variant A"; see below) to be secondary to the form of the legend found in the oriental Christian sources, but he does not know all of those adduced here.

6. The most frequently consulted edition and translation of the Slavonic text was prepared by Jagič, "Die altkirchenslavischen Texte des Adamsbuche," 1–104; see also the review by E. Schürer, *Theologische Literatur-Zeitung* 16 (1893), 398–399. An English translation of the beginning of this work is given by L. S. A. Wells, "The Books of Adam and Eve," in *The Apocrypha and Pseudepigrapha of the Old Testament,* ed. R. H. Charles, vol. 2, 123–154. A Romanian version of the Slavonic *Life of Adam and Eve* exists, called "Legend of Adam." This probably originates from the start of the seventeenth century: see M. Gaster, *Chrestomathie roumaine* (Leipzig: Brockhaus, 1891), vol. 1. lvii, and text on pp. 63–65.

7. Sofia, National Library no. 433, pp. 12–20 (Ms P below). Ivanov, *Livres et Légendes Bogomiles,* 198–204; this book was first published in Bulgarian in 1925. See also Turdeanu, *Apocryphes slaves,* 82. Information on the Old Church Slavonic Adam material and associated Bulgarian texts is to be found in Aleksander E. Naumow, *Apokryfy w Systemie Literatury Cerkiewnosłowiánskiej* (Warsaw: Polish Academy of Sciences, 1976), 82–94.

8. I am lately informed that in the Slavonic version of Pseudo-Methodius there exists another distinct variant of this story. The devil will not allow Adam to bury Abel until Adam has given his cheirograph (*rukopisanie*) in his own hand that "the living are yours and the dead are mine" (N. S. Tikhonravov, *Pamiatniki otrechennoi russoi literatury* [*Monuments of Russian Rejected Literature*] [St. Petersburg: V Tip. Obshchestvenaia pol'za 1863], 2.249). The expression "heaven is yours and earth is mine" is used by the devil in the dialogue of Jesus and the devil in the wilderness (ibid. 282, 286).

9. Jagič, "Die altkirchenslavischen Texte des Adambuches," 3.

10. C. Fuchs, "Das Leben Adams und Evas." in *Die Apokryphen und Pseudepigraphen des Alten Testaments, Band 2, Die Pseudepigraphen* ed. E. Kautzsch (Tübingen: Mohr, 1900), 507.

11. Ivanov, *Livres et Légendes bogomiles,* 206. The Greek text of the *Palaea* was edited more than a century ago by A. Vassiliev; by now a new edition, a translation, and more extensive investigation are very desirable. See A. Vassiliev, *Anecdota Graeco-Byzantina* (Moscow: Imperial University, 1893), and also the study by David Flusser, "Palaea Historica: An Unknown Source of Biblical Legends," in *Essays in Aggadah*

and Folk-Literature, Scripta Hierosolymitana, 22 (Jerusalem: Magnes, 1971), 48–79. See further on the Palaea the study by Turdeanu, "La *Palaea* byzantine chez les Slaves et chez les Roumains," in *Apocryphes slaves,* 392–403.

12. The Slavonic versions of many apocryphal books are preserved in the *Historical Palaea.* See preceding note.

13. A substantial discussion of the Slavonic version is to be found in M. Nagel, "La Vie grecque d'Adam et d'Eve" (doctoral dissertation, Strasbourg, 1974), 1.91–112. On textual grounds, he connects it with his Family II of the Greek manuscripts (Vat. gr. 119, fifteenth century; and Patmos, St. John, 447, sixteenth century). The Greek manuscripts as a whole range from the eleventh to the seventeenth centuries. They are divided by Nagel into three families, of which he considers Family I to be the most important.

> Family I   D S V K (14:3–43:5) P G B A T L C
> Family II   R M
> Family III *N I K* (Title–17:2) Q Z H E X F U W

For full details of the manuscripts and other textual particulars, see Stone, *History of the Literature of Adam and Eve,* 8–11. Nagel's discussion is oriented mainly to the issues of textual relationship, but he does attempt to isolate criteria by which the independent developments of Slavonic may be distinguished from developments of its Greek *Vorlage.* He does not, however, dedicate any extensive discussion to the cheirograph pericope.

14. A list of sigla and of technical and bibliographic data is to be found in appendix 1.

15. in order to obtain nourishment] om pp pp′ tr pr pr′ | nourishment] house t

16. paradise] om m

17. paradise] om t pp pp′ tr pr pr′ Fr Fr′ | sea m S

18. i.e., cheirograph; a literal translation of the Greek term

19. would take on himself the form of a man and would tread the devil under his feet] to be born from the Virgin pp′ tr pr pr′ Fr Fr′

20. + and he said, "For me, the Lord, this handwriting" t (corruption?) | + and he took a board pp pp′ tr | and Adam took ink pr Fr | and Adam took moisture (?urine) pr′

21. kept it [or owned him] power Fr + and the devil took Adam's handwriting and kept it [or owned him] pp pp′ pr pr′

22. This reverses the motivation in the other versions of the *Life of Adam and Eve,* where it is Eve who apologizes and initiates the penance. These sections correspond to pericopes 17–27 of Anderson and Stone, *Synopsis of the Books of Adam and Eve: Second Revised Edition.*

23. Moreover, as a result of the structure presented here, the curse and judgment precede Eve and Seth's quest; again, this differs from the other versions.

24. A brief discussion of this issue is to be found in chapter 1.

25. As we will see below, some of the Romanian rewritings of the cheirograph story have the angel Michael instead at this juncture.

26. Here, and in *Death of Adam,* Adam is taught "Cainite" skills. In the Slavonic *Life of Adam and Eve,* it is agriculture, which is the sacrifice Cain brought; in *Death*

of Adam §§2–3, Cain is taught ironworking, which, according to Genesis 4:22, was invented by his descendants. An ancient Jewish development of the "culture hero" theme may be found in the *Book of the Watchers* in *1 Enoch,* but agriculture does not figure there.

27. Nagel, *Vie grecque,* 93.

28. Ibid, 92–93.

29. This text is parallel to 1:1–3:4 of Latin, Armenian, and Georgian, but is somewhat shorter.

30. We quote the Armenian version, but the others resemble it.

31. On this matter, see Anderson, "The Penitence Narrative," 9–19. He provides a detailed analysis of the theme of the food and its different types. See also the earlier discussion by Stone, *The Penitence of Adam,* vol. 2, x–xvii.

32. The angels were not always considered to eat; compare *Testament of Abraham,* 4:9. E. P. Sanders has written a detailed note on this matter with a number of references from Rabbinic literature in Charlesworth, *The Old Testament Pseudepigrapha,* 1.884. Those texts that do say that angels eat, attribute heavenly food to them; see, e.g., *Wisdom of Solomon* 16:20 (manna) and *Joseph and Asenath* 16:8 (wondrous honey).

33. The negative biblical attitude to Cain's sacrifice of agricultural produce may have contributed to this view, although that probably originated in traditional views estimating animal herding higher than the settled life; see note 26. In addition, the incident in §§33–34 = Variant A, §§2–4 of the devil standing before the oxen is in some measure reminiscent of the angel standing before Balaam's donkey (Numbers 24:23), but what significance could this have?

34. Tr. J. Goldin, *The Fathers According to Rabbi Nathan* (New York: Schocken. 1974), 11.

35. Ibid, 14.

36. It is intriguing to recall that, Daniel 4:25, interpreting Daniel 4:15–16, reads, "You [i.e., Nebuchadnezzar] shall be driven away from human society, and your dwelling shall be with the wild animals. You shall be made to eat grass like oxen. . . ." To eat the food designated for animals signals reduction to a subhuman level. Although the text does not mark Nebuchadnezzar's return to human status explicitly by reversing the change in food, the ranking of varieties of food is clear. A number of passages regard milk and honey as ideal foods; see Isaish 7:15–16, *Sibylline Oracles* 5:281–2, 3:743–746; E. A. W. Budge, *The Alexander Book In Ethiopia* (London: Oxford University Press, 1933), 157–158, says that the angels eat grapes.

37. This is probably to be explained by the Latin version's concern to reduce the role of the search for food and to replace it with a search for forgiveness in general; see Stone *Penitence of Adam,* 2.x–xvii.

38. Compare also §2 of that work. In §3 of *Death of Adam,* Adam is also taught ironworking. With that idea, compare Armenian *4 Ezra* 8:62M. In chapter 5 below, a separate discussion is devoted to *Adam, Eve, and the Incarnation.*

39. This situation was a partial reversal of the curse, for in the Garden, according to 1.1–1.4 (unique to the Slavonic version), Adam's control of the animals was so utter that "apart from Adam's command nothing was allowed to move around, or land, or eat anything before Adam permitted it. It was the same with Eve."

40. This corresponds to §44[29] of the other versions, but the incident itself is also unique to the Slavonic version.

41. Is the opposition of divine justice and mercy implied by this formulation? It reads as if, having asserted his justice, God then proceeds to act with mercy. See Stone, *Commentary on 4 Ezra,* Index, s. v.

42. The more common form in Greek is Ἰαήλ. Is Joël < *Yeho-el really another way of talking of Michael, whose name means "who is like God"? Their functions are rather similar both here (cf. Georgian 20:1b) and elsewhere. On this angel, see Stone, *History of the Literature of Adam and Eve,* 46 n. 14, and references there. Note that in 44(33).5, the angels pray for Adam's forgiveness.

43. The same intermediate status, between the paradisiacal state and the completely unprivileged, emerges from an analysis of the incident of Eve and Seth's fight with the beast, chaps. 37–39 = Slavonic 11–15. Humans have forfeited the right of absolute authority over the animals; nonetheless, the image of God in them makes them superior to the animals. See further chapter 2, note 41, and note 50 below.

44. See chapter 2, "Culpability."

45. The devil's distinctive footprints are a common folk theme; see the Rabbinic sources cited by L. Ginzberg, *The Legends of the Jews* (Philadelphia: Jewish Publication Society, 1928), 6.301.

46. This phrase recurs in many of the Slavonic and Balkan forms of the story discussed in chapter 4. See also note 8.

47. In Tikhonravov's edition, the text bears the further superscription "About the confession of Eve and about the question of her grandchildren and about the sickness of Adam."

48. These last words are crossed out in the original. Another translation of this passage is by F. H. Marshall, *Old Testament Legends from a Greek Poem on Genesis and Exodus by Georgios Chumnos* (Cambridge: Cambridge University Press. 1925), xxviii–xxix. The term "cheirograph" is discussed below.

49. Adam's lamentation forms a major theme of the Romanian Adamic literature discussed in chapter 4. It is also prominent in the Armenian *Repentance of Adam and Eve.*

50. It is intriguing to note that there are various levels of light, just as there are various levels of food. The night, the absence of light, corresponds to the absence of food, just as the light of this world corresponds to the food given to humans. In both cases, the this-worldly phenomena are pallid reflections of the paradisiacal ones. See also note 43.

51. This formulation is typical of the Slavonic-Balkan tradition represented both by the Slavonic *Life of Adam and Eve* and by the Bulgarian and Romanian texts presented in the next chapter. The similarity of the formulae in Variants A and B suggests their mutual influence.

52. Of course, even more may have been omitted than the elements we have adumbrated. No clue to Variant B's literary source is evident.

53. See chapter 2, "Dragon Heads in the Jordan," 22–24.

54. Just as the Slavonic form of the legend relating to the death and burial of Abel is another reuse of its basic structure; see note 8.

55. See his note on the text of Variant A, appendix 1.

56. See the study by B. Moncó, which is published as appendix 3.

57. See chapter 1, p. 3, and also appendix 3.

58. Nearly all the sentences in the document start with the word "and." We have omitted it throughout for stylistic reasons.

59. See Psalm 74(73):13.

60. Two different Old Russian words are used here, порода and раи, and both are translated "paradise."

61. See Tikhonravov, *Pamiatniki,* 1.6; he states that this was from an old parchment book, a common Old Believer strategy for claiming antiquity for their writings. The West Russian (Catholic) *Passion of Christ* [*Strasti khristovy*] from the fifteenth century, published in 1901, does not contain our story. Tikhonravov was apparently acquainted with another version of this work (A. Kulik).

62. See chapter 2, note 39.

63. Ibid.

64. See "Dragon Heads in the Jordan" in chapter 2.

65. Another variant is Megas's tale; see chapter 6.

66. This is reminiscent of Genesis 37:31, in which Joseph's brothers slaughter a goat for blood to stain his coat of many colors.

67. See Tikhonravov, *Pamiatniki,* 2.249. The exact translation reads, "And Adam and Eve began to dig in the earth in their desire to lay Abel their son there. The devil came and said to Adam, 'The earth is mine. Give me your cheirograph written by your hand. The living are yours and the dead are mine.' Adam gave him the cheirograph written by his hand and he concealed his son Abel." The expression "heaven is yours and earth is mine" is also used by the devil in the dialogue of Jesus and the devil in the wilderness (ibid., 2.282, 286).

68. See, e.g., *Life and History of Abel,* 4–6.

69. This incident does not occur in the Slavonic *Life of Adam and Eve.*

4. THE LEGEND IN BALKAN ART, FOLKLORE, AND TRADITION

1. Unfortunately, not all the bibliography was available to me. It is most probable that a thorough search of ethnographic and literary resources in Romanian would uncover yet further significant literary uses of the story. See Turdeanu, *Apocryphes slaves;* Leopold Kretzenbacher, *Teufelsbünder und Faustgestalten im Abendlande* (Klagenfurt: Verlag des Geschichtsvereines für Kärnten, 1986), 42–51; Leopold Kretzenbacher, *Bilder und Legenden: Erwandertes und erlebtes Bilder-Denken und Bild-Erzählen zwischen Byzanz und dem Abenland* (Klagefurt: Geschichtverein für Kärnten, 1971), 49–73, "Jordantaufe und dem Satansstein."

2. He drew it from P. Comarnescu, *Rümanische Kunstschätse. Voroneţ. Fresken aus dem 15. und 16. Jahrhundert* (Bucharest: Verlag für fremdsprachige Literatur, 1959), 24–25 [*non vidi*].

3. For further discussion both of Bulgarian and of Romanian (Transylvanian, Moldavian, and Bucovinan) tales, see the remarks of P. Henry. "Folklore et iconographie religieuse; Contribution à l'étude de la peinture moldave," *Melanges: Bibilothèque de l'Institut français de hautes études en Roumanie* 1 (1927), 88–91. See further references, particularly ibid., 90.

4. E. Barsov, *Chteniia v. imper. obshchestve istorii i drevnostei* 2 (1886), 7. A German translation was published by Jagič "Die altkirchenslavischen Texte des Adambuches" 42.

5. V. Mochulskii, *Istoriko-literaturnyi analiz stixa: "O golubinoi knige"* (Warsaw, 1886), 237; quoted by Jagič, "Die altkirchenslavischen Texte des Adambuches," 43.

6. See chapter 2, note 37.

7. Turdeanu, *Apocryphes slaves*, 126, note 96 gives an extensive bibliography of publications of one recension. This recension does not contain the cheirograph material.

8. See Turdeanu, ibid., 123. This is also true of the Greek liturgy; see chapter 6.

9. See chapter 5.

10. Turdeanu, *Apocryphes slaves*, 127.

11. Ibid., 130–131.

12. See the documentation assembled by Turdeanu, ibid., 127, note 100, and see further p. 128.

13. N. Roddy graciously prepared the following translation from Romanian. The Romanian text is to be found in Nicolae Cartojan, *Cărţile populare în literatura românească*, 2 vols. (Bucharest: Editura enciclopedica româna, 1974, originally published in 1929). Dr. Roddy stresses the localization of the tradition here. "For the medieval Romanian reader or listener, Adam is simply the first Romanian peasant who has wandered away from his landlord (rather, was expelled) and trespassed on another" (private communication September 1, 1999).

14. Note Slavonic Variant A §3, "Or, will you be God's, then go to Paradise!"

15. A French translation by Turdeanu is found in *Apocryphes slaves*, 128.

16. In the fifth recension of the poem, cited by Turdeanu, ibid., 136, a redactor has replaced the Jordan with the Black Sea. This type of domestication of traditions has been shown to exist in other instances in apocryphal texts. Thus, N. Roddy has highlighted similar processes in the Romanian version of the *Testament of Abraham*; see Nicolae Roddy, "Scribal Intent: Sociocultural Appropriation of the Testament of Abraham in Eighteenth-Century Romanian Lands," *Journal of Religion and Society* 1 (1999); e-journal available at <http://www.creighton.edu/JRS/>.

17. Is this reminiscent of the creation of Adam in Genesis 2:7?

18. Turdeanu, ibid., 134. The brick, baked in fire, also occurs in two other Romanian sources.

19. Turdeanu, ibid., 129.

20. Turdeanu, ibid., 133. The detail of the floating up of the cheirograph occurs in no other source. Turdeanu also refers to Maxim the Greek, sixteenth-century Greco-Russian humanist, *Skazanije o rukopisanii grěhovněm* "Discourse on the 'Cheirograph of Sins.'" *Apocryphes slaves*, 115, no. 57. No further reference is given there. This is apparently more about Colossians 2:14.

21. Kretzenbacher, *Bilder und Legenden*, 64–65, citing A. Dima, *Rumänische märchen; in deutscher übersetzung nach Haupttypen ausgewählt und mit Anmerkungen versehen* (Leipzig: O. Harrassowitz, 1944).

22. See the comment in chapter 1, note 18. This is another example of the "Romanianization" of the story remarked upon in note 16 above. N. Roddy has commented, in private communication, "Adam, the Jordan river, etc. occupy the same Romanian mythic corridor as its own historical and geographical persons and places."

23. Ivanov, *Livres et Légendes bogomiles*, 311–313.

24. Ibid., 300–301, no. 6.

25. Ibid., 309–310.

26. See iconographic type 6, which has the same element.

27. This is one interpretation of the scroll. As with other biblical figures, it could also represent a book, in this case the Gospels.

28. Dionysius of Fourna, 5.12.22 (cited in Megas, "Das χειρόγραφον Adams," 314). Turdeanu, *Apocryphes slaves,* 115–122, discussed the iconography of the contract in some detail. See also Paul Hetherington, *The "Painters Manual" of Dionysius of Fourna* (London: Saggitarius Press, 1974), 53. This description is related to iconographic type 6, presented below.

29. G. G. Meersseman, *Der Hymnos Akathistos im Abendland,* 2 vols., Spicilegium Friburgense, 3 (Freiburg [Ch]: Universitätsverlag, 1960), 1.37–38; Egon Wellesz, *The Akathistos Hymn,* Monumenta Musicae Byzantinae Transcripta, 9 (Copenhagen: Munksgaard, 1957), viii.

30. See, e.g., Princeton, Garrett 13, fol. 23r, and the study by Μαρίας Άσπρα Βαρδαβακή, ΟΙ ΜΙΚΡΟΓΡΑΦΕΙΣ ΤΟΥ ΑΚΑΘΙΣΤΟΥ ΣΤΟΝ ΚΩΔΙΚΑ GARRET 13, PRINCETON (Athens, 1992), 155–156 (English summary) and plate 23. An example from Mount Athos is given by her on plate 129, from the Sanctuary of the Laura Monastery. See Megas, "Das χειρόγραφον Adams," 314, and his comments, ibid., 317–318, touching on the relationship of the χειρόγραφον with the baptism, as well as the Armenian texts given below.

31. Χάριν δοῦναι θελήσας ὀφλημάτων ἀρχαίων | ὁ πάντων χρεωλύτης ἀνθρώπων, | ἐπεδήμησε δι' ἑαυτοῦ | πρὸς τοὺς ἀποδήμους τῆς αὐτοῦ χάριτος· | καὶ σχίσας τὸ χειρόγραφον, | ἀκούει παρὰ πάντων οὕτως, Ἀλληλούϊα. Wellesz, *The Akathistos Hymn,* lxxix. Megas cites the Greek text of stanza 22 of the Hymnos Akathistos with the following description of the scene by Dionysius: χάριν δοῦναι θελήσας. »Σπίτια καὶ ἐν αὐτοῖς ὁ Χριστὸς ἱστάμενος, σχίζων χαρτὶ μὲ τὰ χεριά του, γράμμενον μὲ γράμματα ἑβραϊκά· καὶ εἰς τὸ τέλος τοῦ χαρτίου ταῦτα τὰ γράμματα·ὠτὸ τοῦ Ἀδὰμ χειρόγραφον«. Καὶ ἀπὸ τὰ δύο μέρη αὐτοῦ ἄνθρωποι γονατισμένοι, νέοι καὶ γέροντες (p. 314).

32. See chapter 2, note 6.

33. The idea is often also designated by διαρρήγνυμι; cf., e.g., Chrysostom, *Baptismal Homily* 3.21: Διὰ τοῦτο οὐκ ἀπήλειψεν ἀλλὰ διέρρηξεν· οἱ γὰρ ἧλοι τοῦ σταυροῦ διέρρηξαν αὐτὸ καὶ διέφθειραν ἵνα ἄχρηστον γένηται τοῦ λοιποῦ "This is why He did not erase it, but tore it to pieces. The nails of the cross tore up the decree and destroyed it utterly, so that it would not hold good for the future." Note also pseudo-Athanasius, *Quaestiones in scripturam sacram,* PG 28,763–4: *Quaest.* CX: Αὐτὸς γὰρ ὁ διάβολος ὁ κρατῶν τὸ χειρόγραφον τῆς παραβάσεως τοῦ Ἀδάμ, αὐτὸς ἔσχισεν, ἐπειδὴ ὑπὸ Χριστοῦ ἐδεσμεύθη ἐπὶ τοῦ σταυροῦ. "The devil, holding the cheirograph of the transgression of Adam, tore it himself, when he was shackled by Christ upon the Cross." Paintings reflecting this description are presented as iconographic type 6.

34. See further above, start of iconographic type 1.

35. Turdeanu, *Apocryphes slaves,* 119–120, remarks that this iconography has no roots in the Slavonic *Vita Adam et Evae.* We can now state that his statement is not precise, because we can adduce Variants B and C of the Slavonic *Life of Adam and Eve.* Megas, "Das χειρόγραφον Adams," 314, mentions a painting of Martin de Vos, which also shows the χειρόγραφον.

36. So Turdeanu, *Apocryphes slaves,* 121; contrast Kretzenbacher (next note).

37. See Kretzenbacher, *Bilder und Legenden,* color plate IV, opposite p. 72; description on p. 73.

38. See ibid., color plate V, opposite p. 74; description on p. 73.

39. Turdeanu, *Apocryphes slaves,* 120. Compare R. Röhricht, *Bibliotheca Geographica Palestina,* rev. ed. by D. Amiran (Jerusalem: Universitas, 1963), 550.

40. E. Smirnova, *Moscow Icons, Fourteenth to Seventeenth Centuries* (Leningrad: Aurora Art Publishers, 1989), 279 and plate 99. She also mentions as examples icons in the Cathedral of the Annunciation in Moscow and the Cathedral of the Trinity in Zagorsk.

41. The manuscripts are Suceviţa no. 24 (1607), fol. 11, and Suceviţa no. 23, fol. 10 (ca. 1568).

42. S. Der Nersessian, "Une nouvelle réplique slavonne de Paris gr. 74 et les manuscrits de Anastase Crimcovici," in *Etudes Byzantines et Arméniennes* (Louvain: Imprimerie orientaliste, 1973), 265–278 and figs. 164 and 166.

43. Turdeanu, *Apocryphes slaves,* 121.

44. Kurt Weitzmann et al., *Frühe Ikonen. Sinai, Griechenland, Bulgarien, Jugoslawien* (Wien-München: Schroll, 1965), 81. See Kretzenbacher, *Bilder und Legenden,* p. 55, note 13. He mentions another seventeenth-century Bulgarian icon there. A similar composition with seven or eight serpents and a square stone is shown by Weitzmann et al., *Frühe Ikonen,* 146. See Figure 4. This icon is by Gorma Oryahovitsa, from the first half of the seventeenth century. See also no. 76 in Kostatinka Paskaleva, *Bulgarian Icons through the Centuries* (Sofia: Soyat, 1987).

45. Kretzenbacher, *Bilder und Legenden,* color plate II, opposite p. 52, description pp. 51–52; also reproduced in G. Ristow, *Die Taufe Christi* (Recklinghausen: Bongers, 1965), frontispiece.

46. No. 420, shown by K. Weitzmann et al., *Frühe Ikonen,* no. 81.

47. Described by Kretzenbacher, *Bilder and Legenden,* 55, from K. Miiatev, *Ikonen aus Bulgarien,* xliiiff. [*non vidi*]. Kretzenbacher remarks on p. 55, "Sehr fraglich bleibt es, ob die weißen Zackenlinien auf dem Stein etwa die Reste von Schriftzeichen darstellen sollen" (p. 55). Another Bulgarian icon with the same scene, undated, is mentioned by Kretzenbacher, *Bilder und Legenden,* 57, from the catalogue of an exhibit held in Essen in 1964: *Kunstschätze in bulgarischen Museen und Klöstern* (Essen: Villa Hügel, 1964), nos. 163 and 279 [*non vidi*]. It shows Christ on a flat stone in the Jordan with seven serpents' heads.

48. Paskaleva, *Bulgarian Icons,* fig. 76. Compare Weitzmann et al., *Frühe Ikonen,* no. 142. See Kretzenbacher, *Bilder und Legenden,* 55, note 13. A similar icon, of the seventeenth century from Prissovo monastery (Bulgaria), is in the National Church Museum in Bulgaria. It is illustrated in A. Tschilingnov, *Die Kunst des christlichen Mittelalters in Bulgarien: 14. bis 18. Jarh* (Berlin: Union, 1978), plate 274. This shows Christ in the baptism, standing on an irregular stone cheirograph with seven black snakes issuing from under it.

49. G. Millet, *La peinture du Moyen Age en Yougoslavie* (Paris: E. de Boccard, 1954), vol. 3, plate 52.1. Millet discusses the date on p. xvi. Lynn Jones kindly verified this reference for me.

50. These are Xenophontou, Esphigmenou, and the Baptistery of the Laura of St.

Athanasius. They are mentioned by Turdeanu, *Apocryphes slaves,* 120, citing M. Didron, *Manuel d'iconographie chrétienne* (Paris: Imprimerie Royale, 1845), 164–165 note. Didron claims to have seen at least twenty instances of this scene in Greece. See further Turdeanu, *Apocryphes slaves,* 120–121. The material is discussed by Kretzenbacher, *Bilder und Legenden,* 56–57, and the frescoes are described by G. Schäfer, *Das Handbuch der Malerei von Berge Athos* (Trier: Fr. Lintz, 1855), in his edition of Dionysius of Fourna, 179–180.

51. G. Schäfer, *Das Handbuch der Malerei von Berge Athos,* 179. Schäfer also had in his possession a wooden cross of Athonite provenance with Christ standing on a stone, but without serpents.

52. Kretzenbacher, *Bilder und Legenden,* 67–71. See also Valeriu Anania, *Cerurile Oltului: Scolile Arhimandritului Bartolomeu la imaginile fotografice ale lui Dumitru F. Dumitru* (Episcopate of Rîmnicului and Argeţ, 1990). On p. 202 is found Archimandrite Bartholemew's commentary on the scene, which shows complete familiarity with the cheirograph legend. He is commenting on an icon in Brâncoveanu Monastery in the County of Olt, dated to 1702. In that commentary, another example in the monastery of Cozia is mentioned (N. Roddy).

53. Upper margin: Ս̅ր̅. յովանէս. որ մկրտի զքրիստոս: Ս̅ր̅. Հոգին աղաւսակերպ իջեալ ի յերկնից. The lower margin reads: Գէսն յորդանան. ստանալայն է կերպ վիշապ աւձի. որ պահէ ի մէջ շրոյն. աղաանա՛ ձեռագիրն:

54. See chapter 2, page 22.

55. I am grateful to Dr. G. Ter Vardanian and Dr. Armen Malkhasian, who kindly provided me with technical information about this manuscript. Dr. Emma Korkhmazian first drew my attention to it.

56. P. Henry, *Les Eglises de la Moldavie du Nord des origines à la fin du XVIe siècle* (Paris: Librairie Ernest Leroux, 1930), 246, from Voroneţ. Henry gives a drawing of the scene. The legend is discussed by Henry there, with some confusion of the different senses of cheirograph. A further discussion and description of the Voroneţ frescos may be seen in Kretzenbacher, *Teufelsbünden,* 42ff. He refers also to Comarnescu, *Rumänische Kunstschätze* [*non vidi*]. This scene is preceded by one of Adam plowing; see Kretzenbacher, *Teufelsbünden,* 43.

57. V. Drăgut and Petre Lupan, *Die Wandmalerei in der Moldau* (Bucharest: Merideane, 1983), 198.

58. The Genesis stories formed an inseparable part of the Romanian fresco cycles; see Henry, *Les Eglises de la Moldavie du Nord,* 245.

59. Drăgut and Lupan, *Die Wandmalerei in der Moldau,* plate 197, also reproduce the picture of Adam plowing.

60. See P. Henry, "Folklore et iconographie religieuse," especially 82–92; his drawing is on p. 83.

61. Henry, *Les Eglises de la Moldavie du Nord,* 246; Turdeanu, *Apocryphes slaves,* 117.

62. Henry, "Folklore et iconographie religieuse," 84.

63. Turdeanu, *Apocryphes slaves,* 118, note 69. It is probable that the Mount Athos fresco, of which we have been unable to see an illustration, is the same one we referred to in note 49. Turdeanu cites O. Tafrali, "Iconografia Imnului Acatist," *Buletinul Comissiunii monumentelor istorice* 7 (1914), Figs. 39 and 40 [*non vidi*].

64. We have seen no representation of it.

65. Weitzmann et al., *The Icon,* 283: from the A. Morozov collection in the Tetriakov Gallery, Moscow. See a later Serbian icon of the same scene in ibid, 321. Of course, the scroll might simply represent the Gospels.

66. H. F. von Mauchenheim, *Russische Ikonen* (Alphen aan den Rijn: Atrium, 1987), 157, and R. Lange, *Die Auferstehung* (Recklinghausen: Bongers, 1966), 72. Another seventeenth-century icon of this scene, with the rolled-up scroll, is in ibid, 73. Adam can be seen below and to the right of Christ, holding the second part of this document. This is clearly a representation of an image that developed from Colossians 2:14. V. I. Antonova and N. E. Mneva, *Katalog drevnerusskoii zhivopisi* [*Catalogue of Old Russian Paintings*] (Moscow: Iskusstvo, 1963), 2.261–262, describe a seventeenth-century Muscovite Anastasis, where Jesus holds a torn scroll inscribed as the cheirograph. They relate this feature to the *Hymnos Akathisos,* and see above in section "Iconographic Types," 8.1. They also note another Muscovite icon of the same iconography, of the year 1659. N. V. Pokrovskii, *Evangelie v pamiatnikakh ikonografii preimushchestvenno vizantiiskikh i russkikh* [*The Gospel in Iconography, Primarily Byzantine and Russian*] (St. Petersburg: Tip. Departamenta udelov, 1892), 495, mentions a third, undated icon showing a torn scroll with the words "He tore the handwritings of Adam [and] by this destroyed the powers of darkness."

67. An unusual iconography is observed in a painting by J. F. Brémond, titled *Descent de Jésus-Christ aux Enfers* (1845), which shows Christ standing on the floor of Hades, with a figure, probably Adam, opposite him holding a book in his hand.

68. In a parallel formulation, Satan is proclaimed lord of the dead, and God, lord of the living in Slavonic Variant C §6 and in Bulgarian stories nos. 7, 8, and 9.

5. ARMENIAN APOCRYPHAL TALES

1. On the disjunction between conciliar and other lists of canonical books and the actual usage of the Armenian Apostolic Church, see M. E. Stone, "Armenian Canon Lists III: The Lists of Mechitar of Ayrivankʻ," *HTR* 69 (1978), 299–300. A catalogue of Armenian biblical manuscripts, listing all works (not just canonical books) contained in them, is S. Ajamian, Ցուցակ Աստուածաշունչ մատեանի Հայերէն ձեռագիրներուն [*Catalogue of Armenian Manuscripts of the Bible*] (Lisbon: C. Gulbenkian Foundation, 1992).

2. M. E. Stone, "Two Armenian Manuscripts and the *Historia Sacra,*" in *Apocryphes arméniens: transmission—traduction—création—iconographie,* ed. V. Calzolari Bouvier, J.-D. Kaestli, and B. Outtier (Lausanne: Zèbre, 1999), 21–36; M. E. Stone, "The Study of the Armenian Apocrypha," in *A Multiform Heritage: Studies on Early Judaism and Christianity in Honor of Robert A. Kraft,* ed. B. G. Wright, Scholars Press Homage Series (Atlanta: Scholars Press (1999), 139–148.

3. The most recent list is M. E. Stone, "The Armenian Apocryphal Literature: Translation and Creation," in *Il Caucaso: Cerniera fra Culture dal Mediterraneo alla Persia (Secoli I–XI),* Settimane di Studio dal Centro Italiano de Studi sull'Alto Medioevo, XLIII (Spoleto: Presso la Sede del Centro, 1996), 612–646. A number of additional compositions have been edited since that list was prepared.

4. S. Yovsēpʻianc̣, Անկանոն Գիրք Հին Կտակարանաց [*Uncanonical Books of the Old Testament*] (Venice: Mechitarist Press, 1896).

5. J. Issaverdens, *The Uncanonical Writings of the Old Testament Found in the Armenian MSS. of the Library of St. Lazarus,* 2nd ed. (Venice: Mechitarist Press, 1934).

6. E. Preuschen, "Die apokryphen gnostischen Adamschriften, aus dem Armenischen übersetzt und untersucht," in *Festgruß B. Stade* (Giessen: Ricker, 1900), 163–252 and *separatim*.

7. W. L. Lipscomb, *The Armenian Apocryphal Adam Literature*, University of Pennsylvania Armenian Texts and Studies, 8 (Atlanta: Scholars Press, 1990).

8. Stone, *History of the Literature of Adam and Eve*, 101–110. See also Stone, "The Armenian Apocryphal Literature: Translation and Creation."

9. See Lipscomb, *Armenian Apocryphal Adam Literature*, 16–20. He drew information on available manuscripts chiefly from H. S. Anasyan, Հայկական Մատենագիտութիւն Ե-ԺԸ դդ [*Armenian Bibliology, Fifth–Eighteenth Centuries*] (Erevan: Academy of Sciences, 1959), 1, 240–241.

10. W. Lüdtke, "Georgische Adam-Bücher," *Zeitschrift für die alttestamentliche Wissenschaft* 38 (1911), 155–168. See also Stone, *History of the Literature of Adam and Eve*, 110.

11. Yovsēpʻianc̔, *Uncanonical Books*, 307–311; Issaverdens, *Uncanonical Writings*, 39–45; Preuschen, "Die apokryphen gnostischen Adamschriften," 29–30; Lipscomb, *Armenian Apocryphal Adam Literature*, Recension 1, 108–127; Recension 2, text 241–245, translation 261–266.

12. Yovsēpʻianc̔, *Uncanonical Books*, 312–314; Issaverdens, *Uncanonical Writings*, 47–51; Preuschen, "Die apokryphen gnostischen Adamschriften," 31–33; Lipscomb, *Armenian Apocryphal Adam Literature*, Recension 1, 128–141; Recension 2, text 246–248, translation 267–269.

13. Yovsēpʻianc̔, *Uncanonical Books*, 314–319; Issaverdens, *Uncanonical Writings*, 53–61; Preuschen, "Die apokryphen gnostischen Adamschriften," 33–36; Lipscomb, *Armenian Apocryphal Adam Literature*, Recension 1, 142–171; Recension 2, text 249–254, translation 270-275; further collations, Stone, *Armenian Apocrypha Relating to Patriarchs and Prophets*, 33–38.

14. Yovsēpʻianc̔, *Uncanonical Books*, 319–324; Issaverdens, *Uncanonical Writings*, 63–70, Preuschen, "Die apokryphen gnostischen Adamschriften," 36–40; Lipscomb, *Armenian Apocryphal Adam Literature*, Recension 1, 172–205; Recension 2, text 255–260, translation 276–282. This information is drawn from Stone, *History of the Literature of Adam and Eve*, 102–103. Information about the manuscripts may be found in appendix 1.

15. A similar form of the legend occurs in a Russian variant of the Slavonic *Life of Adam and Eve*, published by Pypin, *Loniia i otreennyia knigi russkoi stariny*, 2 (*apud* Turdeanu, *Apocryphes slaves*, 116). This is Variant B, presented in chapter 3. Turdeanu's remark that the Armenian *Expulsion* is "une version arménienne du même apocryphe" is not correct (116). It is an Armenian version of the same story, not of the same apocryphon.

16. The translation is reproduced by permission.

17. See the miniature of the baptism from Matenadaran M10806 of 1587, which was discussed in the preceding chapter, Figure 6.

18. The section is indebted to Psalm 90:4, which is also used in 2 Peter 3:8. The six eons are the six thousand years of the world; see Stone, *Armenian Apocrypha: Relating to Adam and Eve*, 87–88, 135. Traditionally, Christ was thought to be born in the middle of the last of these six millennia.

19. See *Adam, Eve, and the Incarnation,* §20. We have found no known parallels to this idea outside the Armenian tradition. The fall of the protoplasts into a dark place also penetrated Armenian iconography, and may be seen in the miniature from Matenadaran manuscript M4280, shown below.

20. In Recension 2, it is explicitly a teaching of agriculture, while in Recension 1, the angel is said to show them the fruit trees. The mention of fruit trees immediately evokes the Edenic state. The Armenian concern for the fruit trees of Eden is evident in the Armenian Enoch stories. According to them, Enoch learned that Adam and Eve had sinned by eating fruit. He planted an orchard and refrained from eating its fruit, so as to avoid their sin. See, in detail, Lipscomb, *Armenian Apocryphal Adam Literature,* 62–68; Stone, *Armenian Apocrypha: Relating to Adam and Eve,* 107, 153. A number of variant forms of this incident occur.

21. Some new texts relating to this tradition will be published in the writer's sourcebook on the *Stories of Adam and Eve in the Armenian Tradition,* currently in preparation.

22. E. Tayec 'i, Անկանոն Գիրք Նոր կտակարանաց [*Uncanonical Books of the New Testament*] (Venice: Mechitarist Press, 1898), 46–52.

23. Tayec 'i, *Uncanonical Books,* 46–47. On this and allied documents, see Anasyan, *Bibliology,* 1,243, no. 13; Matenadaran, manuscript no. M2111, 299v (being edited by the present writer); Venice, Mechitarist manuscript no. V240, 10v–11. That latter text bears the title սակաւ բան վասն թղղթոյն՝ զոր եւ Աստուած Ադամայ, "A small discourse concerning the epistle which God gave to Adam."

24. See, for example, *Questions of Ezra,* Recension B, §§10–12:

> 10 The prophet said, "If the sinner's soul has no good memorial which helps him, what will become of that soul?" 11 The angel said, "Such a one remains in the power of Satan until the coming of Christ, when the trumpet of Gabriel sounds. 12 Then the souls are freed from the power of Satan and soar down from that atmosphere."

This language is central to the Armenian baptismal liturgy. See F. C. Conybeare, *Rituale Armenorum: Being the Administration of the Sacraments and the Breviary Rites of the Armenian Church Together with the Greek Rites of Baptism and Epiphany Edited from the Oldest Mss.* (Oxford: Oxford University Press, 1905), 92–93. Of course, the exorcism of Satan and the rejection of service to him are far from unique to the Armenians as part of the baptismal liturgy. See further Gabriele Winkler, *Das Armenische Initiationsrituale,* Orientalia Christiana Analecta, 217 (Rome: Pont. Institutum Studiorum Orientalium, 1982), 196–197 and 378–383. For current Greek practice, liturgical and popular, see Charles Stewart, *Demons and the Devil: Moral Imagination in Greek Culture* (Princeton: Princeton University Press, 1991), 199. Further ancient Christian sources are discussed by Thomas M. Finn, *The Liturgy of Baptism in the Baptismal Instructions of St. John Chrysostom,* Catholic University of America Studies in Christian Antiquity, 15 (Washington, D.C.: Catholic University of America, 1967), 95–98. There he deals with the renunciation of Satan. On the language of "bondage" in baptism, see his comments on pp. 102–104.

25. See Նոր Բառգիրք Հայկազեան Լեզուի [*New Dictionary of the Armenian Lan-*

guage] (Venice: Mechitarist Press, 1836), 1.288, col. 3 (*NBH*), and M. Ormanian, *Dictionary of the Armenian Church* (New York: St. Vartan Press, 1948), 35. We noted above the connection of the Romanian *Plaint of Adàm* and its cheirograph legend with the Sunday before Lent, and in the Greek liturgy the Sunday before Lent is dedicated to Adam's expulsion.

26. That passage might be the source, however, of the word "annul" (§24). It is the same as that which translates ἐξαλείψας in Colossians, which actually means "rub out." Still, this is not a strong connection.

27. This extensive text is published in Stone, *Armenian Apocrypha: Relating to Adam and Eve,* 20–79. The translation given below is drawn from that work by permission.

28. Stone, "Two Armenian Manuscripts and the *Historia Sacra*."

29. See the preceding section.

30. The period of forty days in the Paris manuscript must be secondary. This is a standard period for abstinence from eating, from Moses' time on Mount Sinai on. The time of Christ's temptation was also forty days. On this number, see M. E. Stone, *Commentary on 4 Ezra* (Hermeneia; Minneapolis: Augsberg-Fortress, 1990), 431. It is, of course, the number of days of Lent.

31. This theme is discussed at p. 70.

32. L. Zak'arian, *History of the Miniatures of Vaspurakan* (Yerevan: Academy of Sciences, 1980), plate III, opposite p. 36 (in Russian).

33. In a related painting, mentioned in note 35, the serpent's tail is actually looped around this frame, even more like what is described in *Penitence of Adam.*

34. See Adolfo Roitman, "'Al Geḥonka Telek' (Gen. 3.14): Hamareh haḥiṣoni šel naḥaš gan ha'eden befaršanut hayehudit ha'atiqa" ("'On your belly you shall go' [Gen. 3:14]: The External Appearance of the Eden Serpent in Ancient Jewish Exegesis"), *Tarbiẓ* 64 (1995), 157–182 (in Hebrew).

35. Another almost identical painting exists, M316 (thirteenth to fourteenth century), with the same captions, illustrated in H. Hakobian, *The Medieval Art of Artsakh* (Erevan: Parberakan Press, 1991), 80. This painting does not have the small figures of the fallen Adam and Eve. A picture of the expulsion, similar in many ways to the above two pictures, is a miniature in M7633 (1629), fol. 2. In it, Christ is standing on the left, expelling Adam and Eve, both of whom have halos and are dressed. Outside the frame, in the same place as in the preceding pictures, is the serpent lying along the frame, with his body looped around it. His inscription here differs and reads "the deceiving serpent." Under the picture we read, "Adam's Garden: Christ's [lacuna] of Adam and Eve." We assume the missing word was "expulsion."

36. In Satan's discussion with Adam and Eve in *Adam, Eve, and the Incarnation,* he initiates the idea of the subjugation of the offspring; in *Expulsion,* it is Adam and Eve who first propose this idea, as a result of Satan's prompting. The formulation of §9 is as a legal asseveration.

37. Compare the words for "tearing" discussed in chapter 4, note 33, and in chapter 7, note 6. The word in Colossians 2.14 means "to erase," not "to tear," and the introduction and use of the words σχίζω and διαρρήγνυμι reflect an ancient development as Colossians 2:14 was modified by the tradition of the descent into Hades. In Pseudo-Cyprian, *Adversus Iudaeos,* line 254, we find the words *hic est qui rupit uetus testamentum et scripsit nouum,* "This is he who tore the Old Testament and wrote

the New"; see D. van Damme, *Pseudo-Cyprian Adversus Iudaeos,* Paradosis: Beiträge zur altchristlichen Literatur und Theologie, 22 (Freiburg: University Press, 1969), 129, and his discussion of this phrase on pp. 22–23.

38. See chapter 5, p. 72 (at note 24), where language of enslavement and freeing from Satan is discussed.

39. J. D. Kaestli, "Témoignages anciens sur la croyance en la descente du Christ aux enfers," 135–142.

40. In P306, §27, the idea of Satan's gospel is stressed. The good tidings of light are to be given by Satan according to §28. In M5913, §31, Adam and Eve are told by Satan, "believe in me!" In §30 Adam and Eve subjugate themselves to Satan and his gospel. This "anti-gospel," and in a sense "anti-Christ," language is highly suggestive.

41. This issue is discussed above in connection with *Expulsion.*

42. In general, the language of "deed of obligation" here seems to accord with the attitude to the "deed of obligation" = cheirograph, according to *Adam Story 1,* given below.

43. See chapter 3, pp. 39–40.

44. See chapter 2, p. 22.

45. See chapter 2, ibid, and chapter 2, note 53.

46. See chapter 2, Satan's Form and the Baptism of Christ.

47. See pp. 54–57 and Figure 6.

48. See chapter 5, p. 72.

49. Translated from Winkler, *Das Armenische Initiationsrituale,* 196.

50. Based on Gen 3:18, in §18. "Immortal plant" means the plant that gives immortality.

51. M. E. Stone and G. A. Anderson published synoptic texts of the "primary" Adam books in *A Synopsis of the Books of Adam and Eve. Second Revised Edition.* The "Primary Adam Books" are the *Apocalypse of Moses* (Greek) and the parallel Latin, Armenian, Georgian, Slavonic, and fragmentary Coptic works.

52. The text of *Adam, Eve, and the Incarnation* here uses a number of verbs that show no particular relationship either to Psalm 114 or to Colossians 2:14.

53. Kaestli, "Témoinages anciens sur la croyance en la descente du Christ aux enfers," 135–142.

54. In note 37, we discussed the source of the Armenian verb պատառեաց, "tear up," used by *Adam, Eve, and the Incarnation.*

55. Stone, *Armenian Apocrypha Relating to Adam and Eve,* 103–107.

56. The same Armenian word is used above, once in §9 ("condition") and twice in §10, where it has been translated once as "condition" and once as "agreement"; cf. Stone, *Armenian Apocrypha Relating to Adam and Eve,* 105–106. A similar development takes place in the modern Greek stories; see chapter 5.

57. A second expression in this context is թոյլ տալ "to give release" (§20). See the discussion of this terminology on p. 72 at note 24 above.

58. Sacrificing to demons; see Deuteronomy 32:17 and LXX, Psalm 106:37–38, 4QpsDaniel, Baruch 4:7, 1 *Enoch* 99:7, cf. 19:1.

59. See Stone, *Armenian Apocrypha Relating to Adam and Eve,* 107 note.

60. See ibid, 103.

6. THE STORY IN GREEK

1. See Megas, "Das Χειρόγραφον Adams," 311–312. He discusses this text and points out the existence of two further copies of it. F. H. Marshall published the text of part of it from British Library Add 40724. He knew of two further manuscripts, one in Venice and one in Vienna; see Marshall, *Greek Poem on Genesis and Exodus,* xi. Stone, *History of the Literature of Adam and Eve,* 88, pointed out the existence of a fourth manuscript, in the Library of St. Catherine's monastery at Mount Sinai. Intriguingly, the manuscript that Marshall published and translated also hails from St. Catherine's monastery, as is clear from the colophon (p. xiii). Like it, the Sinai manuscript is heavily illustrated.

2. Marshall, *Greek Poem on Genesis and Exodus.*

3. Lipscomb, *Armenian Apocryphal Adam Literature,* 211–214 (text); 222–225 (translation).

4. See chapter 4. Marshall, *Greek Poem on Genesis and Exodus,* points out the role of such a plaint in the Greek liturgy (p. xxix).

5. This is not specified in the other texts.

6. Note Genesis 3:21, where we have בגדי עור, "garments of skin," which becomes בגדי אור, "garments of light," by paronomasia in Rabbinic exegesis.

7. Megas, "Das Χειρόγραφον Adams," 314–315. The elements paralleled in the liturgy are in fact references to the tradition in Colossians, not to the legend of the cheirograph.

8. See Marshall, *Greek Poem on Genesis and Exodus,* xxi–xxxii.

9. Lieberman, "Zeniḥin," *Tarbiz* 62 (1972), 46–48 (in Hebrew).

10. See *Berešit rabbati,* ed. Albeck, 26, 5, 85.

11. Eli Yassif, *Sipurei Ben Sira Biymei habeynayyim* (Jerusalem: Magnes, 1984), 289.

12. See note 10.

13. These tales here were drawn from the reprinting in *Laographia* 20 (Athens, 1962), 567–572. The English translations were prepared by B. Moncó, while M. H. Bakker and N. Constas illuminated some obscure points. Leopold Kretzenbacher, *Teufelsbünder und Faustgestalten im Abendland,* 45–46, gives one of these modern Greek tales, recorded in the Peloponnesus ca. 1930. See, in further detail, Leopold Kretzenbacher, *Bilder und Legenden,* 64.

14. In spite of the Slavic invasion of Crete in 623, which was subsequently a Byzantine possession until 1214.

15. Observation of B. Moncó. This is reminiscent of the Armenian *Adam Story 1,* which also has a different word for contract. In all cases, it may be due to the fact that the word "cheirograph" was no longer clear to the tellers.

16. Told by N. Laskaris; taken from *Laographia,* 1962, 569–570. It is drawn from the daily *Morea of Tripoli,* 6 January 1929. The superscription reads: "Because at this time the [feast of the] Holy Theophany is drawing near, I decided to send forth for publication the following tradition about the Protoplasts."

17. Literally, "follow."

18. The same word is used for the tablets of the law. Dr. N. Constas remarks, "Note the inversion of the Mosaic tablets inscribed by God's finger, and the Adamic tablet signed with the blood from Adam's palm, a foreshadowing, it seems, of Christ's wounded palms" (private communication). Above, in discussion of the Armenian

sources, we observed the inversion of the Gospels and of the cheirograph itself; see chapter 6, pp. 84–85.

19. Compare Luke 3:16, "I baptize you with water, but he who is mightier than I is coming . . . he will baptize you with the Holy Spirit and with fire."

20. Actually sung on the evening of Holy Thursday.

21. The translation of Homer is that of Chapman. Here it is selected because it stands in contrast to the style of the translation of the story, just as the Greek of Homer stands in contrast to the Greek of the story.

22. The relationship between Greek popular belief and the Greek church is explored by Stewart in his book *Demons and the Devil: Moral Imagination in Modern Greek Culture.*

23. *Laographia,* p. 569. Translation by B. Moncó. The teller of the tale, which is reported by Antonios Michalakas, was from Basara in the Poloponnesus, and the story was told in Kalamata.

24. Verse from the fifteenth antiphon of Holy Thursday. Note that this hymn is mentioned in the previous story, from the *Morea of Tripoli.*

25. A third story, *Laographia,* pp. 567–568, deals with a contract between a young man and Satan. It is one of many such stories, which are widespread in the Mediterranean countries. Just how such stories are related to the specific morphology of the legend of the cheirograph is unclear.

26. Megas, "Das Χειρόγραφον Adams."

27. This text is discussed in detail by Megas in "Das Χειρόγραφον Adams," 305–320. He deals with a number of issues related to this story. He connects it with Colossians 2:14 and then relates it to the Slavonic *Life of Adam and Eve.* He also notes the connection with Chumnos and with medieval ideas of covenant of humans with Satan. The oldest form is the fourth-century *Martyrdom of Cyprianus and Justina,* which has been remarked upon in note 25. On p. 314, he deals with Greek liturgical sources and then with Dionysius of Fourna. His pioneering work is laudable, although he did not clarify the differences between the meaning of the term cheirograph in Colossians and in the legend.

28. Perhaps "within."

29. Megas: die dienten nicht zum Guten.

30. I.e., you will find no rest.

31. Uncertain (N. Constas).

32. Literally, "cut, incised."

33. Or, perhaps, "made them do what he wished" (N. Constas).

34. A further paragraph of text follows, which is not relevant to our study.

7. THE CHEIROGRAPH ACCORDING TO COLOSSIANS

1. As has been observed, the term is strikingly absent from the Greek folktales, which indicates that its meaning was no longer clear by the time they were told.

2. The issues are well summarized in Kittel and Friedrich, eds., *Theological Dictionary of the New Testament s.v.* χειρόγραφον. This Greek word is calqued into Armenian as ձեռագիր (jeṙagir) in a number of the texts, both in the sense of Adam's contract with Satan and in the sense of the bill of indebtedness Adam incurred.

3. Tertullian, *de pudicitia* 19.19–20. The patristic evidence related to Colossians

2:14 is surveyed by Eugene C. Best, *An Historical Study of the Exegesis of Colossians* *2,14.*

4. The seventeenth-century texts are published in Stone, *Armenian Apocrypha: Relating to Adam and Eve,* 44–146, from manuscripts. J840 and M10200. I am indebted to Dr. Roberta Ervine, who informed me about Vanakan *vardapet's* use of this text, which she is preparing for publication.

5. The translator here has rendered two different verbs by English as "do away." The first occurrence is τοῦ ἀφανισθῆναι, and the second is ἔλυσε.

6. Greek ἔσχισεν, which is not in the New Testament passage; see chapter 5, note 37. The introduction of language of tearing the bill goes along with the introduction of the descent to the underworld into the tradition.

7. Ποῖον χειρόγραφον; Ἢ τοῦτό φησιν, ὃ ἔλεγον πρὸς τὸν Μωυσέα, ὅτι Πάντα ὅσα εἶπεν ὁ Θεὸς ποιήσομεν, καὶ ἀκουσόμεθα· ἢ εἰ μὴ τοῦτο, ὅτι ὀφείλομεν τῷ Θεῷ ὑπακοήν· ἢ εἰ μὴ τοῦτο, ὅτι κατεῖχεν ὁ διάβολος τὸ χειρόγραφον ὃ ἐποίησε πρὸς τὸν Ἀδὰμ ὁ Θεὸς, εἰπών· Ἧι ἂν ἡμέρᾳ φάγῃς ἀπὸ τοῦ ξύλου, ἀποθανῇ. John Chrysostom, *Homily 6 on Colossians 2 (PG* 62: 337–344). English translation from *The Nicene and Post-Nicene Fathers,* ed. P. Schaff (repr., Peabody: Hendrickson, 1995), series 1, vol. 13, 286. These notions are explored by Finn, *The Liturgy of Baptism in the Baptismal Instructions of St. John Chrysostom,* 93–95.

8. Beck, ed., *Des Heiligen Ephrems des Syrers Hymnen de Nativitate (Epiphania),* CSCO, 186–187 (Leuven: Peeters, 1959), 1.24 (p. 194).

9. Beck, ed., *Carmina Nisibena,* 48.

10. Ibid. 36.17.

11. Thanks are expressed to E. Mathews, who kindly reviewed the translations of the citations from Ephrem. The late J. C. Greenfield also made some helpful proposals, particularly relating to the translation of the *Carmina Nisibena.*

12. See M. Borret, ed., *Origène, Homélies sur l'Exode,* Sources Chrétiennes, 321 (Paris: Editions du Cerf. 1985), 194–195; Ronald E. Heine, *Origen: Homilies on Genesis and Exodus,* The Fathers of the Church (Washington, D.C.: Catholic University, 1981), 295–296.

13. M. Gronewald, ed., *Didymos der Blinde, Psalmenkommentar (Tura-Papyrus),* vol. 5: *Kommentar zu Psalm 40–44* (Bonn: Habelt Verlag, 1970), 142–145 to Ps 43.13, ἁμαρτίᾳ πέπρακεν ἑαυτὸν καὶ χρεώστην πεποίηκεν. αὐτίκα γοῦν τὸ δι᾽ οὗ κατέχει ὁ ἐχθρὸς βασιλεὺς τῶν ψυχῶν, λέγεται χειρόγραφον. χειρόγραφον δέ ἐστιν, ὃ συνεστήσατό τις ταῖς ἑαυτοῦ χερσί[ν]."ἦρεν" οὖν "αὐτὸ ἐκ μέσου", ἵνα μηκέτι κρατῇ ἡμᾶς τῷ χειρόγραφῳ ᾧ ἡμεῖς συνεστησάμεθα κατα[γρά]ψαντες ἑαυτοὺς αὐτῷ.

14. Note, for example, Epiphanius, *pan. haer.* 69.66.6.

15. Pseudo-Macarius of Egypt, *Homily* 11.10 (*PG* 34.552B–C). We give here a translation of the passage of Pseudo-Macarius, prepared by K. Koblentz (University of Notre Dame) in connection with a seminar held at the Hebrew University in 1995. This and the translation by Steven C. Smith at the end of this chapter were stimulated by joint research then being carried out by the writer and Professor Gary Anderson. Compare also *Homily* 19:2, *Homily* 10, *Homily* 53. John Chrysostom, *de coemetrio et de Cruce* (*PG* 49:398); *Baptismal Homily* 3: 20–22, etc.; Augustine, *Against Julian* 1.6.2, *On Forgiveness of Sins* 49; Theodoret of Cyrrus, *Interpretatio epistulae ad Coloss.* 2:14 (*PG* 82: 611A); Narsai, *Homily II on Epiphany,*

248–257, 370–374, 525–535, *Homily III on the Passion,* 670–680, *Homily IV on the Resurrection,* 41–55, 80–82, 107–108, 135–138, 179–180, 289–293, 301–310, etc.

16. Compare Ephrem, *Carmina Sogyata* 9 and *Carmina Nisibena* 48.9, which describes how Christ forced the devil to annul or change the bill of indebtedness.

17. Assuming that *iecitur foras* is a reference to John 12:31.

18. *Exsuens se carne,* "putting off the flesh," is the translation of ἀπεκδυσάμενος τὰς σάρκας—a misreading of ἀπεκδυσάμενος τὰς ἀρχάς, "disarming the powers."

19. I.e., the Jews and the gentiles?

20. Literally, "separative" or "disjunctive."

21. I.e., Jesus?

8. CONCLUSION AND IMPLICATIONS

1. It is true that manuscripts of Georgios Chumnos's *Poem on Genesis and Exodus* were copied at the monastery of St. Catherine in the Sinai, but that was an expression of its spread in the area dominated by the Greek Orthodox Church.

2. The role of the very much smaller Chalcedonian Armenian confession might be significant in this connection, but it is very poorly documented.

3. I saw an eighteenth- or nineteenth-century baptism with the cheirograph on stone on the iconostasis of a Greek church on one of the Prince's Islands in the Sea of Marmora, and a photograph of a modern example was given me, from the Cypriot Monastery of St. George of the Cats.

4. Stewart, *Demons and the Devil.*

APPENDIX I

1. The edition and presentation of the Slavonic text have been prepared by Alexander Kulik. I am indebted also to Constantine Zuckerman and Alexei Krokhmalnikov, who assisted me in a number of matters relating to the Slavonic version.

2. This manuscript was also the basis of Yovsēpʻiancʻ's text. The homilies were not published by Yovsēpʻiancʻ.

3. Stone, *Armenian Apocrypha Relating to Patriarchs and Prophets,* 33–38.

4. This was subsequently reprinted thrice: Constantinople, 1730 (fols. 1–39); Constantinople, 1747 (fols. 1–36); and Constantinople, 1793 (fols. 1–35).

5. Stone, *Armenian Apocrypha: Relating to Adam and Eve,* 41–59, 64–67.

6. See O. Eganyan, A. Zeytʻunyan, and P. Antʻabyan, Ցուցակ Ձեռագրաց Մաշտոցի Անվան Մատենադարանի [*Catalogue of Manuscripts of the Maštocʻ Matenadaran*] (Erevan: Academy of Sciences, 1970), vol. 2, cols. 869–870. The text is drawn from Stone, *Armenian Apocrypha Relating to Adam and Eve,* 103–107.

7. See Stone, *Armenian Apocrypha Relating to Patriarchs and Prophets,* 2–11.

8. See Stone, *A History of the Literature of Adam and Eve,* 88. This is manuscript no. 1187 of St. Catherine's Library: see K. W. Clark, *Checklist of Manuscripts in St. Catherine's Monastery, Mount Sinai* (Washington, D.C.: Library of Congress, 1952), 28–31.

9. βυθόν

10. Two different words for garden are used. The first is κῆπο, Classical Greek κῆπος. The second one is μπαχτσιά, presumably of Turkish origin. It is striking that the word παράδεισος, which is the only word found in Genesis, is not used

here. It is, however, widespread in Modern Greek with the connotation of "paradise." The word κῆπος appears thirty-five times in Septuagint, but it never appears in the Genesis story. Its Hebrew correlate is *gan*. The word παράδεισος appears forty-six times, fourteen of them in Genesis. Its principal Hebrew correlate is also *gan* (BM).

11. στενοχωρήθηκε. This and the other glosses in notes 14, 18–26, 28–29, 31–35, 37 are embedded in Megas's text in brackets.

12. The Greek form of Eve is Εὖα in the Septuagint and in all ecclesiastic literature. Here we find Γεύα, which is pronounced *yéva* (BM).

13. The word γυναῖκα also means "wife." We have translated γυναῖκα as "woman" because a different word for spouse does exist: σύζυγος, without distinction of gender. The closeness of Adam and Eve is strengthened by the verb πλαγιάζω, which means "to lay on the side" (BM).

14. νὰ συνομιλοῦν.

15. I translate the verb βόσκω as "to harvest fruit." It means also "to harvest from nature" and thus "to eat like animals" (BM).

16. γελάω "to laugh" means "to be deceived" in the middle voice (BM).

17. When the protoplasts were expelled from the Garden, they lost their garments of light, in Hebrew בגדי אור. Here they lose their fur, that is, their עור בגדי (BM).

18. ἅμα εἶδαν ὁ ἕνας τὸν ἄλλον γυμνόν.

19. ἀπέμεινε.

20. τινάχτηκε.

21. τὸ μαχαιράκι τους.

22. ξυλόκαρφα.

23. τἀπόκρυφα μέρη.

24. ἀντικρυστά.

25. χωροῦσε.

26. κατάρα.

27. The verb σκοτώνω, "to kill, to harass," has the secondary meaning "slave away" (BM).

28. σκόνη.

29. ἔφυγε.

30. The verb πολεμώ also conserves its ancient meaning of "make the war" or "believe" (BM).

31. ἀπόκει βασανιζόμαστε.

32. μὲ δυσκολίαν.

33. Turkish word: document (Urkunde).

34. μέτωπο.

35. στρατό.

36. γῆς οἰκουμέν': The oikoumene, the inhabited world, may also be understood as the "community of believers" (BM).

37. λειψό.

APPENDIX 2

1. S. C. Malan, *The Book of Adam and Eve, Also Called The Conflict of Adam and Eve with Satan* (London: Williams and Norgate, 1882).

2. For all the references, see Stone, *History of the Literature of Adam and Eve,* 98–101, where the relevant bibliography is to be found.

3. Marshall, *Greek Poem on Genesis and Exodus,* xxix.

APPENDIX 3

1. I am grateful to M. Stone, who helped me with the Armenian, and to I. Fikhman, for his assistance in Russian.

2. On agentive nouns, see P. Chantraine, *La formation des noms en Grec ancien* (Paris: Librairie ancienne Honoré Champion, 1933), 8–12.

3. H. G. Liddell and R. Scott et al., *A Greek-English Lexicon,* revised and augmented throughout by Sir H. Stuart Jones, with the assistance of R. McKenzie and with the cooperation of many scholars with a revised supplement (Oxford: Clarendon Press, 1996) 1985, s.v.

4. See A. Vendryès, *Traité d'accentuation grecque* (Paris: Klinsieck, 1945), 188. For nominal composition, see E. Schwyzer, *Griechische Grammatik auf der Grundlage von Karls Brugmanns griechische Grammatik* (München: Beck, 1968–1971), vol. 1, 425–455.

5. See J. F. Niermeyer, *Mediae Latinitatis Lexicon Minus* (Leiden: Brill, 1976), 649–650.

6. I owe this clear observation to my colleague and friend Aldina Quintana.

7. See O. Bloch, *Dictionnaire étymologique de la Langue Française,* 6th ed. (Paris: Presses universitaires de France, 1975), 389.

8. See M. Cortelazzo, *Dizionario etimologico della lingua italiana* (Bologna: Zanichelli, 1979–1988), 75.

9. See J. Corominas, *Breve Diccionario etimológico de la lengua castellana,* 3rd ed. (Madrid: Gredos, 1973), 379.

10. See M. Jastrow, *A Dictionary of the Targumim, The Talmud Babli and Yerushalmi, and the Midrashic Literature* (Luzac, N.Y.: G. P. Putnam, 1903), I. 679.

11. This formulation is not quite accurate. In fact, the type of contract designated by Latin *chirographum* is different from the Greek χειρόγραφον.

12. This is the result of a search in the *Thesaurus Linguae Graecae* (TLG) database.

13. See note 3.

14. Ibid.

15. J. H. Moulton and G. Milligan, *The Vocabulary of the Greek Testament: Illustrated from the Papyri and Other Non-literary Sources* (London: Hodder and Stoughton, 1915), 687. This is considered to be the best dictionary of Greek of the Hellenistic and Greco-Roman periods.

16. See M. Amelotti, "Συγγραφή, χειρόγραφον *-testatio, chirographum.* Osservazioni in tema di tipologie documentali," in *Scritti giuridici,* ed. L. Migliardi Zingale (Turin: G. Giappichelli Editori, 1984), 134.

17. H. Ch. Youtie and J. Garret Winter, *Papyri and Ostraca from Karanis,* Michigan Papyri, 8 (Ann Arbor, University of Michigan Press, 1951), 69–71, doc 480.

18. D. Barthélemy and J. T. Milik, eds., *Qumran Cave I,* Discoveries in the Judean Desert, 1 (Oxford: Clarendon Press, 1955), 240 (1Q 114).

19. See note 16.

20. F. Preisigke, *Wörterbuch der griechischen Papyruskunden* (Berlin: Erben, 1925–1931), II.732–733.

21. F. Pringsheim, *The Greek Law of Sale* (Weimar: H. Bohlaus Nachfolger, 1950), 65.

22. See G. W. H. Lampe, ed., *A Patristic Greek Lexicon* (Oxford: Clarendon Press. 1961), 1522. Lampe's lexicon is designed to complement Liddell and Scott. It covers mainly the patristic literature, that is, from the Greco-Roman to the Transitional period.

23. See note 17.

24. See Amelotti, "Συγγραφή, χειρόγραφον -*testatio, chirographum,*" 134–135.

25. See P. G. W. Glare et al., eds., *The Oxford Latin Dictionary* (Oxford: Clarendon Press, 1968–1976), vol. 1, 310.

26. See D. R. Shackleton Bailey, ed., *Cicero: Epistulae ad familiares* (Cambridge: Cambridge University Press), vol. 1, 99 (text), and vol. 1, 342 (notes).

27. F. Frost Abbot, *Selected Letters of Cicero* (Norman: University of Oklahoma Press, 1964), 104.

28. Another possible interpretation is that here, *Graeculam chirographum* refers to the ancient form of the cheirographon, that is, the Ptolemaic chirographum, which was an absolutely private document. It is opposed to the Roman chirographum from the period of the Principate, when a copy was deposited in the archives. See H. J. Wolff, *Das Recht der griechischen Papyri Aegyptens in der Zeit der Ptolemaeer und des Prinzipats* (Munich: Verlag C. H. Beck, 1978), 129–130.

29. See note 25.

30. *Papyri, Greek and Egyptian. Edited by Various Hands in Honour of Eric Gardner Turner* (London: The Egypt Exploration Society, 1981), 83–88; J. Enoch Powell, *The Rendell Harris Papyri* (Cambridge: Cambridge University Press, 1936), 47–48.

31. For different types of documents, see I. Fikhman, Ббедеуе Б Докъментаюъг Папуролойуг [*Introduction to Documentary Papyrology*] (Moscow: Academy of Sciences, 1987), 215–230. On the cheirograph, see pp. 224–225.

32. See H. J. Wolff, *Das Recht der griechischen Papyri Aegyptens in der Zeit der Ptolemaeer und des Prinzipats*, 129.

33. H. Idris Bell and C. H. Roberts, *A Descriptive Catalogue of the Greek Papyri in the Collection of Wilfred Merton, F.S.A.* (London: Emery Walker, 1948), vol. 1, 91–92.

34. E. Lobel and C. H. Roberts, *The Oxyrhynchus Papyri XXII* (London: The Egypt Exploration Society, 1954), 147–150.

35. ἐξαλείφω still bears the meaning "to erase" in Modern Greek.

36. G. Milligan, *Selections from the Greek Papyri* (Cambridge:Cambridge University Press, 1912), xxii note 2.

37. See, for instance, Pap. Mich 44, in: D. S. Crawford, *Papyri Michaelidae* (Aberdeen: The Egypt Exploration Society, 1955), 99–101. It is dated to 527 C.E.

Bibliography

This bibliography does not contain the works cited only in appendixes 1 and 3; i.e., the editions of the texts in the various languages and papyrological sources. Those are given in full in the appendixes.

[n.a.] (1964). *Kunstschätze in bulgarischen Museen und Klöstern.* Essen: Villa Hügel.

Ajamian, S. (1992). Յուցակ Աստուածաշունչ մատենանի Հայերէն ձեռագիրներուն [*Catalogue of Armenian Manuscripts of the Bible*]. Lisbon: C. Gulbenkian Foundation.

Anania, V. (1990). *Cerurile Oltului: Scolile Arhimandritului Bartolomeu la imaginile fotografice ale lui Dumitru F. Dumitru.* Episcopate of Rîmnicului and Argeţ.

Anasyan, H. S. (1959). Հայկական Մատենագիտութիւն. Ե-ԺԷ դդ. [*Armenian Bibliology, Fifth–eighteenth Centuries.*] Erevan: Academy of Sciences.

Anderson, G. A. (1993). "The Penitence Narrative in the *Life of Adam and Eve.*" *Hebrew Union College Annual* 63, 1–38.

Anderson, G. A. (2000). "The Punishment of Adam and Eve in the *Life of Adam and Eve.*" In *Literature on Adam and Eve: Selected Essays,* ed. G. Anderson, M. Stone, and J. Tromp SVTP, 14. Leiden: Brill, 57–81.

Anderson, G. A., and M. E. Stone (1999). *A Synopsis of the Books of Adam and Eve: Second Revised Edition.* Early Jewish Literature, 17. Atlanta: Scholars Press.

Antonova, V. I, and N. E. Mneva (1963). *Katalog drevnerusskoi zhivopisi* [*Catalogue of Old Russian Paintings*]. Moscow: Iskusstvo.

Βαρδαβακη, Μ. Α. (1992). *ΟΙ ΜΙΚΡΟΓΡΑΦΕΙΣ ΤΟΥ ΑΚΑΘΙΣΤΟΥ ΣΤΟΝ ΚΩΔΙΚΑ GARRET 13, PRINCETON.* Athens: Hē en Athēnais Archaiologikē Hetaireia.

Barsov, E. (1886). *Chteniia v imper. obshchestve istorii i drevnostei* 2.

Beck, E., ed. (1959). *Des Heiligen Ephrems des Syrers Hymnen de Nativitate (Epiphania).* CSCO, 186–187. Leuven: Peeters.

Beck, E., ed. (1963). *Des Heiligen Ephrems des Syrers Carmina Nisibena.* CSCO 240–241. Leuven: Peeters.

Best, E. C. (1956). *An Historical Study of the Exegesis of Colossians 2, 14.* Rome: Pontifica Universitas Gregoriana.

Bischoff, B. (1966). "Zur Frügeschichte des mittelalterlichen Chirographhum." In *Mittelalterliche Studien.* Stuttgart: Huersmann, 118–121.

Borret, M. (1985). *Origène. Homélies sur l'Exode.* Sources Chrétiennes, 321. Paris: Editions du Cerf.

Breen, A. (1992). "Anonymous, Liber Commenei. The Liturgical Materials in Ms Oxford, Bodleian Library, Auct. F.4/32." *Archiv für Liturgie-Wissenschaft* 34, 121–153.

Breeze, A. (1995). "Master John of St. Davids, Adam and Eve, and the Rose among the Thorns." *Studia Celtica* 29, 225–235.

Budge, E. A. W. (1933). *The Alexander Book in Ethiopia.* London: Oxford University Press.

Cartojan, N. (1929). *Cărţile populare în literatura românească.* 2 vols. Bucharest: Editura enciclopedica româna, repr. 1974.

Cavarnos, G. (1993). *Guide to Byzantine Iconography.* Boston: Holy Transfiguration Monastery.

Charles, R. H., ed. (1913). *The Apocrypha and Pseudepigrapha of the Old Testament.* 2 vols. Oxford: Oxford University Press.

Charlesworth, J. H., ed. (1983, 1985). *The Old Testament Pseudepigrapha.* 2 vols. Garden City, N.Y.: Doubleday.

Christ, W., and M. Paranikas (1871). *Anthologia Graeca Carminum Christianorum.* Leipzig: Teubner.

Clark, K. W. (1952). *Checklist of Manuscripts in St. Catherine's Monastery, Mount Sinai.* Washington, D.C.: Library of Congress.

Comarnescu, P. (1959). *Rümanische Kunstschätze. Voroneţ. Fresken aus dem 15. und 16. Jahrhundert.* Bucharest: Verlag für fremdsprachige Literatur.

Conybeare, F. C. (1905). *Rituale Armenorum: Being the Administration of the Sacraments and the Breviary Rites of the Armenian Church Together with the Greek Rites of Baptism and Epiphany Edited from the Oldest Mss.* Oxford: Oxford University Press.

Cross, F. L., and E. A. Livingstone (1990). *The Oxford Dictionary of the Christian Church.* Oxford: Oxford University Press.

Der Nersessian, S. (1973). "Une nouvelle réplique slavonne de Paris gr. 74 et les manuscrits de Anastase Crimcovici." In *Etudes byzantines et arméniennes.* Louvain: Imprimerie orientaliste.

Didron, M. (1845). *Manuel d'iconographie chrétienne.* Paris: Imprimerie Royale.

Dima, A. (1944). *Rumänische märchen; in deutscher übersetzung nach Haupttypen ausgewählt und mit Anmerkungen versehen.* Leipzig: O. Harrassowitz.

Drăguţ, V., and P. Lupan (1983). *Die Wandmalerei in der Moldau.* Bucharest: Merideame.

Eganyan, O., A. Zeyt'unyan, and P'. Ant'abyan (1965, 1970). Ցուցակ ձեռագրաց Մաշտոցի անվան մատենադարանի [*Catalogue of Manuscripts of the Maštoc' Matenadaran*]. Erevan: Academy of Sciences.

Elliott, J. K. (1993). *The Apocryphal New Testament.* Oxford: Clarendon Press.

Erffa, Hans Martin von (1989). *Ikonologie der Genesis: Die christlichen Bildthemen aus dem Alten Testament und ihre Quellen.* Munich: Deutschen Kunstverlag.

Evans, J. M. (1968). *Paradise Lost and the Genesis Traditions.* Oxford: Clarendon Press.

Finn, T. M. (1967). *The Liturgy of Baptism in the Baptismal Instructions of St. John Chrysostom.* Catholic University of America Studies in Christian Antiquity, 15. Washington, D.C.: Catholic University of America.

Flusser, D. (1971). "Palaea Historica: An Unknown Source of Biblical Legends." In *Essays in Aggadah and Folk-Literature.* Scripta Hierosolymitana, 22. Jerusalem: Magnes, 48–79.

Fraade, Steven D. (1984). *Enosh and His Generation: Pre-Israelite Hero and History in Postbiblical Interpretation.* Society of Biblical Literature Monograph Series, 30. Chico, Calif.: Scholars Press.

Fuchs, C. (1900). "Das Leben Adams und Evas." In *Die Apokryphen und Pseudepigraphen des Alten Testaments, Band 2, Die Pseudepigraphen,* ed. E. Kautzsch: Tübingen: Mohr, 506–528.

Gaster, M. (1891). *Chrestomathie roumaine.* 2 vols. Leipzig-Bucharest: Brockhaus and Socecu.

Gaster, T. (1974). "Satan." In *Interpreter's Dictionary of the Bible.* New York: Abingdon Press.

Ginzberg, L. (1928). *The Legends of the Jews.* Philadelphia: Jewish Publication Society.

Goldin, J. (1974). *The Fathers According to Rabbi Nathan.* New York: Schocken.

Gronewald, M. (1970), *Didymos der Blinde. Psalmenkommentar (Tura-Papyrus).* Vol. 5, *Kommentar zu Psalm 40–44.* Bonn: Habelt.

Hakobian, H. (1991) *The Medieval Art af Artsakh.* Yerevan: Parberakan Press.

Halford, M. E. B. (1981). "The Apocryphal Vita Adae et Evae: Some Comments on the Manuscript Tradition." *Neuphilologische Mitteilungen* 82, 417–427.

Halford, M. E. B. (1982). "The Apocryphal Vita Adae et Evae: Some Comments on the Manuscript Tradition—A Correction." *Neuphilologische Mitteilungen* 83, 222.

Heine, R. E. (1981). *Origen: Homilies on Genesis and Exodus.* The Fathers of the Church. Washington, D.C.: Catholic University.

Heist, W. W. (1952). *The Fifteen Signs before Doomsday.* East Lansing: Michigan State College.

Hennecke, E., and W. Schneemelcher (1991–1992). *The New Testament Apocrypha.* Cambridge and Louisville: J. Clarke & Co. and Westminster/John Knox Press.

Henry, P. (1927). "Folklore et iconographie religieuse: Contribution à l'étude de la peinture moldave." *Melanges: Bibliothèque de l'Institut français de hautes études en Roumanie* 1, 64–82.

Henry, P. (1930). *Les Eglises de la Moldavie du Nord des origines à la fin du XVIe siècle.* Paris: Librairie Ernest Leroux.

Hetherington, P. (1974). *The "Painters Manual" of Dionysius of Fourna.* London: Saggitarius Press.

Issaverdens, J. (1934). *The Uncanonical Writings of the Old Testament Found in the Armenian MSS. of the Library of St. Lazarus.* 2nd ed. Venice: Mechitarist Press.

Ivanov, J. (1976). *Livres et Légendes Bogomiles (Aux Sources du Catharisme).* Paris: Maisonneuve et Larose.

Jagič, V. (1893). "Slavische Beiträge zu den biblischen Apocryphen, I, Die altkirchenslavischen Texte des Adamsbuche." In *Denkschr. kais. Akademie der Wissenschaften, philos.-hist, Classe.* Vienna, 1–104.

James, M. R. (1924). *The Apocryphal New Testament.* Oxford: Clarendon.

Jonge, M. de, and J. Tromp (1997). *The Life of Adam and Eve and Related Literature.* Sheffield: Sheffield Academic Press.

Kaestli, J.-D. (unpublished draft). "Le mythe de la chute de Satan: est-il d'origine juive?"

Kaestli, J.-D. (1993). "Témoignages anciens sur la croyance en la descente du Christ aux enfers." In *L'évangile de Barthélemy d'après deux écrits apocryphes,* ed. J.-D. Kaestli and P. P. Cherix. Turnhout: Brepols, 135–142.

Kister, M. J. (1993) "Ādam: A Study of Some Legends in *Tafsīr* and *Ḥadīṭ* Literature." *Israel Oriental Studies* 13, 113–174.

Kittel, G., and G. Friedrich, eds. (1974). *Theological Dictionary of the New Testament.* Grand Rapids: Eerdmans.

Kontoglu, P. (1960). Ἔκφρασις τῆς ὀρθόδοξου εἰκονόγραφιας. Athens: Aster.

Kretzenbacher, L. (1971). *Bilder und Legenden: Erwandertes und erlebtes Bilder-Denken und Bild-Erzählen zwischen Byzanz und dem Abendland.* Klagefurt: Geschichtverein für Kärnten.

Kretzenbacher, L. (1986). *Teufelsbünder und Faustgestalten im Abendlande.* Klagenfurt: Verlag des Geschichtsvereines für Kärnten.

Kvam, K. E., L. S. Schearing, and V. H. Ziegler, eds. (1999). *Eve and Adam: Jewish, Christian and Muslim Readings on Genesis and Gender.* Bloomington and Indianapolis: Indiana University Press.

Lafontaine-Dosogne, J. (1988). "La tradition byzantine des bapistères et de leur décor, et les fonts de Saint-Barthélemy à Liège." *Cahiers archéologiques* 36, 53–56.

Lange, R. (1966). *Die Auferstehung,* Recklinghausen: Bongers.

Lazar, M. (1960). "La Légende de l'Arbre de Paradis ou bois de la croix." *Zeitschrift für Romanische Philologie* 76, 34–63.

Levison, J. R. (1988). *Portaits of Adam in Early Judaism: From Sirach to 2 Baruch.* Journal for the Study of the Pseudepigrapha Supplement Series, 1. Sheffield: JSOT Press.

Levison, J. R. (1989). "The Exoneration of Eve in the *Apocalypse of Moses* 15–30." *Journal for the Study of Judaism* 20, 135–150.

Liddell, H. G., and R. Scott et al. (1961). *A Greek-English Lexicon.* Oxford: Oxford University Press.

Lieberman, S. (1972). "Zeniḥin." *Tarbiz* 62, 46–48 (in Hebrew).

Lipscomb, W. L. (1990). *The Armenian Apocryphal Adam Literature.* University of Pennsylvania Armenian Texts and Studies, 8. Atlanta: Scholars Press.

Lüdtke, W. (1911). "Georgische Adam-Bücher." *Zeitschrift für die alttestamentliche Wissenschaft* 38, 155–168.

Malan, S. C. (1882). *The Book of Adam and Eve, Also Called The Conflict of Adam and Eve with Satan.* London: Williams and Norgate.

Marshall, F. H. (1925). *Old Testament Legends from a Greek Poem on Genesis and Exodus by Georgios Chumnos.* Cambridge: Cambridge University Press.

Mauchenheim, H. F. von (1960). *Russische Ikonen.* Alphen aan den Rijn: Atrium.

Meersseman, G. G. (1960). *Der Hymnos Akathistos im Abendland.* 2 vols. Spicilegium Friburgense, 3. Freiburg (Ch): Universitätsverlag.

Megas, G. (1928). "Das Χειρόγραφον Adams. Ein Beitrag zu Col 2: 13–15." *Zeitschrift für die Neutestamentliche Wissenschaft* 27, 305–320.

Mellinkoff, R. (1970). *The Horned Moses in Medieval Art and Thought.* California Studies in the History of Art, 14. Berkeley: University of California Press.

Meyer, W. (1878). "Vita Adae et Evae." *Abhandlungen der königlich bayerischen Akademie der Wissenschaften, Philosophische-philologische Klasse* 14.3, 185–250.

Millet, G. (1916). *Recherches sur l'Iconographie de l'Evangile aux XIVᵉ, XVᵉ et XVIᵉ siècles d'après les monuments de Mistra, de la Macédoine et du Mont-Athos.* Paris: E. de Boccard.

Millet, G. (1962). *La peinture du Moyen Age en Yougoslavie (Serbie, Macedoine et Montenegro) Album presenté par A. Frolow.* Paris: E. de Boccard.

Mochulskii, V. (1886). *Istoriko-literaturnyi analiz stixa: "O golubinoi knige."* Warsaw.

Mozley, J. H. (1929). "The Vitae Adae." *Journal of Theological Studies* 30: 121–149.

Mozley, J. R. (1930). "A New Text of the Story of the Cross." *Journal of Theological Studies* 31, 113–127.

Murdoch, B. (1972). *The Fall of Man in the Early Middle High German Biblical Epic: The "Wiener Genesis" the "Vorauer Genesis," and the "Anegenge."* Göppinger: Arbeiten zur Germanistik, 58. Göppinger: Kümmerle.

Murdoch, B. (1994). "Sethites and Cainites: The Narrative Problem of Adam's Progeny in the Early Middle High German Genesis Poems." In *German Narrative Literature of the Twelfth and Thirteenth Centuries: Studies Presented to Roy Wisbey on His Sixty-fifth Birthday,* ed. M. H. Jones, Volker Hönemann, Adrian Stevens, and David Wells. Tübingen: Max Niemeyer, 83–97.

Murdoch, B. O. (1976). *The Irish Adam and Eve Story from Saltair na Rann.* Vol. 2, *Commentary.* Dublin: Dublin Institute for Advanced Studies.

Murdoch, B. O. (1978). "Eve's Anger: Literary Secularization in Lutwin's 'Adam und Eva.'" *Archiv* 215, 256–271.

Murdoch, B. O. (2000). *Adam's Grace: Fall and Redemption in Medieval Literature.* Cambridge: D. S. Brewer.

Nagel, M. (1974). "La Vie grecque d'Adam et d'Eve." Doctoral thesis. Strasbourg.

Napier, A. S. (1894). *History of the Holy Rood Tree.* London: Kegan Paul.

Naumow, A. E. (1976). *Apokryfy w Systemie Literatury Cerkiewnosłowiańskiej.* Warsaw: Polish Academy of Sciences.

NBH (1836). Նոր Բառգիրք Հայկազեան Լեզուի [*New Dictionary of the Armenian Language*]. Venice: Mechitarist Press.

Oblensky, D. (1987). *The Bogomils: A Study in Balkan Neo-Manicheanism.* Twickenham: Hall.

Ohly, F. (1976) *Der Verfluchte und der Erwählte: Vom Leben mit der Schuld.* Opladen: Westdeutscher Verlag.

Ormanian, M. (1948). *Dictionary of the Armenian Church.* New York: St. Vartan Press.

Paskaleva, K. (1987). *Bulgarian Icons through the Centuries.* Sofia: Soyat.

Petkovi, Sr. (1987). "Slikarstvo Spolašne Priprate Gračanice" [Painting of the Exo-Narthex of Gračanice]. In *Bizantiyska Umetnost Počerkom XIV veka* [Byzantine Art from Its Inception Down to the Fourteenth Century], *Symposium Gračanica 1973.* Belgrade, 201–212 and 8 plates.

Pettorelli, J.-P. (1998). "La Vie latine d'Adam et Ève." *Archivum Latinitatis Medii Aevi* 61, 5–104.

Pettorelli, J.-P. (1999). "La vie latine d'Adam et Eve; Analyse de la tradition manuscrite." *Apocrypha* 10, 195–296.

Pokrovskii, N. V. (1892), *Evangelie v pamiatnikakh ikonografii preimushchestvenno vizantiiskikh i russkikh* [*The Gospel in Iconography, Primarily Byzantine and Russian*]. St. Petersburg: Tip. Departamenta udelov.

Preuschen, E. (1900). "Die apokryphen gnostischen Adamschriften, aus dem Armenischen übersetzt u. untersucht." In *Festgruss B. Stade.* Giessen: Ricker, 163–252.

Quinn, E. C. (1962). *The Quest of Seth for the Oil of Life.* Chicago: University of Chicago Press.

Ristow, G. (1965). *Die Taufe Christi.* Recklinghausen: Bongers.

Roddy, N. (1999). "Scribal Intent: Sociocultural Appropriation of the Testament of Abraham in Eighteenth-Century Romanian Lands," *Journal of Religion and Society* 1. E-journal available at <http://www.creighton.edu/JRS/

Röhricht, R. (1963). *Bibliotheca Geographica Palestina.* Rev. ed. by D. Amiran. Jerusalem: Universitas.

Roitman, A. (1995). "'Al Geḥonka Telek' (Gen. 3.14): Hamareh haḥiṣoni šel naḥaš gan ha'eden befaršanut hayehudit ha'atiqa." *Tarbiẓ* 64, 157–182.

Rosenstiehl, J. M. (1983). "La chute de l'Ange, Origines et développement d'une légende, ses attestations dans la littérature copte." *Journée d'études coptes. Strasbourg 28 mai 1982.* Cahiers de la Bibliothèque copte 1. Louvain, 44–47.

Schäfer, G. (1855). *Das Handbuch der Malerei von Berge Athos.* Trier: Fr. Lintz.

Schäfer, P. (1977). "Adam II. Im Frühjudentum." In *Theologische Realenzyklopädie.* Berlin: de Gruyter, 1, 424–427.

Schäfer, P. (1986). "Adam in jüdischen Überlieferung." In *Vom alten zum neuen Adam:*

Urzeitmythos und Heilsgeschichte, ed. W. Strolz. Freiburg, Basel, and Vienna: Herder, 69–93.

Schaff, P. (1995 repr.). *The Nicene and Post-Nicene Fathers.* Series 1, vol. 13. Peabody: Hendrickson.

Schürer, E. (1893). Review of Jagič. *Theologische Literatur-Zeitung* 16, 398–399.

Smirnova, E. (1989). *Moscow Icons, Fourteenth to Seventeenth Centuries.* Leningrad: Aurora Art Publishers.

Smith, J. I., and Y. Y. Haddad (1982). "Eve: Islamic Image of Women." *Women's Studies International Forum* 2, 135–144.

Sparks, H. D. F., ed. (1984). *The Apocryphal Old Testament.* Oxford: Oxford University Press.

Stewart, C. (1991). *Demons and the Devil: Moral Imagination in Greek Culture.* Princeton: Princeton University Press.

Stichel, R. (1990). *Die Geburt Christi in der russischen Ikonenmalerei.* Stuttgart: Franz Steiner Verlag.

Stone, M. E. (1978). "Armenian Canon Lists III: The Lists of Mechitar of Ayrivank'." *Harvard Theological Review* 69, 289–300.

Stone, M. E. (1981). *Signs of the Judgment, Onomastica Sacra and the Generations from Adam.* University of Pennsylvania Armenian Texts and Studies, 3. Chico, Calif.: Scholars Press.

Stone, M. E. (1981). *The Penitence of Adam.* CSCO, 429–430. Leuven: Peeters.

Stone, M. E. (1982). *Armenian Apocrypha Relating to Patriarchs and Prophets.* Jerusalem: Israel Academy of Sciences.

Stone, M. E., ed. (1984). *Jewish Writings of the Second Temple Period.* Compendia Rerum Iudaicarum ad Novum Testamentum, 2.2. Philadelphia and Assen: Fortress and van Gorcum.

Stone, M. E. (1990). *Commentary on 4 Ezra.* Minneapolis: Augsberg-Fortress.

Stone, M. E. (1992). *A History of the Literature of Adam and Eve.* Early Judaism and Its Literature, 3. Atlanta: Scholars Press.

Stone, M. E. (1993). "The Fall of Satan and Adam's Penance: Three Notes on *The Books of Adam and Eve.*" *Journal of Theological Studies* 44, 143–156.

Stone, M. E. (1996). *Armenian Apocrypha Relating to Adam and Eve.* Studia in Veteris Testamenti Pseudepigrapha, 14. Leiden: Brill.

Stone, M. E. (1996). "The Armenian Apocryphal Literature: Translation and Creation." In *Il Caucaso: Cerniera fra Culture dal Mediterraneo alla Persia (Secoli I–XI).* Settimane di Studio dal Centro Italiano de Studi sull'Alto Medioevo, XLIII. Spoleto: Presso la Sede del Centro, 612–646.

Stone, M. E. (1999). "The Study of the Armenian Apocrypha." In *A Multiform Heritage: Studies on Early Judaism and Christianity in Honor of Robert A. Kraft,* ed. B. G. Wright. Scholars Press Homage Series. Atlanta: Scholars Press, 139–148.

Stone, M. E. (1999). "Two Armenian Manuscripts and the *Historia Sacra.*" In *Apocryphes arméniens: transmission — traduction — création — iconographie.* ed. V. Calzolari Bouvier, J.-D. Kaestli, and B. Outtier. Lausanne: Zèbre, 21–36.

Stone, M. E., and J. Strugnell (1979). *The Books of Elijah, Parts 1 and 2.* Texts and Translations, 5. Missoula: Scholars Press.

Stone, M. E., and T. A. Bergren (1999). *Biblical Figures outside the Bible.* Philadelphia: Trinity Press International.

Stone, M. E., B. G. Wright, and D. Satran (2000). *The Apocryphal Ezekiel.* Early Judaism and Its Literature, 18. Atlanta: Society for Biblical Literature.

Stoyanov, Y. (1994) *The Hidden Tradition in Europe.* London: Arkana-Penguin.

Sweet, A. M. (1992) "A Religio-Historical Study of the Greek *Life of Adam and Eve.*" Ph.D. Thesis, Notre Dame.

Tafrali, O. (1914). "Iconografia Imnului Acatist." *Buletinul Comissiunii monumentelor istorice* 7, figs. 39 and 40.

Tayec'i, E. (1898). *Անկանոն Գիրք Նոր Կտակարանաց* [*Uncanonical Books of the New Testament*]. Venice: Mechitarist Press.

Tikhonravov, N. S. (1863), *Pamiatniki otrechennoi russkoi literatury* [Monuments of Russian Rejected Literature]. St. Petersburg: V Tip. Obshchestvennaia pol'za.

Tschilingnov, A. (1978). *Die Kunst des christlichen Mittelalters in Bulgarien: 14. bis 18. Jarh.* Berlin: Union.

Turdeanu, É. (1981). *Apocryphes slaves et roumains de l'Ancien Testament.* Studia in Veteris Testamenti Pseudepigrapha, 5. Leiden: Brill.

van Damme, D. (1969). *Pseudo-Cyprian Adversus Iudaeos.* Paradosis: Beiträge zur altchristlichen Literatur und Theologie, 22. Freiburg: University Press.

Vassiliev, A. (1893). *Anecdota Graeco-Byzantina.* Moscow: Imperial University.

Weitzmann, K., et al. (1982). *The Icon.* London: Evans.

Weitzmann, K., M. Chatzidakis, et al. (1965). *Fruhe Ikonen. Sinai, Griechenland, Bulgarien, Jugoslawien.* Wien-München: Schroll.

Wellesz, E. (1957). *The Akathistos Hymn.* Monumenta Musicae Byzantinae Transcripta, 9. Copenhagen: Munksgaard.

Wells, L. S. A. (1913). "The Books of Adam and Eve." In *The Apocrypha and Pseudepigrapha of the Old Testament* ed. R. H. Charles. Oxford: Oxford University Press, 123–154.

Winkler, G. (1982). *Das armenische Initiationsrituale.* Orientalia Christiana Analecta, 217. Rome: Pont. Institutum Studiorum Orientalium.

Yassif, E. (1984). *Sippurei Ben Sira Biymei habeynayyim.* Jerusalem: Magnes.

Yovēp'ianc', S. (1898). *Անկանոն Գիրք Հին Կտակարանաց* [*Uncanonical Books of the Old Testament*]. Venice: Mechitarist Press.

Zak'arian, L. (1980). *History of the Miniatures of Vaspurakan.* Yerevan: Academy of Sciences (in Russian).

Index

To avoid confusion all book titles are italicised, including biblical books. The lists of manuscripts in Appendix 1 are not included in this index.

MICHAEL E. STONE was educated at the University of Melbourne and holds the degrees of Ph.D. from Harvard University and D. Litt. from the University of Melbourne. He has, since 1965, been on the faculty of the Hebrew University of Jerusalem, where he holds the double appointment of Gail Levin de Nur Professor of Religion and Professor of Armenian Studies. He is the author of more than 40 books and 250 articles in the fields of ancient Judaism and Armenian studies. His work has encompassed Jewish literature of the Second Temple Period, including the Dead Sea Scrolls, and many aspects of Armenian studies, with special emphasis on the Bible and biblical traditions in Armenian, the Armenians in the Holy Land, and the history of Armenian writing.